EMPLOYEE'S GUIDE TO NEW JERSEY WORKERS' COMPENSATION LAW

Protect Your Rights When Injured at Work

Lisa Pezzano Mickey, Esq.

ISBN: 978-1-941645-44-4

Design and Published by:

Speakeasy Publications

73-03 Bell Blvd, #10

Oakland Gardens, NY 11364

www.SpeakeasyMarketingInc.com

888-225-8594

DISCLAIMER

This publication is intended to be informational only. No legal advice is being given, and no attorney-client relationship is intended to be created by reading this material. If you are facing legal issues, whether criminal or civil, seek professional legal counsel to get your questions answered.

Pezzano Mickey & Bornstein, LLP

224 Roseberry Street, Suite 4

Phillipsburg, NJ 08865

908-332-5552

www.pmblawfirm.com

TABLE OF CONTENTS

ATTORNEY INTRODUCTION

Lisa Pezzano Mickey was born and raised on Long Island, New York. In 1988, she graduated from Villanova University and thereafter received her law degree, with honors, from George Washington Law School in 1991.

She first began practicing law for a non-profit organization in Newark, New Jersey. She thereafter became the senior associate in a prominent Central New Jersey law firm, where she represented several different insurance carriers in the defense of workers' compensation claims. In 2001, she opened her own practice in Central New Jersey, until founding the partnership of Pezzano Mickey & Bornstein in 2012.

As the daughter of a New York City police officer and stay-at-home Mom turned real estate agent, Lisa grew up with an extended family which includes electricians, stone-cutters, carpenters, baggage handlers, and office workers.

Her grandmother had to work the midnight shift to support her four children after the untimely death of her grandfather, instilling a strong work ethic in her family. Through these examples, Lisa developed great respect for hard-working Americans whose toil and sweat built this great country. It is thus fitting that she now represents injured workers, and has dedicated herself to helping them obtain the justice they deserve.

CHAPTER 1

OVERVIEW OF THE NEW JERSEY WORKERS' COMPENSATION SYSTEM

The N.J. Workers' Compensation Act provides injured employees with three types of benefits: (1) medical treatment related to the work injury; (2) temporary disability benefits of up to 70% of wages while out of work under the care of a doctor; and (3) an award of permanent partial or total disability benefits if there is objective evidence of a permanent loss of function.

Medical Benefits

The workers' compensation insurance carrier must pay 100% of all related medical treatment. The injured employee does not owe any co-payment or deductible. However, that treatment must be pre-authorized by the employer's workers' compensation carrier. The drawback for injured workers is that the employer's carrier chooses the doctor.

Temporary Disability Benefits

The Workers' Compensation Act provides that an employee is entitled to receive 70% of his average weekly wage, up to the state maximum, for the period of time that the authorized treating physician indicates he is unable to work and needs active medical treatment. The average weekly wage is calculated based upon the employee's gross wages before taxes, and it is generally although not always computed over the six month period immediately prior to the date of the accident.

The average wage includes all overtime paid during that six month period. For accidents which occurred in 2018, the state minimum temporary disability rate is $241 per week, and the maximum temporary disability rate is $903 per week. The maximum and minimum temporary disability rates change every year, based upon the state average weekly wage.

Permanent Disability Benefits

Once the injured worker has been discharged from medical treatment, the permanent disability phase of the workers' compensation claim begins. In order to preserve the right to receive permanent disability benefits, a Claim Petition must be filed with the Division of Workers'

Compensation (hereinafter "DWC") within two years of the date any benefits were paid by the workers' compensation insurance carrier. See, sample Claim Petition at Appendix A.

The filing of the Claim Petition starts an adversarial proceeding in the DWC between the injured worker (known as the "petitioner" in the DWC) and the employer (known as the "respondent"). In order to evaluate the degree of permanent disability sustained by the petitioner, both the carrier and petitioner's attorney will retain medical experts who are familiar with the New Jersey disability schedule. Both experts will provide exaggerated estimates of the disability for the purposes of negotiating a settlement of the claim. Most claims settle prior to trial, at a percentage of permanent partial disability benefits somewhere between the estimates of the medical experts.

The workers' compensation system in New Jersey is far from perfect. Especially when the employer does not carry the required insurance coverage, injured employees often face long delays in treatment and benefits. For the majority of claimants with minor injuries, the system runs smoothly and fairly. However, if you sustained a serious injury, you may find that the treatment you receive from the workers' compensation system is substandard since the care will be micromanaged by insurance bureaucrats, whose main goal is to patch you up quickly in order to stop your benefits. If you fall into this

category, it is essential for you to retain competent legal counsel as early in the process as possible.

CHAPTER 2

WHAT TYPES OF CLAIMS ARE COVERED BY N.J. WORKERS' COMPENSATION?

The simple answer is that if you were hurt during the course of your employment, you most likely have a valid workers' compensation claim.

Do I Still Have A Claim If My Employer Did Not Cause The Accident?

In New Jersey, workers' compensation is basically a no fault system. In other words, an employee does not need to prove that an employer committed negligence in order to obtain workers' compensation benefits. You can trip over your own two feet and still collect workers' compensation as long as you weren't engaging in behavior which could be construed as a major deviation from your employment.

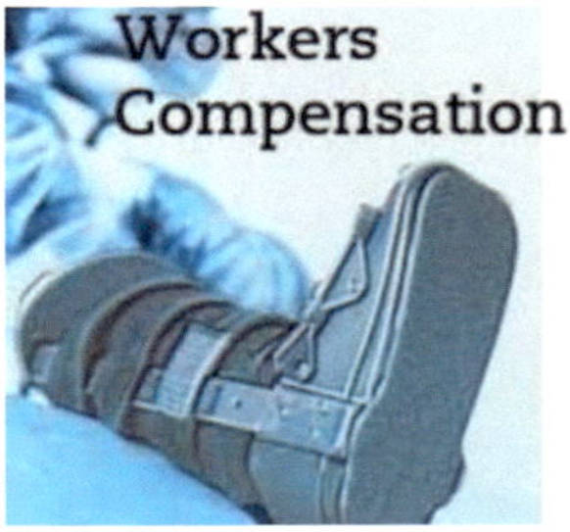

What Industries Are Covered by N.J. Workers' Compensation Laws?

All industries which perform work in the state are covered by the New Jersey Workers' Compensation Act. Even out-of-state employers may need workers' compensation coverage if a contract of employment was signed in New Jersey, or if the work is performed in New Jersey. Virtually all individuals who work in the state are covered by the Act, with the exception of longshoremen and employees of the United States government, who are protected by separate compensation systems.

Does the N.J. Workers' Compensation Act Cover Only Accidents or Does It Also Cover Long Term Problems and Illnesses?

The Act applies to both traumatic injuries from specific accidents as well as occupational injuries which occur over time as a result of the work effort. Examples of occupational injuries include carpal tunnel syndrome caused by repetitive typing, pulmonary disability of a fireman who repeatedly suffered from smoke inhalation, or a factory worker who experiences hearing loss due to constant loud noises. Back injuries may also be caused by years of heavy labor in the construction industry. Shoulder impingement may be caused by the repetitive use of tools. Any activity which requires the use of the same muscles repeatedly has the danger of causing an occupational injury.

Occupational claims are generally more difficult to prove than specific accident claims. Many insurance carriers in New Jersey automatically deny occupational claims as a matter of course. With all occupational claims, the personal risk factors of the injured worker, such as smoking, are always at issue. It is undoubtedly more difficult to prove that an employee with a 30 year smoking industry developed a pulmonary disability due to chemical exposure, than it is to prove causal relationship in a case involving a non-smoker.

How Can Someone Prove That an Injury Is Related to Their Current Occupation?

It is critical for the injured worker to be able to demonstrate that his activities on the job were more taxing than those outside of his employment, to successfully litigate an occupational claim. Therefore, it is important to have a very specific list of job duties at work, with a description of each duty (for example, how much is lifted, what tools/machines are utilized, and a log showing the length of time of each activity). The injured worker should be prepared to provide her doctors with a complete description of the activities which led to the symptoms, to enable the physician to document how the injury is related to her employment. Since litigation often takes years to

conclude, and memories fade, it is advisable to write down the job duties while still employed or shortly after employment ends. If a formal job description from the employer is available, that document should also be obtained. If possible, it is helpful to save the names and contact information of co-workers who would be able to corroborate your testimony regarding the nature of the work.

What Injuries Might Not Be Covered By Workers' Compensation?

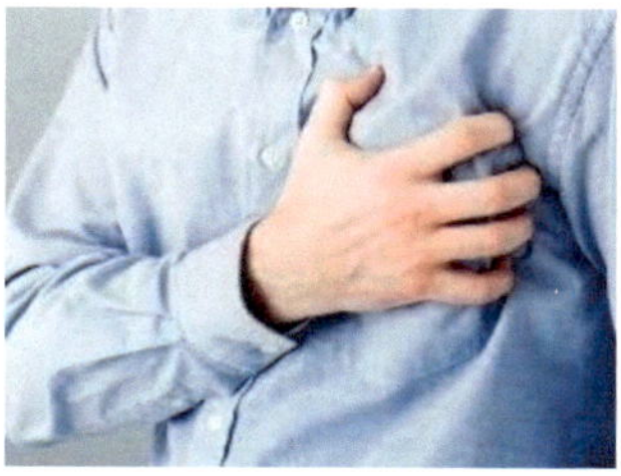

(1) A heart attack or a stroke on the job will only be covered under certain circumstances. If the heart attack was not brought on by the work effort, it is not compensable. In other words, if the employee just happened to be at work at the time of the heart attack, and could have just as easily suffered a cardiac arrest if he had been relaxing at home at the time, then workers' compensation benefits are not available. On the other hand, if you experience chest pain due to the strain of lifting a 200-pound box at work, then the injury would come under the purview of the Workers' Compensation Act.

(2) Pre-existing injuries are not covered. However, pre-existing injuries which are exacerbated by the accident should be paid by workers' compensation.

(3) Self-inflicted injuries are not compensable.

(4) Injuries which are caused solely due to the intoxication of the employee are not covered.

(5) While psychiatric disability may be covered by workers' compensation, such claims are notoriously difficult to pursue. All jobs are stressful in some respect, so the Courts have held that the mere stress of performing one's job duties and/or personality disputes with co-workers or supervisors is not enough to make an employer liable for a psychiatric condition, such as anxiety, depression, or a mental breakdown. There must be some unusual, objectively stressful work condition, peculiar to the workplace, which would have mentally affected any reasonable person. It is often very difficult for an employee with a pre-existing psychiatric problem to meet this burden. In addition, the employee must be prepared to disclose sensitive, personal information, such as the records of a therapist, to pursue a psychiatric claim.

What If a Work Accident Irritates or Exacerbates a Preexisting Condition?

Insurance carriers are notorious for pointing to a pre-existing injury as the cause of an employee's symptoms. However, if a pre-existing condition was asymptomatic prior to the work accident, it should not be used as a basis to deny workers' compensation benefits. For example, if you were diagnosed with pre-existing arthritis which never caused any symptoms before the accident, the carrier should not use that condition as a basis to deny benefits, although they often try to do so. In short, while workers' compensation insurance will not cover the arthritis which existed prior to the accident, it should cover any exacerbation or acceleration of the arthritis which became symptomatic because of the work injury.

The difficulty of proving that a pre-existing condition was aggravated by a work injury usually depends upon the severity of the trauma and a review of the medical reports. For example, it is undeniable that arthritis may be present yet asymptomatic for years. Whether or not medical treatment becomes necessary due to a traumatic event often boils down to the strength of the medical testimony and how persuasive the employee is in explaining how active he was prior to the accident.

Employees must be prepared to release copies of all prior medical records which are relevant to the work injury in order to pursue a claim.

CHAPTER 3

QUESTIONS REGARDING SCOPE OF EMPLOYMENT

What If I Did Not Have a Traditional 9 – 5 Job When I Was Injured?

If you were not employed at the time of the accident then the injuries will not be covered through workers' compensation. For instance, if you were injured while assisting a friend with a project, even if you received some sort of payment for your services, you may be considered a "causal employee," and not covered by the N.J. Workers' Compensation Act.

Are Independent Contractors Entitled to Receive Workers' Compensation?

If you were an "independent contractor," rather than an employee, then your injuries will fall outside of the protection of the Act. It should be noted however, that even if you signed an agreement which declares that you are an independent contractor, that agreement does not end the inquiry. Nor does the fact that you pay all taxes yourself establish that you are an independent contractor. Instead, the Courts will look to both the "control test" and the "relative nature of the work test" to determine whether you are an independent contractor or an employee. If the company directs the details of how you perform your job and you are economically dependent upon the company, then you are more likely than not an employee as opposed to an independent contractor, entitled to the protection of the Workers' Compensation Act. On the other hand, if you work on a contractual basis with many different customers, and can take projects on at your discretion, you will most likely be considered an independent contractor. If so, you should speak to an insurance agent about taking out your own workers' compensation policy which contains sole proprietorship coverage.

Are Undocumented Immigrants Covered by the New Jersey Workers' Compensation Act?

Yes, undocumented aliens who are in the country in violation of the federal immigration laws may still obtain benefits under the New Jersey Workers' Compensation Act. Accordingly, unless the law is changed, an employer currently cannot deny medical treatment, temporary disability, or permanent disability benefits to a worker on the basis of her immigration status.

What If I Was Injured While I Was Traveling to Work or When I Was Away from My Usual Job Site?

Injuries which occur while traveling to/from work are not covered by workers' compensation. Accordingly, if you were involved in a motor vehicle accident on your way to work, the injuries would not come under the purview of workers' compensation. This concept is referred to as the "going and coming rule." The critical question in such cases is "when" the employee actually arrives at the workplace. For instance, does he arrive at work when he pulls into the parking lot, a job site, enters the front door of the office building, or an interior office suite? This area of the law is shifting rapidly, but New Jersey Courts have in general held that if the employer owns the premises where the accident occurred (known as the "premises rule") then the injuries will be considered work-related.

There are several exceptions to the "premises rule" and the "going and coming rule," which entitle employees to obtain workers' compensation benefits, despite being outside of the normal workplace when the injuries occurred. One such exception is if the injuries occurred while the employee was on a "special mission." For instance, a salesman who was injured while traveling to a meeting would be entitled to receive workers' compensation benefits. If the salesman's injuries occurred when he took a detour for personal reasons, then the injuries may fall outside of the protection of workers' compensation, unless it was such a minor deviation to be considered insignificant by the Court.

Are Workers' Compensation Benefits Available If the Injury Occurs During Lunch?

Generally, lunch break accidents are covered *if* they occur on the employer's premises, unless the injury was sustained as a result of an activity which did not benefit the employer, such as smoking. If an employee goes off premises for lunch, then the injury would not be compensable unless the off-premises luncheon was scheduled at the request of the employer, or the lunch otherwise qualifies as a "special mission" which benefited the employer. For instance, if the injury occurred during the course of taking a customer of the company out to lunch, the accident should be covered by workers' compensation.

Similarly, the fact that an employee has not officially "clocked in" or "clocked out" of work is irrelevant. For example, if an employee who arrives at work early in order to have a cup of coffee and socialize before clocking in has an accident, that injury will be covered by workers' compensation.

CHAPTER 4

RESPONSIBILITIES OF THE EMPLOYER

An employer must post the name of its workers' compensation insurance carrier in a conspicuous place at the workplace. In order to avoid denial of insurance coverage, the employer must also place the workers' compensation carrier on notice of any work accidents or claims of injury. After notifying the insurance carrier of the accident, the employee should receive a claim number from the carrier, which must be used to obtain medical treatment.

Can an Employer Send an Injured Worker to a Doctor Following an Accident?

Of course, in the case of an emergency, an employer should call an ambulance or otherwise transport the injured worker to a hospital. If the injury does not require emergent medical care the employer may instruct the employee to make an appointment with a "company doctor," until the workers' compensation insurance carrier directs the employee to a specific physician within their network. If the employer does not have a company doctor, then the employer may advise the injured worker to go to his own doctor, until the insurance carrier directs treatment elsewhere. The employer should not instruct the injured worker to use his health insurance to obtain medical treatment– to do so potentially constitutes insurance fraud.

What Information Should the Employer Gather After a Work Accident?

The terms of the workers' compensation insurance policy require the employer to cooperate in providing investigation regarding the accident, as well as wage information, so that benefits may be paid promptly to the injured employee. The employer should prepare an accident report to document the injury. In addition, employers must file a "First Report of Injury" form, which may be found on the New Jersey Department of Labor's website.

If there is some question about whether an accident occurred, it is advisable for the employer to investigate the accident by obtaining witness statements and then turning the investigation over to its workers' compensation insurance carrier. The bottom line is that even if an employer does not believe that an injury occurred, it is incumbent upon the employer to report the accident to the workers' compensation carrier. The carrier will then continue the investigation started by the employer and will refuse to pay the claim if it is not legitimate.

The employer should provide the carrier with a copy of the accident report, if any, and pass on any statements made by the employee and co-workers regarding complaints of injury before or after the accident. If the accident was a result of negligence by an outside company or individual, the employer should share that information with the claims adjuster.

The carrier will ask the employer to complete a 26 week wage statement, listing the employee's weekly salary for the 6 month period prior to the accident. Overtime pay must be included in the wage calculation. Unfortunately, it is not uncommon for benefits to be delayed because an employer fails to complete the required forms to the carrier on a timely basis. Injured workers' may speed up the process by providing their attorney with a complete copy of their paystubs.

Do The Fraud Provisions Of The Workers' Compensation Act Apply to Employers?

Yes; it is important to remember that the fraud provisions of the Workers' Compensation Act apply to employers as well as employees. Accordingly, if the employer knowingly reports incorrect information to the workers' compensation carrier, to deny a legitimate claim, the employer could potentially be charged with a crime in the fourth degree, and subjected to civil penalties and attorneys' fees.

Who Pays the Workers' Compensation Benefits?

If an employer has a valid workers' compensation insurance policy, then the insurance carrier alone will be held responsible for the payment of benefits to the injured worker. However, if an employee is a minor, insurance coverage will only be extended if the employer obtained "working papers" for the minor. If not, the employer could potentially be held directly liable for double benefits to be paid to the underage employee. Accordingly, employers of teenagers must confirm that the appropriate paperwork is kept on file.

Is The Employer Obligated To Provide An Employee With Light Duty Work?

The Workers' Compensation Act does not require employers to accept an injured employee back to the workforce if she is medically unable to perform all of her job duties. However, insurance carriers often encourage employers to offer "light duty" work, in an effort to stop payment of temporary disability benefits. Many businesses financially suffer from such an arrangement, if they are forced to pay a salary to an employee who is unproductive due to injury. An employer may and should stand up to the insurance carrier's efforts to hoist this cost onto its business. Employers generally pay high premiums to the insurance industry and should not be fooled into putting injured employees back to work prematurely, to the detriment of their businesses and the health of their employees. If the employer refuses to offer light duty work, the injured worker will continue to receive temporary disability benefits from the insurance carrier until she is released to return to work full duty, or is discharged from active medical treatment.

Is an Employer Required to Keep an Injured Workers' Position Open?

The Workers' Compensation Act does not prohibit an employer from terminating an employee who is injured during the course of employment. However, it is illegal for an employer to take any adverse employment actions against a worker in retaliation for reporting a work accident or applying for workers' compensation benefits.

Employers should also keep in mind that other state and federal laws may be implicated in the termination of an injured employee. For example, both the federal Americans with Disabilities Act and the New Jersey Law Against Discrimination require employers to provide "reasonable accommodations" to injured workers, which could include unpaid medical leave time, or to hold a position for an employee who is medically unable to perform the "essential functions" of her job. The safest course of action for employers considering the termination of an injured worker is to consult with an attorney who specializes in employment law.

What Should An Employer Do When An Injured Worker Is Medically Released To Return To Work?

When the employee is released to return to work by her doctor the insurance carrier will terminate payment of temporary disability benefits, often the same day. Accordingly, employers should allow the injured worker to return to work as soon as possible. The employer should immediately advise the employee if the position is no longer available because it has been filled or eliminated, so that she may apply for unemployment compensation benefits. On the flip side, employers should immediately advise the workers' compensation carrier of the date when an injured worker returns to work, to avoid the overpayment of temporary disability benefits by the insurance carrier.

CHAPTER 5

THE WORKERS' COMPENSATION CLAIMS PROCESS: STEP BY STEP

The claims process should start immediately after an accident occurs at work. The following is a rudimentary roadmap of a claimant's usual journey through the workers' compensation system:

(1) Report the Accident / Injury

It is sometimes uncomfortable for employees to report a work accident. They may be fearful of being reprimanded for failing to follow safety protocol, or they may not want to be viewed as a "complainer." Get over it! You must report the accident to your supervisor or risk being left with no job and no benefits. If you work for a small company which does not prepare accident reports, keep a diary on your own of the date of the accident, who you told, what you said, and seek medical attention if needed. Injured workers must place employers on notice of an accident within 90 days. The notice may be informal and need not even be in writing. However, if your employer fails to obtain a claim number from a workers' compensation carrier within the first month following an accident, it would be wise to formally place the employer on notice of the accident. Obtaining the employer's accident report is sufficient to prove notice, as well as an emailed response from a supervisor acknowledging the incident.

(2) Request Medical Treatment

You should ask your employer where to schedule an appointment for medical treatment. If you need emergent medical treatment of course, go straight to the emergency room. If your employer thereafter fails to give you any direction, then you may see the doctor of your choice, and obtain a copy of the doctor's notes regarding your injury before leaving the physician's office.

(3) Obtain a Claim Number from the Workers' Compensation Insurance Carrier

After your employer reports the injury to the workers' compensation carrier, the carrier should provide you with a claim number and authorize a doctor. If your employer fails to report the injury, then you should schedule an appointment with a workers' compensation attorney.

Your attorney may report the injury directly to the insurance carrier if your employer fails to do so. The name of the insurance carrier should be posted in a common area at work, such as a lunch room, copy room, or supply room. Every insured employer's workers' compensation carrier is supposed to also be listed online at the website for the New Jersey Compensation, Ratings, and Inspections Bureau, at www.njcrib.com.

If your employer is uninsured, your attorney should file a Motion to Join the Uninsured Employers' Fund ("UEF"). Unfortunately, the UEF only pays medical and temporary disability benefits. It does not pay any permanent disability benefits. The process of obtaining benefits from the UEF is often long and arduous.

(4) Your First Medical Appointment Before Workers' Compensation Assigns a Physician

You may see your own doctor to document your injuries and to obtain a treatment recommendation, until the insurance carrier directs you to a particular physician. If you are forced to make an appointment with your family doctor, it's preferable to ask the doctor refer you to a specialist for treatment of the work-related injuries. You should advise the doctor that the injury is work related, but provide your health insurance as "secondary coverage," if you have it.

Some physicians will actually refuse to provide treatment for work injuries, fearing that their bill will not be paid by health insurance on that basis. However, health insurance may always be utilized as secondary coverage. Accordingly, if your doctor refuses to provide you with at least an initial evaluation, find another doctor!

(5) <u>Contact with the Workers' Compensation Insurance Claims Adjuster</u>

You should receive a letter, or at least a phone call, from a claims adjuster, who is a representative of the workers' compensation insurance carrier. The adjuster may request a statement from you regarding the accident, which you should supply, while keeping your answers short and to the point. Remember that the claims adjuster wields a great deal of power over the medical treatment and benefits you receive, so it is important to treat her respectfully. If the carrier has not yet directed you to a doctor, tell the claims adjuster that you will see your own doctor until she authorizes a workers' compensation physician. If you are unable to work because of the injuries, you should also ask her when she will be sending you a check for temporary disability benefits.

(6) Medical Treatment with the Workers' Compensation Physician

Unfortunately, some physicians who regularly treat injured workers forget that their first obligation is to their patient, and not the workers' compensation insurance carrier. These unscrupulous physicians may care more about pleasing the insurance carrier in order to maintain their referral relationship, than they do about your individual care. You should be mindful of that possible bias when you speak with the doctor.

During the first visit with the workers' compensation physician it is critical to discuss every part of your body which was injured in the accident. It is common for the insurance carrier to limit treatment authorization to a specific body part (i.e.: your right arm). If so, the doctor may completely ignore any other complaint. Do not let that happen! Ask the doctor to confirm that he is able to treat every area of the body which was injured. If she advises you that she is only authorized to treat your right arm, ask her to at least make a note that you are also experiencing pain in another body part (i.e.: your neck). If you feel that you are physically unable to work due to your injuries, you should also ask the doctor for an "out of work" note to provide your employer.

If possible, request a copy of the doctor's notes before leaving each and every medical appointment. It is common for workers' compensation physicians to instruct employees that their records will be forwarded directly to the insurance carrier. However, New Jersey law provides that patients may obtain a copy of all medical records. Do not be shy about reminding the doctor's office that their policy is incorrect. Review the office notes immediately to make sure they are accurate and reflect a history of the work accident. If the office notes contain any errors or omissions, bring them to the doctor's attention right away, and ask him to issue a correction.

For further information regarding medical treatment under the New Jersey Workers' Compensation Act, please refer to Chapter 6.

(7) Temporary Disability Benefits

If the workers' compensation physician takes you out of work, then you are entitled to receive temporary disability benefits of up to 70 percent of your average weekly wage, until the time you're released to return to work, or have been released from active medical treatment. For further information regarding temporary disability please refer to Chapter 7.

(8) Release from Medical Treatment

Once you have been released from authorized medical treatment, your temporary disability benefits will stop, even if you have not been released to return to the same line of work, or if your position is no longer available with the same employer. If you disagree with the assessment of the workers' compensation physician you should seek a second opinion with another doctor. The second opinion doctor's note may be utilized as a basis to obtain more treatment and temporary disability benefits. If you are unable to return to the same job and there is no physician indicating that you need more medical treatment, then you should then apply for unemployment benefits, while searching for alternate employment.

(9) Filing a Claim Petition

In order to preserve your right to receive additional benefits, a Claim Petition must be filed with the Division of Workers' Compensation within two years of the date of the date you were last paid workers' compensation benefits, including medical treatment authorized through the workers' compensation insurance carrier. If no treatment or temporary disability benefits were paid by workers' compensation, the deadline is two years from the date of the accident.

It should be noted that the fact that an employer condoned or even encouraged you to obtain medical treatment after an accident does not mean that the treatment was authorized through workers' compensation. If the medical treatment was paid through health insurance, that treatment generally cannot be used as a basis to extend the two year statute of limitations. The rare exception to this rule is if the employer purposely directed you to utilize health insurance rather than workers' compensation. In such a situation, your attorney may argue that the two-year deadline does begin to run until medical treatment for the injury ended.

Figuring out the deadline for filing occupational claims is more difficult. The general rule is that a Claim Petition must be filed within two years of the date the employee knew or should have known that the injuries occurred as a result of the employment. If there is a question about whether the injury is causally related to your occupation, the safest course of action is to file a Claim Petition within two years of the last date of employment. If the symptoms arose years after the employment ended, the medical records will be critically important in determining whether the Claim Petition was filed on a timely basis. New Jersey Courts have held that the two-year deadline begins when medical records reference the employment as a cause of the injuries.

(10) Permanent Disability Evaluations

Several months after you have been discharged from authorized medical treatment both your attorney and the insurance carrier will schedule you for evaluations with workers' compensation medical experts who will estimate your degree of permanent disability related to the accident. The opinions of the two experts will vary widely, and will set the stage for settlement of your claim. More information is provided regarding permanency evaluations in Chapter 9.

(11) Settlement of Your Permanent Disability Claim

Settlement negotiations may begin once you have been evaluated by experts for both the insurance carrier and your attorney, and both sets of reports have been received. If you are not satisfied with the insurance carrier's settlement offer your attorney may request a conference with the Judge of Compensation. The Judge will review the expert reports and provide a recommendation for settlement. If the parties agree to settle the claim consistent with the Judge's recommendations, then you must appear at a Hearing to place the details of the settlement on the record. Chapter 10 includes a discussion regarding the types of settlements available under New Jersey law, as well as the settlement hearing process.

(12) Trials in the Division of Workers' Compensation

If the parties are unable to reach an agreement regarding all aspects of the claim, the Court will schedule a Trial. At the Trial, the injured worker will testify, as well as the medical experts. Generally, the same Judge who evaluated the claim for settlement will preside over the Trial. There is no jury – only a Judge of Compensation will hear the evidence and issue a decision. Please see Chapter 11 for more information regarding Trials.

(13) Right to Reopen Your Claim

You may not reopen a claim which was resolved on a "lump sum" basis, which is also referred to a "Section 20 award" under the Workers' Compensation Act. However, if you received a judgment or entered into a settlement which includes the right to receive future medical treatment then you may reopen your claim within two years of the date you received your last workers' compensation benefits, including authorized medical treatment. "Reopener" claims are discussed more fully in Chapter 12.

CHAPTER 6

MEDICAL TREATMENT UNDER WORKERS' COMPENSATION

The New Jersey Workers' Compensation Act provides that an employer must provide all medical treatment necessary to "cure and relieve" the effects of a work injury. The employer or its insurance carrier must pay 100% of the medical bills, with no co-payment or deductible owed by the injured worker.

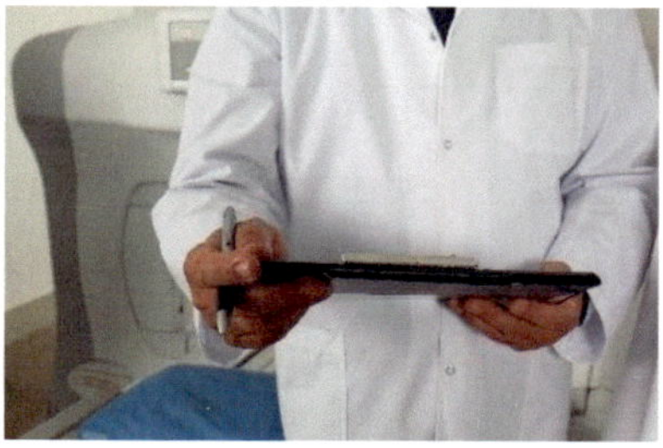

Can You Be Treated by Your Own Doctor?

The insurance carrier has the right to assign a specific physician to treat the work injury. While you may request authorization to be treated by your own doctor, most insurance carriers will not permit ongoing treatment by a personal physician. Some carriers provide injured workers with a list of "network" physicians who are authorized to provide treatment, while others direct treatment to a specific physician.

If the insurance carrier authorizes medical treatment through a particular physician and you reject that treatment, choosing instead to seek treatment with your own physician, you may be held personally liable for those medical bills.

If you fail to advise your physician that the injury occurred at work and the bills are submitted to your health insurer for payment, you could technically be charged with committing insurance fraud. The health insurance carrier may also seek reimbursement for the medical bills, to be paid out of the proceeds of any settlement or judgment you receive from workers' compensation.

If the workers' compensation insurance carrier denied your claim, or failed to assign a physician, you may seek treatment through your health insurance. However, it is advisable to first send a formal request for treatment in writing to the workers' compensation carrier, indicating that unless you are directed to a particular physician you will seek treatment with the physician of your choice. Preferably, you should seek advice from an experienced workers' compensation attorney, who would serve a formal demand for medical treatment upon the insurance carrier.

I Am Afraid to Go to The Doctor Because I Cannot Afford to Pay Medical Bills Which Are Not Paid by Workers' Compensation Insurance.

An injured employee is not personally liable for medical treatment which was authorized under workers' compensation. It is illegal for a medical provider to sue a patient for unpaid medical bills which are the subject of a workers' compensation claim. If you are receiving medical benefits through workers' compensation it is advisable to check your credit scores periodically, to make sure that your credit has not been negatively affected by a carrier's failure to pay your medical bills on a timely basis. If a physician files a small claims action against you, or reports an unpaid bill to the credit agencies, your attorney should forward a letter reminding the doctor that all medical bills are the responsibility of the workers' compensation carrier and no "balance billing" is permitted under New Jersey law.

Special Considerations for Recipients of Medicare/Medicaid

If your medical coverage is through Medicare/Medicaid, federal law provides that the parties must check with those federal programs before settling any claim, in order to determine whether the government paid any claims related to the work accident. If so, Medicare/Medicaid must be reimbursed out of the proceeds of any settlement, if the workers' compensation carrier is not held responsible for the payment of the lien.

Can I Trust the Workers' Compensation Doctor?

The short answer is that it depends upon the doctor. There are many physicians in New Jersey who have ongoing business relationships with workers' compensation carriers, and it is their financial interest to keep the insurance carriers satisfied, to ensure the assignment of the next "customer". Some of these physicians forget that their patient is the injured worker and not the insurance carrier. You must strive to make the workers' compensation physician your advocate to the insurance carrier by clearly communicating your injuries and physical complaints. It may seem silly, but if your doctor likes you and believes you, he is more likely to advocate on your behalf. On the other hand, if you are a difficult patient to deal with (demanding, nasty, or seem to be embellishing your injuries), it is doubtful that a physician or his staff will go the extra mile for you. Never forget that doctors are human beings, with their own set of biases.

How Important Is Your Medical History in A Workers' Compensation Case When You Have Suffered from An Injury in The Past?

Even if you have an entirely unrelated prior injury to a different body part you should still inform your physician of your complete medical history. If you fail to provide a complete history you may be accused of trying to "cover-up" a prior injury. Take care though, not to over-emphasis a prior ache or pain which was not serious enough to warrant a trip to the doctor. Generally speaking, if a prior injury was not significant enough to warrant medical attention, you do not need to bring it up.

If I Had an Injury in The Past and Re-Injured The Same Body Part At Work Will My Medical History Be Used to Deny Me Benefits?

Absolutely; the insurance carrier will seek to limit or even deny a claim on the basis of a prior injury. If you sustained a prior injury to the same part of the body it is critical to obtain all medical records regarding the prior injury, to demonstrate your prior condition at the time you were discharged from treatment. Do <u>not</u> attempt to hide your prior injury. If you do fail to acknowledge a prior injury, you could be accused of fraud. That being said, if you disclose a prior injury for which medical treatment was sought, having a prior injury alone is not a basis upon which a workers' compensation carrier may legitimately deny medical treatment. However, your workers' compensation permanent disability award will be reduced by the percentage your condition is deemed to be pre-existing.

What If the Workers' Compensation Physician Recommends Surgery and I Do Not Want It?

You have the right to reject any medical treatment which you do not want. However, unless you are under active medical treatment, you are not entitled to receive workers' compensation temporary disability benefits. Accordingly, if the authorized physician recommends surgery, you should first inquire about whether less invasive measures could provide you with relief. If you have already gone through conservative treatment, such as physical therapy, medication, and/or injections, and the doctor advises that surgery is the only remaining option, then you are faced with an important decision. You may either go forward with the surgery or request a second opinion through workers' compensation. The majority of insurance carriers will gladly schedule an appointment for a second opinion, which is much less costly than paying for surgery. However, there is a risk that the second opinion examination will be scheduled with a physician who will not truly provide an independent opinion, and will merely provide the carrier with a perfunctory report indicating that no further medical treatment is necessary.

What Is the Proper Role of a Nurse Case Manager?

In cases involving serious injuries, the insurance carrier will often assign a "nurse case manager," who should not be confused with the "claims adjuster." All workers' compensation claimants are assigned a claims adjuster, whose responsibility is to investigate the accident, issue temporary disability benefits, direct medical treatment, gather medical records, and to negotiate the ultimate settlement of the claim. If the injuries are complex, the claims adjuster may request

the assistance of a nurse case manager, who will handle communications between the injured worker, the physician, and the insurance carrier.

There are some kind and decent nurse case managers out there. However, you should never forget that the nurse case manager is a representative of the insurance carrier, and her first allegiance is to the carrier. Her goal is simply to save the insurance carrier money on the claim by limiting expensive medical treatment and facilitating your return to work as soon as possible. Therefore, you must take care when communicating with the nurse case manager not to disclose unnecessary information which may be used against you.

It is unfortunately quite common for nurse case managers to pressure doctors into prematurely releasing patients from medical treatment and/or to return to work. You may make it more difficult for the nurse case manager to put undue pressure on your physician by insisting on your right to privacy during medical appointments. Under no circumstances should you allow the nurse case manager to accompany you into the examination room during visits with your physician. The nurse case manager's role should be limited to scheduling medical appointments, and facilitating the authorization of medical testing and procedures.

What Is An "Independent Medical Examination" and How Does It Affect Medical Treatment?

The term independent medical examination ("IME") is really a misnomer. The physician who performs such an examination is anything but "independent," in that he is merely a hired gun of the carrier. It would be more accurate to refer to this carrier tool as a "defense medical examination." Such examinations are often scheduled by insurance claims adjusters to provide them with the opinion that they want to hear, which is that no further treatment is necessary and/or related to the work accident.

If the carrier believes that the authorized physician is over-treating the patient, or is not returning him to work quickly enough, the carrier may choose to schedule an IME. New Jersey law gives carriers the right to schedule such examinations as often as they deem necessary. The purpose of the IME may be to direct the treatment to a more appropriate medical expert. Unfortunately though, more often than not the IME is specifically scheduled to create a basis for cutting off medical and/or temporary disability benefits to an injured worker.

Unless there is a reason to question the competence of the authorized treating physician, some workers' compensation attorneys refuse to allow their clients to attend an IME prior to being discharged from the authorized treating physicians. The decision of whether or not to attend an IME is a strategic one. The law provides the carrier with the right to schedule these exams, and if a claimant refuses to attend such an exam his benefits may be terminated. However, if the independent medical consultant finds that no further treatment is necessary or related to the accident, the carrier may terminate further benefits on that basis anyway. If benefits are terminated following an IME the claimant's attorney should file a "Motion for Medical and Temporary Benefits." The Court will generally accept the opinion of the authorized treating physician, who followed the patient over a course of time, over the opinion of an "independent" expert who performed a cursory examination.

What Is A "Functional Capacity Evaluation," and Should I Attend One?

A Functional Capacity Evaluation ("FCE") consists of a series of physical tests conducted by a therapist, to measure a claimant's ability to perform tasks necessary for employment. Many attorneys refuse to allow their clients to attend FCEs, since the results may be manipulated and are often used to force claimants to return to work prematurely. If the workers' compensation carrier schedules an FCE while you are still under medical treatment and has not yet been released to return to work by the doctor, there is absolutely no reason for you to attend the FCE. However, you must be aware of the dangers of refusing to attend it outright. If you refuse to attend the FCE, the claims adjuster may accuse you of failing to cooperate with medical treatment and terminate your benefits on that basis. An aggressive workers' compensation attorney will remind the adjuster that an FCE does not cure or relieve any symptoms, so it therefore does not fall under the category of medical treatment.

In order to avoid a confrontation on this issue, if your doctor anticipates releasing you from care in 4-6 weeks anyway, another tactic is to simply reschedule the FCE until you have been medically cleared to return to work. At that point, if your employer requires you to attend an FCE in to determine your permanent work restrictions, you should cooperate with the FCE if you wish to continue working with that employer.

What if the Workers' Compensation Carrier Fails to Pay Bills for Authorized Medical Treatment?

Whenever you appear for an appointment for authorized medical treatment you should provide the claim number of the workers' compensation carrier, and direct all bills to be sent to that carrier. If a claim number has not yet been assigned you should provide the name of your employer. You will not be turned away at

the emergency room just because a claim number has not been assigned, or if the cause of the injury is in dispute.

If you provide the workers' compensation claim number and continue to receive bills from medical providers, you should call the billing office of the hospital or physician to confirm that the bills are being submitted to the workers' compensation carrier. Forward the bills to the workers' compensation carrier, with a copy to your attorney. If the treatment was authorized, the final Court Order Approving Settlement or Judgment will include a provision indicating that all bills for authorized medical treatment were paid, or will be paid by the workers' compensation carrier.

You should not discontinue your medical treatment out of fear that your medical bills are not being paid. As long as the medical treatment was authorized through workers' compensation the bills will be paid. It is unlawful in New Jersey for medical providers to seek payment from workers' compensation claimants or "balance bill" them. If you receive a collection's notice you should check your credit score to make that the outstanding bill has not been reported to the credit agencies. If the medical bill appears on your credit report than you should write a letter to the credit agencies, explaining that the bill was the responsibility of the workers' compensation insurance carrier, and enclose a copy of the letter you received from the carrier directing you to treat with that physician, as well as the Claim Petition filed with the Division of Workers' Compensation. It is advisable to send this information to the three major credit agencies: Equifax, Experian, and TransUnion. As of the writing of this manual, the credit agencies may be reached at the following addresses:

Equifax Credit Information Services, LLC
P.O. Box 740241, Atlanta, GA 30374
866-349-5186: Dispute Credit Report Items

Experian National Consumer Assistance Center
P.O. Box 4500, Allen, TX 75013
800-509-8495: Dispute Credit Report Items

TransUnion Consumer Relations
P.O. Box 2000, Chester, PA 19016-2000
800-916-8800: Disputes Items & Status Checks

If you are served with a Summons and Complaint, seeking collection of a bill for authorized treatment, you should immediately provide it to your workers' compensation attorney. Your attorney should file a Motion to Dismiss the Complaint filed by the medical provider, on the basis that the issue of medical treatment is within the sole jurisdiction of the Division of Workers' Compensation.

The medical providers also have a direct remedy against the workers' compensation carrier. In New Jersey, physicians have the right to file their own claim for the payment of medical bills in the Division of Workers' Compensation.

CHAPTER 7

TEMPORARY DISABILITY - WAGE REPLACEMENT BENEFITS

The New Jersey Workers' Compensation Act provides that temporary disability benefits equaling 70% of the employee's gross average weekly wages (up to the state maximum rate) shall be paid if the employee is unable to work as a result of a work accident, until he has reached maximum medical improvement from treatment.

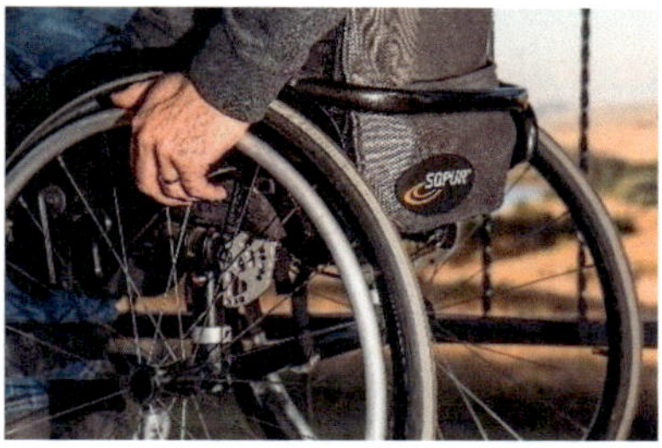

How Long After a Workers' Compensation Claim Is Filed Will an Employee Begin Receiving Wage Replacement for Time Out of Work?

Temporary disability benefits are payable when the employee is out of work for seven consecutive days, although it often takes longer for the insurance carrier to actually administer the benefits. In other words, if you are sent back to work by your doctor in less than a week, you are not entitled to receive workers' compensation lost wage benefits. Once seven days has passed though, benefits are payable starting on the first day you were unable to work.

How Can I Prove That I Am Unable to Return to Work?

After an accident or injury occurs at work, it is not enough to just advise your employer that you do not feel well, and need to take off a few days to recover from work, in order to collect temporary disability benefits. Of course, if your company has a sick leave policy, you may be entitled to receive sick pay, even without a doctor's note. However, you may not collect workers' compensation temporary disability unless you receive an "out of work" note from a doctor, who confirms that your inability to work is related to the work accident. You should transmit the medical note to your employer, but be sure to keep a copy of it.

How is the Temporary Disability Rate Calculated?

In order to figure out if the workers' compensation carrier is paying you at the correct temporary disability rate you must first calculate your "average weekly wage," including overtime. Take a look at your paystub. Do you make the same amount every week or does your salary vary? If you earn an annual salary, your weekly wage should be the same every week. Your temporary disability rate is thus easy to compute at 70% of your gross weekly wage before tax.

If your wages vary every week, your rate is based upon your average earnings, which is generally, although not always computed over the six (6) month period immediately prior to the date of the accident. It is recommended that you gather all of your paystubs for the last twenty-six (26) weeks prior to the accident, in order to compute your average pre-tax wage. Do not count the week of the accident if you only worked a partial week due to your injuries. Likewise, if you took an unpaid leave during that six (6) month period, do not include those weeks when calculating your average wage. It is common for insurance carriers to mistakenly include these unpaid weeks, which thereby lowers your rate unfairly. However, you cannot exclude those weeks in which you simply worked less hours, just as the carrier cannot exclude those weeks when you worked more overtime than usual.

What is the Significance of the New Jersey Maximum and Minimum Temporary Disability Rates?

If you are a high wage earner, your temporary disability benefits are capped at the State maximum rate. In 2018, the maximum rate in New Jersey is $903/week. Some employers may voluntarily offer to pay the difference between the workers' compensation rate and your salary.

However, they are not required to do so. Speak with your human resources department to inquire about whether your company offers such a benefit.

If you earn only the minimum wage and/or work part-time, you may be entitled to receive more than your average weekly wage if you are hurt on the job and unable to work. New Jersey law establishes a *minimum* weekly rate, which may exceed your part-time wages. In 2018, the minimum rate in New Jersey is $241/week.

What Happens If the Doctor Puts Me Back to Work on a Light Duty Basis?

The workers' compensation carrier may encourage the physician to release you back to work, at least on a light duty basis. While you are still receiving medical treatment, you should provide the doctor with a copy of your job description. You should explain exactly what job duties you feel that you cannot perform due to your injury. If the doctor releases you to return to work on a light duty basis, ask him to write down your limitations with as much specificity as possible, such as: no bending, no overhead work, no use of machinery, no lifting over a certain weight, or mandatory breaks every 30 minutes.

If you are placed on light duty, then you should bring a copy of the "return to work" note with restrictions to your supervisor or human resources department. If your employer does not offer light duty work, ask your supervisor to provide you with a written note to that effect. If no light duty work is available, then your temporary disability benefits should continue until you are released to return to work full duty *or* you have been discharged from medical treatment.

What Steps Should I Take If My Supervisor Directs Me to Perform Tasks in Excess of the Light Duty Restrictions Listed by the Workers' Compensation Doctor?

If your employer does have a light duty work program, then you must attempt to return to work, since your temporary disability benefits will be terminated. Given the difficult job market, it is advisable to make yourself useful to the company when you return. However, do not be afraid to refuse to perform a task which clearly requires you to perform work in excess of the light duty restrictions set forth by your physician. Keep a copy of your light duty note with you at work, and politely remind your supervisor that you need to follow your doctor's orders to avoid reinjuring yourself.

At the next doctor's visit following your return to work, you should discuss the activities which you have been requested to perform at work, and explain the symptoms you are experiencing as a result. Ask the physician to make a note if you are being forced to work beyond your light duty restrictions. The doctor will hopefully either reiterate that the light duty restrictions must be enforced, or give you a new "out of work" note.

If your supervisor continually requests that you perform tasks in excess of your physical capabilities, then you should keep a log of those activities to refresh your memory in the event it is necessary to explain these examples to the Court in the future. Your attorney should send a letter to the carrier explaining that the light duty restrictions are not being respected by your employer, and requesting the resumption of temporary disability benefits until light duty work is provided. If it is too difficult for the company to provide continued light duty work, your employer should so advise the insurance carrier. If you anticipate being able to work full duty in the future, it may also be helpful for your attorney to forward a letter to the employer, or the employer's attorney, reminding the company that it must merely advise the insurance carrier if it has become too difficult from a business perspective to provide you with continued light duty work, thereby triggering the recommencement of temporary disability benefits. However, if it appears that you may be permanently be restricted to working light duty, and you want to keep your job, it may not be the best long-term strategy for you to discourage your employer from offering work which is truly light duty in nature.

I Returned to College After My Injury. Am I Still Entitled to Receive Temporary Disability Benefits?

Generally, if you return to school on a full-time basis then you are not entitled to receive continued temporary disability benefits, on the basis that you have removed yourself from the workforce. However, if you are able to prove that you worked at the same time that you attended college prior to the injury, an argument may be made that you are entitled to receive temporary disability benefits. Unfortunately, the law is unclear on this issue and you should consult with a workers' compensation attorney about your particular circumstances.

What Should I Do if the Workers' Compensation Doctor Prematurely Sends Me Back to Work Full Duty?

If you are released to return to work full duty then you should at least attempt to return to work, even if you do not feel able to do so. If you try to work and cannot perform your job duties, advise your employer if you experience additional pain while working. If you are "written up," for failing to perform certain physical activities due to your injuries you should obtain a copy of that report, and immediately forward a copy of it to your attorney.

If you have not exhausted all medical options available to enable you to work at your pre-injury level, then you should request to return to the workers' compensation physician. Explain to the doctor what occurred when you performed a particular activity at work, and why you feel that you need more time off to recuperate. If the doctor recommends additional treatment to help you improve function and directs you to postpone returning to work, then you are entitled to receive continued temporary disability benefits.

If the insurance carrier ignores your request, then you may seek a second opinion through your health insurance, to determine whether you need additional treatment. Remember, you are only entitled to receive temporary disability if you are unable to work and are receiving active medical treatment. Your attorney may utilize the office note of your second opinion doctor to file a "Motion for

Medical and Temporary Disability Benefits." See, Appendix B. The downside to using a treating medical doctor is that it is difficult and expensive to persuade a doctor with an active medical practice to testify in Court on your behalf. However, at least obtaining such a report can get your attorney in front of a Judge of Compensation, to discuss your injuries. If you do not have health insurance, then your attorney may send you to an independent medical examiner who may also provide such a report, although that doctor would not render medical treatment. Such experts may charge up to $600 for the examination and a report. The benefit of using an independent medical examiner is that he usually has more experienced testifying in Court, and it is practically easier and less expensive to get such an expert into the courthouse, as opposed to a doctor who treats patients on a daily basis.

Are There Any Lost Wage Benefits Available After Workers' Compensation Stops Payment of Temporary Disability Benefits?

Yes, there is an alternate source for you to obtain some financial relief if your workers' compensation temporary disability benefits are terminated and you are medically unable to return to work. Your employer may have purchased a disability plan through a private insurance company, or you may be qualified to receive benefits through the State if New Jersey. You should ask your company's human resources department whether the company's disability insurance is through a "state plan" or a "private plan." If your company purchased a private plan, you must apply for benefits through that insurance company.

If your employer is covered by a state plan, you may qualify for state temporary disability insurance benefits [hereinafter referred to as "TDI"], if you have earned the threshold amount of wages in New Jersey covered employment during the 52 weeks immediately prior to the date your disability began. You must have earned at least $168 per week in the last 20 weeks, OR earned at least $8,400 during the year in which the disability occurred to qualify for benefits.

You may apply for TDI benefits while you are waiting for the Division of Workers' Compensation to hear the Motion for Temporary Disability Benefits which your attorney filed on your behalf. Please note that filing a Motion for Temporary Disability Benefits is not a prerequisite for obtaining TDI benefits. However, it is advisable to file a Motion in order to increase the chances of forcing the workers' compensation carrier to pay the lien which will ultimately be placed on your workers' compensation case by the State of New Jersey, for the benefits it paid to you.

The quickest way to obtain TDI benefits is to file an online application. If you do not have internet access, you may mail your completed Application to the Division of Temporary Disability Insurance / P.O. Box 387 / Trenton, NJ 08625-0387 /Fax: 609-984-4138. See, Appendix C for sample Application.

The current Application for State TDI benefits contains three parts. You must complete Part A of the Application. Your physician must complete the Certification found in Part B. You should ask your employer to complete Part C of the Application, which lists your wages in the ten (10) week period immediately prior to your disability. If your employer refuses to complete their portion of the Application you may write "Employer Uncooperative" on Part C, and instead attach a copy of your paystubs over the last ten (10) weeks.

The New Jersey Division of Temporary Disability Insurance provides lost wage benefits for qualified individuals who are unable to work due to non-occupational causes. Accordingly, if your disability is related to a work injury your application for TDI benefits will initially be denied. Do not be alarmed. Upon receipt of a denial, you must simply complete a "Certification of Contested Workers' Compensation Claim" form. See, Appendix D. In order to qualify for TDI benefits, your attorney must first file a Claim Petition in the Division of Workers' Compensation, and provide you with the Claim Petition number which must be noted in the Certification form. The State will then assert a lien for any benefits it paid on your behalf, to be paid out of the proceeds of any award you obtain in the Division of Workers' Compensation.

State TDI pays qualified applicants two-thirds (2/3) of their average wage, up to a maximum benefit rate which changes annually. The maximum weekly benefit rate is $633 for disabilities which begin on or after January 1, 2017. There is a seven (7) day waiting period before you are eligible to receive benefits, and TDI benefits are available for up to six months, as long as a physician continues to certify that you are unable to work.

I Worked at Two Different Jobs at the Time of My Work Accident. How Do I Obtain Compensation for Lost Wages at My Second Job?

With stagnant wages these days, many people find it necessary to work at a second job in order to make ends meet. But what happens if you get hurt at one job, and can't work at the other because of your injury? Workers' compensation will only pay wage replacement benefits for the job in which you were injured. You may apply for benefits from the State of New Jersey if you are disabled from working at the second job. However, there are many exceptions and pitfalls to be aware of when collecting both workers' compensation and State temporary disability benefits [hereinafter referred to as "TDI"].

When applying for TDI benefits for part-time employment, you must take special care in completing Part A of the Application. You must indicate on the form whether or not the injury was caused by your employment. This question continues to cause much confusion for applicants with multiple jobs, in which only one job caused the injury. Some attorneys advise their clients to check off "no" to this answer, if the injury was not caused by the specific job for which you are claiming benefits, but to add a note clarifying that the injury is related to your job with a completely different employer. The reason for going through this seemingly unnecessary step is to avoid the bureaucratic red tape which will be unleashed if the injury is listed as work related, to avoid the State from paying you duplicate benefits. If your injury is reported as work-related, then you must list all of your employments at the time the disability arose, so that all of your wages are taken into account to compute your TDI rate. Your rate will then be reduced by the amount you receive for workers' compensation. Unfortunately, the State continues to mistakenly place TDI liens on the unrelated workers' compensation case. Your attorney must then try to persuade the State to lift the lien, resulting in unnecessary delays at the time of settlement.

What Is the Maximum Amount of Time That I May Collect Temporary Disability Benefits Through Workers' Compensation?

Temporary disability benefits are, by their very nature, "temporary." The maximum period of time that you may collect temporary disability benefits is 450 weeks (approximately 8.5 years). However, you must be under active medical treatment during this time period in order to qualify for continued lost wage benefits. In order to be considered "active," the medical treatment must help you progress towards an increase in function, not just alleviate your symptoms temporarily. For instance, injections, physical therapy, or surgical intervention are all modalities which constitute active medical treatment. Going back to your doctor once every three months for prescription medication is generally <u>not</u> sufficient to constitute active medical treatment, to qualify you for continued temporary disability benefits. Accordingly, you should use the time you are out of work wisely by considering other occupations and job opportunities in order to prepare yourself to return to the workforce.

My Employer Offered to Accept Me Back to Work on a Light Duty Basis, But Is Only Providing Me with a Few Hours of Work.

It is common for the workers' compensation carrier to pressure employers into providing a light duty return to work program, even when employers practically do not have such work to offer. If your employer is only able to find a few hours of light duty work for you to perform then you are entitled to receive continued temporary disability benefits which are reduced by the partial salary you are paid by your employer. Unfortunately, many workers' compensation carriers will immediately suspend benefits as soon as the employee returns to work, even if it is only for a few hours. You should provide your attorney with a copy of your paystub, proving that you are not being paid your pre-accident wages for the light duty work. The insurance carrier is obligated to pay you the difference between your part time wages and your workers' compensation rate. If your part-time salary exceeds your temporary disability rate then you are not entitled to any additional benefits from workers' compensation.

What If the Workers' Compensation Doctor Indicates That I Can Never Return to Full Duty Work?

Temporary disability benefits will be terminated once you have reached "maximum medical improvement" from treatment, even if you cannot return to work full duty or even to the same line of work. The New Jersey Law Against Discrimination and the federal American with Disabilities Act require employers to offer "reasonable accommodations" for your disability. A reasonable accommodation may include providing you with help lifting heavy items, allowing you to stand and stretch periodically, or installing an ergonomic keyboard. Keep in mind though, that an employer cannot be forced to keep you on the payroll if you are unable to perform the essential functions of your job.

If you believe that your employer may make simple accommodations for you which would allow you to do your job, without disrupting the business, you should ask your doctor to provide you with a note indicating that such an accommodation is necessary. If your employer refuses to make these adjustments which will permit you to keep working, without disrupting the business, then you should consult with an attorney who specializes in employment law. The Division of Workers' Compensation does not have jurisdiction to decide these issues.

Will The Workers' Compensation Carrier Pay For Me To Obtain Retraining In Another Occupation If I Cannot Return To The Same Type Of Job?

The New Jersey Workers' Compensation Act does not require your employer or the insurance carrier to provide you with retraining. If you are not ready or financially able to retire, you should make plans to start a new career. The New Jersey Division of Vocational Rehabilitation Services ("DVRS") does provide some limited assistance. DVRS provides counseling, training, assistance with job searching and placement. You may contact your local DVRS office to schedule an appointment for an initial interview, at which time your eligibility for services will be evaluated. See, Appendix E, for a list of DVRS field offices.

CHAPTER 8

THE INTERPLAY BETWEEN WORKERS' COMPENSATION AND UNEMPLOYMENT BENEFITS

Both the temporary disability and unemployment programs provide "lost wage" benefits, but for very different reasons. You are generally qualified to receive temporary disability benefits if the authorized physician indicates that you are medically unable to return to work and are receiving active medical treatment. By contrast, you are only eligible for unemployment benefits if you were terminated from your job and you are ready, willing, and able to work. In addition, you must have worked within the last two years to qualify for unemployment benefits. Accordingly, unemployment is not an option for the long-term disabled, who should apply for social security disability.

What Happens If I Return to Work but I Am Fired Because I Am Physically Unable to Do My Job?

You should apply for unemployment benefits if the authorized workers' compensation physician indicates that you are medically able to return to work but you are fired because you cannot physically perform all of your job duties. Your attorney may also use your termination as evidence that the workers' compensation physician sent you back to work prematurely. However, you would not be entitled to receive additional temporary disability benefits unless you are able to prove that you also require further medical treatment.

If you return to active medical treatment, it is common for physicians to neglect to provide you with an "out of work" note given that you are unemployed. Do not allow your doctor to ignore this issue. In fact, there is no reason for you to volunteer to the doctor that you are collecting unemployment. Rather, remind the doctor of your chosen profession, and explain how you had difficulty performing your job duties. Ask your physician to comment on your ability to work. If the physician indicates that you cannot work in your chosen profession, and you need further medical treatment, then the carrier should resume payment of temporary workers' compensation benefits and your unemployment benefits must stop. If there is any overlap between the temporary disability benefits and unemployment you must reimburse the Division of Unemployment.

If you quit your job, you are not entitled to receive unemployment benefits. Accordingly, do not quit, even if you feel that the physical demands of your job would be too much for you. If your physician released you to return to work you should attempt to do so, to avoid the argument that you abandoned your job. Otherwise, you may be caught in the unfortunate position of being ineligible for either temporary disability or unemployment.

You should attempt to return to work, and take note of those tasks which you have difficulty performing. You know your own body better than any doctor. Although you should try to work, if it is obvious that to continue with a given task will cause you further injury, then stop and inform your supervisor that you need help. You should then return to the doctor if possible to report your progress. Even if you did not receive an official "light duty" note, your employers may try to accommodate you. If not, and you are physically unable to do your job, then it is preferable for you to be fired, rather than quit, so that you may collect unemployment benefits. The bottom line is that you should not resign unless you have another position lined up.

What If I Return to Active Medical Treatment While I Am Collecting Unemployment Benefits?

If your employer terminates you because you were unable to perform the essential functions of your position, you may initially apply for unemployment benefits. You should then request a return visit to the workers' compensation physician, and explain that you attempted to return to work as he recommended but were unable to perform your job duties. Tell the doctor exactly what tasks you had difficulty executing. If you did not do so previously, provide the physician with a copy of the job description from your employer, and ask him to reconsider whether there is any treatment available which could improve your function enough, to allow you to perform your job. You must emphatically express to the doctor that your aim is to return to the same line of work, and you are counting on him to help you so that you may return to work. If an authorized workers' compensation physician indicates that additional medical treatment would help to improve your condition and that you are either unable to work or can only work light duty which is not available, then the workers' compensation carrier should resume payment of temporary disability benefits, since you are no longer eligible for unemployment benefits.

As Long as I Am Being Paid, What Difference Does It Make If I Collect Unemployment Instead of Workers' Compensation?

Unfortunately, there are many applicants who collect unemployment when they are physically unable to work because there is no medical proof that they are disabled, and they are ineligible for workers' compensation benefits since they are no longer receiving active medical treatment. Unemployment runs out quickly, so you should be diligent in your search for work and consider accepting positions which are outside of your field, even if it means taking a substantial pay cut. You may be eligible for partial unemployment if you take a part time job. From a long-term perspective, it is preferable for you to try different jobs and stay in the workforce, then to wait for the perfect job opportunity.

If you collect unemployment benefits in New Jersey for the maximum number of weeks (currently 26 weeks), your benefits will end unless there is federal extension program in place, during periods of high unemployment. It is very difficult to persuade a workers' compensation carrier to restart temporary disability benefits once you fall into the category of long-term unemployed. For this reason, if your condition worsens while you are receiving unemployment benefits it would be wise for you to return to the workers' compensation doctor before your unemployment runs out. If the doctor indicates that you are disabled and additional medical treatment could improve your function, then you should stop collecting unemployment and your attorney should ask the workers' compensation carrier to restart temporary disability benefits. The fact that you were receiving unemployment benefits will prove that you "lost wages," because of your injury, thereby entitling you to receive temporary disability benefits again.

What if I Am Denied Unemployment Benefits?

Your employer may challenge your unemployment application if you were fired "for cause." You cannot be denied unemployment if you were terminated because you were physically unable to perform your job due to your injuries. You should hire an attorney who specializes in unemployment appeals to fight on your behalf if your employer tries to block your application. Besides the short term problem of being left with no source of income, the denial of unemployment benefits may have long-term implications. If the Division of Unemployment finds that you were terminated "for cause," and you do not find alternate employment, then the workers' compensation carrier will likely deny payment of temporary disability benefits should you be taken out of work in the future due to your injury, on the basis that you have not proven a loss of wages.

CHAPTER 9

PARTIAL PERMANENT DISABILITY

Your attorney cannot move forward with a settlement of your claim until you have completed curative medical treatment (in other words – additional care is not going to make you better). Once a physician determines that you have reached maximum medical improvement ("MMI") from treatment, the next phase of your workers' compensation claim then begins: the process of establishing your permanent disability rating.

This phase of the case is often the most difficult financially for the employee who has sustained significant injuries and is unable to return to the workforce. Unless it is absolutely clear that you are totally, permanently disabled, there will be a delay between the time you last collect temporary disability benefits, and when the carrier starts payment of permanent disability benefits.

What Is A Permanent Disability?

The New Jersey Workers' Compensation Act defines a "permanent disability" as follows:

. . . a permanent impairment caused by a compensable accident or compensable occupational disease, based upon demonstrable objective medical evidence, which restricts the function of the body or of its members or organs; included in the criteria which shall be considered

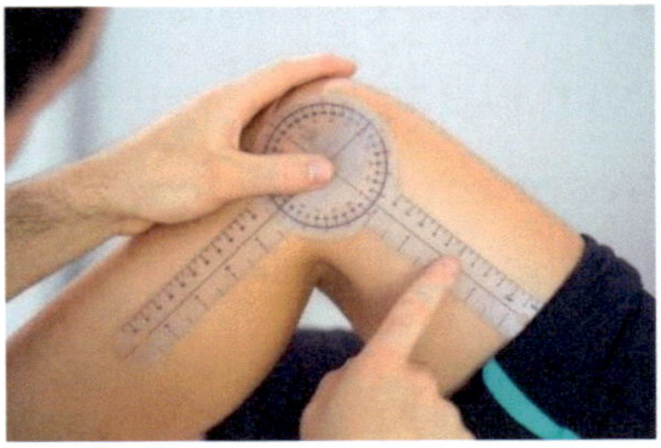

shall be whether there has been a lessening to a material degree of an employee's working ability. Subject to the above provisions, nothing in this definition shall be construed to preclude benefits to a worker who returns to work following a compensable accident even if there be no reduction in earnings. . . ." N.J.S.A. 34:15-36.

Accordingly, you may be entitled to receive an award of partial permanent disability benefits if you suffer from a loss of function, even if you returned to work at the same job.

What is the Process for Determining Permanent Disability?

In order to establish your permanent disability level you will be examined by "independent" medical experts familiar with the New Jersey workers' compensation schedule. The insurance carrier may insist upon waiting six months from the date you are released from active medical treatment to schedule you for a permanency evaluation with its medical expert. The carrier might want to delay scheduling a permanency evaluation to give your body further time to heal and improve function. The claims adjuster will also need time to collect your medical records to provide them to the medical expert.

The workers' compensation insurance carrier may never schedule you for such an examination if you are not represented by an attorney, since the carrier is not required to pay you partial permanent disability benefits. In fact, the vast majority of people who are hurt at work never take advantage of collecting permanent disability benefits since they return to work and the insurance carrier never advises them that they may be entitled to a permanency award. Accordingly, to ensure that you receive a fair award of permanent disability benefits, it is crucial for you to retain a competent workers' compensation attorney.

If you are represented by an attorney, you will be scheduled for permanency evaluations with experts retained by both your attorney and the insurance carrier.

There are a limited number of workers' compensation experts in the State of New Jersey who are familiar with the workers' compensation disability ratings system. Accordingly, you may need to travel across the state to attend these examinations.

The medical experts on both sides will exaggerate and usually have widely divergent opinions regarding your level of disability. For example, it is common for the injured workers' expert to evaluate a disability at over 50% partial total, while the carrier's expert finds zero disability. When both sets of reports have been completed, they will be utilized to negotiate a settlement of your partial permanent disability claim.

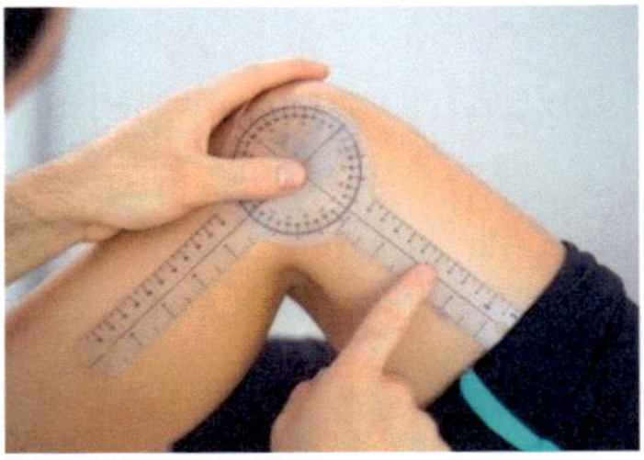

If I Live Out of State Now Am I Required to Return to New Jersey to Attend Permanency Exams?

You are not required to remain in the State of New Jersey to pursue a workers' compensation claim. However, before moving out of state, you should keep in mind that you must return to New Jersey to be evaluated by medical experts who are familiar with the state disability schedule, if you wish to be compensated for your permanent disability. The insurance carrier is not required to cover the cost of you to travel back to the state.

What Is the Cost Associated with Attending a Permanency Examination?

The Workers' Compensation Act currently provides that medical experts retained by injured workers may charge a maximum fee of $600 for an examination and report. This capped fee has discouraged many physicians from conducting workers' compensation examinations. The insurance carrier bears the cost of the examination and report of its own medical expert. There is no cap placed on the amount an insurance carrier may spend on its medical experts, who may charge thousands of dollars for an examination and report. Attorneys representing injured workers, including the author, continue to lobby the state legislature to reverse this inequity.

Most medical experts who perform examinations on behalf of injured workers represent Petitioners exclusively. Some of these experts will wait for their fee to be paid until a settlement is reached on the claim, while others require their $600 fee to be paid at the time of the appointment. If you are out of work and unable to afford the expert's fee, you should ask your attorney to pay the upfront fee, with the understanding that she will be reimbursed at the time of settlement. However, if you are back to work, there are many attorneys who expect their clients to have some "skin in the game," by covering this cost, given that the attorney works without payment until a settlement is reached.

What Should I Bring to the Permanency Examinations?

It is the responsibility of the insurance carrier to provide copies of your medical records to their expert, and your attorney should likewise send all records to the petitioner's expert in advance of the appointment. Accordingly, there is usually no need for you to bring extra copies, unless your attorney directed you to bring new records she was unable to obtain in time for the appointment.

It is important, however, to bring all of your x-rays and/or MRI films of the injury with you to the examinations. If you had a pre-existing injury, you should also bring any prior films with you to the appointment, for the expert to compare. If you fail to bring the MRI films with you to the appointment, the results of the examination may be inconclusive, or the expert's opinion may be easily undermined. If the expert does not have the benefit of the MRI films, you may need to deliver them after the exam, and incur the cost of a supplemental report from your own expert. A settlement of your case will also be delayed if you fail to bring the films with you to the permanency examinations.

If you have a difficult time recalling the names of the medication you are taking for your injury, it is advisable to either make a list of them, or bring the medications with you to the permanency examinations. Even if you are not currently taking prescription medications, you should tell the experts how often you take over-the-counter pain relievers.

If you do not speak English, or if you have a heavy accent and it may be difficult for the doctor to understand you, then you should bring an interpreter to the examination. You may also bring a loved one or friend for "moral support," and to be a witness to the examination by the insurance carrier's expert, which could be beneficial if a Trial is necessary in your case.

How Should I Prepare for My Permanency Examinations?

Prior to your appointment, you should give some thought to your physical complaints and limitations. Since you will only have a limited opportunity to communicate with the doctor, you should be prepared to succinctly explain your pain to him, and what activities you are unable to engage in due to your injuries.

Some insurance carrier experts will provide you with a history form to complete at the time of the appointment. It is inappropriate for the expert to require you to complete any form without the assistance of your attorney. Many attorneys require the form to be produced in advance of the appointment, to assist you in completing it. If a form is first provided at the time of the appointment, you should complete only the general information and contact your attorney's office for further instructions.

You should have your route to the examinations mapped out, and make sure to arrive at your appointments early to check in. It is not uncommon for injured workers to wait months for an appointment with one of these medical experts. Accordingly, do not lose your appointment slot by failing to appear for the examination on time. Although it is important to arrive on time for these appointments, there is often a long wait to see the doctor. Unfortunately, these experts are often over-booked, leading to lengthy waits by patients.

Why Is It Important to Provide a History of The Accident and Medical Treatment If the Expert Has My Medical Records?

Most medical experts rely upon a staff member to obtain a history of the accident and medical treatment from you. You should be prepared to briefly explain how your injury occurred, focusing upon the physical impact to your body, as opposed to the events leading up the accident. For example, if you fell 10 feet off a ladder, spend your time explaining which part of your body impacted with the ground, rather than what caused you to climb the ladder in the first place.

Although your medical records should have been forwarded by the insurance carrier or your attorney in advance of the examination, you should still be prepared to recite a general history of the medical treatment you received following the accident. You do not need to have the date of every appointment memorized. However, you should know the date of any surgeries you underwent, as well as how many weeks you had physical therapy, and the number of injections you tried before resorting to surgery, or any other medical procedure. The expert will also want to know how long you were out of work following the injury. It is important to provide this information in the event that the medical records which the carrier provided to your attorney were incomplete.

What Happens During the Actual Physical Examination with the Workers' Compensation Experts?

The physician's assistant usually stays in the examination room during the examination, as both a witness and to help the doctor. After you provide a history, the medical expert will may only perform a cursory physical exam. Do not be concerned if the examination is very brief. The estimates of disability provided by the expert are largely governed by the physician's review of your medical records.

The expert should perform a battery of physical tests on you, to measure your range of motion, strength, and pain levels. You must speak up if you experience any pain during the testing. However, be aware that the expert will be looking for signs of malingering or exaggeration, which will paint you as less credible to the Court. You should leave the drama at home; it is not helpful for you to grimace in pain at the slightest movement if you do not actually feel severe pain. I have seen the complaints of patients with significant injuries be completely discounted by insurance carrier experts because the expert thought that they were "gilding the lily," by embellishing their injuries. Everyone experiences pain differently. Be yourself – but do not operate under the illusion that you can trick a trained medical expert into believing that your symptoms are worse than they are in reality. You will damage your case if you attempt to put on a show. On the other hand, you will not improve your case by playing the "tough guy," and downplaying your complaints to the doctor.

You should tell the physician about your limitations at work and home due to the injury. Even if you returned to the same job, performing the same work duties, but with pain, explain that to the doctor. Tell the expert if you gave up any recreational activities, have difficulty sleeping, or performing chores around the house. Estimate how many times a week you must take pain medication, even if it is over the counter medication.

If you had a prior injury, it is crucial for you to disclose it to the medical expert. You should explain what medical treatment you underwent for the prior injury, and how you felt in the days immediately before the subject work accident. If you were fully recovered from the prior injury at the time of the work accident, with no limitations, you must highlight that fact. On the other hand, if you still suffered from occasional pain from the prior injury, explain the degree to which the work accident exacerbated your symptoms.

What Steps I Should Take After the Permanency Examination with the Insurance Carrier's Expert?

Do not bother complaining to your attorney that the examination was a sham. Rather, while your memory is fresh, you should make notes regarding the insurance expert's examination. Write down the exact time the physical examination began and ended. Did the expert ignore you when you tried to point out a symptom? What sort of testing was done during the examination? It is common for insurance carrier experts to claim that a Petitioner failed to disclose a prior injury if the carrier neglected to submit any medical records regarding that injury. Be sure to thus make a note of all prior injuries you disclosed at the appointment. If the expert mentions that he did not have the benefit of a particular medical record you should advise your attorney. Send the post-examination notes to your attorney and keep a copy for your own records.

How Many Permanency Examinations Will I Need to Attend?

At a minimum, you will need to attend examinations with two experts – one for the insurance carrier and one scheduled by your own attorney. Depending upon your injury you may need to attend multiple sets of exams. For instance, if you suffered from a fracture, you will be scheduled for examinations with an orthopedist. If you experienced nerve damage due to the accident (i.e.: suffer from numbness or tingling, and underwent an EMG), you should also attend neuropsychiatric evaluations. Neuropsychiatric experts evaluate both neurological deficits, such as those caused by damage to the nerves or a head injury, as well as psychiatric disability arising from depression or anxiety. If you suffer from an occupational pulmonary injury, or were diagnosed with cancer related to chemical exposure, then you will need to be evaluated by an internist. An ENT (ear, nose, and throat specialist) should evaluate you for hearing loss or swallowing difficulties following neck surgery. While they exist, there are few experts who perform permanency evaluations for eye injuries, dental injuries, and urological injuries in New Jersey. Your attorney may recommend limiting the number of exams to those experts who are absolutely necessary to negotiate a settlement of your claim, in order to reduce the expenses which will be deducted from your settlement award.

I Attended Examinations with Both Sets of Experts. Now What?

Do not expect to hear immediate results following the permanency examinations. Some medical experts are so backed up that it often takes over 6 weeks for them to release a narrative report. Many attorneys refrain from even sharing the results of the report with their clients, until a settlement offer has been received. You should request to see a copy of the reports though, to make sure that the doctor did not misrepresent your statements during the examination.

What If the Medical Experts Disagree on My Degree Of Permanent Disability?

The medical expert for the respondent (hired by the employer's insurance carrier) rarely agrees with the level of disability found by the expert retained by the petitioner (hired by your attorney). The experts may even disagree on your diagnosis and its causal relationship to the work accident. Unless you are clearly totally disabled, Respondents' experts generally find a very minimal disability, if any. One popular expert among insurance carriers believes that only a quadriplegic could be 100% totally disabled, while a paraplegic would be only 50% disabled. By contrast, Petitioners' experts typically inflate the permanent disability rating. Accordingly, do not panic and assume that your life is over if your own expert alleges that you are 75% disabled. On the other hand, it would not be unusual for an insurance carrier's expert to estimate your disability at 1%, even when the injuries have had a profound impact on your life.

Your permanent disability level will generally be established somewhere between these opposing estimates of disability. Please see the chapter regarding settlement for details on the process of reaching a compromise with the insurance carrier to resolve your claim in the Division of Workers' Compensation. See, Chapter 10.

How is the Dollar Amount of a Partial Permanent Disability Award Calculated?

The amount of your benefits will be based upon the schedule of disabilities in effect in the year in which your work accident occurred. The benefits will vary based upon your wages, up to the maximum rate at the time of the accident, and the number of weeks of benefits available for the injured body part.

The number of weeks of benefits to be paid depends upon the body part which was injured. The schedule of disabilities in New Jersey sets forth the maximum weeks which shall be paid for total loss of a "member" (hand, arm, foot, leg):

Thumb:	75 weeks
First finger (index):	50 weeks
Second Finger (middle):	40 weeks
Third Finger (ring):	30 weeks
Fourth Finger (pinky):	20 weeks
Great Toe:	40 weeks
Other Toes:	15 weeks
Hand:	245 weeks
Arm:	330 weeks
Foot:	230 weeks
Leg:	315 weeks

Thus, if you lost 100% of use of your hand, you are entitled to receive 245 weeks of benefits. If a body part is amputated, a 30% "bonus" will be added to the award.

More commonly, claimants suffer from a partial loss of use of a member, which would be compensated based upon the above schedule. For example, if the Court determines that you lost 50% of the use of your foot, you would be entitled to receive 115 weeks of benefits. In 2017, at the maximum rate of disability, a 50% disability of the foot equals only $29,345.00, even if it prevents you from working in the same occupation. The pathetically low compensation rates for hand and foot injuries is one of the major injustices in the New Jersey Workers' Compensation Act, in this author's opinion. Unfortunately, efforts to lobby the New Jersey Legislature to change the schedule of disabilities for extremities have failed in recent years.

In addition to scheduling the losses for extremities, the Workers' Compensation Act provides that the total loss of vision in one eye shall be paid 200 weeks of disability benefits. Total hearing loss is limited to 200 weeks of disability benefits.

There is no separate schedule for "partial total" permanent disability – those injuries outside of the above specific body parts. Injuries to the head, neck, shoulder, trunk, back, internal injuries, and psychiatric injuries are paid in terms of partial total disability. The law provides that a disability which is partial total in nature shall be payable in increments of six weeks of benefits for every percentage point of disability, on a 600-week scale. For example, if you have a disability of 10% partial total you would be entitled to receive 60 weeks of benefits. A disability of 20% partial total would pay 120 weeks of benefits, and so on.

The dollar amount of your partial total award is also dependent upon your weekly rate. Ever since the New Jersey Workers' Compensation Act has been in effect, with the exception of 2011, the minimum/maximum rates have increased annually. In 2018, the maximum temporary and permanent disability rate is $903/week.

Although the temporary disability rate is 70% of average weekly wages, up to the maximum rate, your permanent disability rate may be much lower, depending upon your level of disability. For example, the first 90 weeks of benefits are payable at only 20% of the state average weekly wage for that year. The rate increases incrementally after 90 weeks of disability, up to the maximum rate, which is 75% of the state average weekly wage for that year. There are a few large "jumps" in the chart, at which point the rate increases dramatically. Settlement discussions often focus upon these thresholds. For example, after 30% partial total, the rates increase from $282.83/week to $418/week, for injuries occurring in 2017. Thus, an award of 30% partial total would equal $52,710.00, while an award of 31% partial total equals $77,748, for a 2017 accident. Generally, most Judges of Compensation will only award over 30% partial total for injuries which were serious enough to require surgical intervention.

A chart summarizing the various disability levels and rates was published by New Jersey Manufacturer's Insurance, which is used by workers' compensation attorneys to calculate the amount payable for a specific injury. At the first meeting with your attorney, she may show you this chart to educate you about how your award for permanent disability will be calculated. <u>See</u>, Appendix F (Rate Charts for 2012 – 2018)

In 2007, the Division of Workers' Compensation rolled out a computer program, referred to as "OSCAR," which automatically calculates the dollar amount payable to a claimant based upon the year of the accident, wages, and percentage of disability for all types of injuries. The application was published online in 2015 and may be accessed at: https://courtsonline.dol.state.nj.us/OscarCalc.

In order to utilize the OSCAR program to compute the dollar amount of your partial permanent disability award, plug in the year of the accident, your average weekly wage in the year of the accident, and the percentage of disability for each body part injured. If you injured multiple body parts, your disability award will be paid in terms of partial total. Although injuries should be broken down by body part when calculating the dollar value of a claim, keep in mind that the Court will look at your overall level of disability when deciding your level of partial permanent disability. For example, if you injured your hand, leg, and arm in an accident, those multiple injuries taken together will increase your rate of disability. However, if you returned to work with few limitations after an accident involving multiple injuries, the Judge of Compensation would consider it a windfall to combine the full value of each individual injury, if it would exceed your actual overall partial permanent disability level.

How Will My Permanent Disability Benefits Be Calculated If I Suffered From a Prior Injury?

Even if you injured the same part of your body prior to the work accident, you may be entitled to a permanent disability award for your work injury. However, the burden will be on you and your attorney to prove with objective medical evidence that you suffered a permanent disability as a result of the work accident. The respondent is entitled to receive a credit for any "pre-existing functional loss," if you are awarded permanent disability benefits in connection with the work injury. Technically, once an injured worker demonstrates his overall level of disability, the burden shifts to the respondent to prove the degree of permanent disability which should be attributed to the pre-existing condition.

For example, if you underwent back surgery due to a work injury in 2017, but received physical therapy from a lower back strain in 2010, the Court may award you 25% partial total permanent disability benefits, with a credit of 5% for your pre-existing condition. The dollar amount of such an award would depend upon your wages at the time of the accident. The credit for the pre-existing condition is negotiable, unless you received a prior compensation award for it – in that case, the insurance carrier would automatically receive a credit for the percentage of disability you received in the prior award.

After Being Examined by the Insurance Carrier's Medical Expert I Received a Check for Partial Permanent Disability Benefits. Is My Case Now Over?

You may receive a check from the insurance carrier after attending an examination by the respondent's expert, known as a "voluntary tender." The amount of the tender is generally based upon the permanent disability level estimated by Respondent's medical expert. For example, if the Respondent's expert alleges that you sustained a 5% partial permanent disability due to an accident in 2017, the carrier may immediately issue you a check for $7,170.00. You may cash this check without jeopardizing your right to additional benefits. The voluntary tender should be considered an advance on your final settlement or judgment. The value of a claim is generally substantially more than the estimate of the respondent's expert, so your case will continue after you receive a voluntary tender check.

Insurance carriers will generally only schedule a permanency evaluation if you are represented by an attorney and a Claim Petition has been filed in the

Division of Workers' Compensation. Occasionally permanency evaluations are scheduled by the carrier to discourage the injured worker from seeking the advice of an attorney. Thereafter, the carrier may pay the injured worker a "voluntary" settlement, based upon the degree of disability estimated by the carrier's medical expert. Unfortunately, unwitting claimants may believe that they have forfeited their rights to pursue the claim further by cashing the check forwarded by the insurance carrier. However, an injured workers' right to be fairly compensated for his permanent injury cannot be unilaterally limited by the carrier. Rather, a final settlement can only be enforced when it is given the stamp of approval of a Judge of Compensation.

Most claims are worth substantially more than the estimate of the carrier's medical expert. Accordingly, a carrier's voluntary tender of a percentage of permanent disability benefits should be considered only a down payment on the ultimate settlement award. If you receive such a check you may cash it, without fear that doing so constitutes a final settlement of your claim. Thereafter, schedule an appointment with a workers' compensation attorney so that you may obtain the full value of your claim! At the time your case is settled or otherwise resolved, the insurance carrier will receive a credit for the dollar amount it voluntarily paid to you.

Insurance carriers do not issue voluntary tenders to be magnanimous. Rather, their motivation is economical and sometimes vengeful, since the Court will not assess an attorneys' fee on a "bona fide" voluntary tender, which is issued within 26 weeks of the date you were released from medical treatment. The attorney's fees will be based upon the net amount you receive on a settlement award, after the carrier receives a credit for a bona fide voluntary tender. Since the insurance carrier pays more than half of the legal fee on accepted permanency claims, the carrier has an interest in reducing the fees of your attorney. Some carriers also use voluntary tenders to punish attorneys who they view as overly aggressive in protecting the rights of their clients. For example, if your attorney filed several Motions for Medical Treatment on your behalf, an unscrupulous claims adjuster may issue a voluntary payment to both reduce legal expenses on the claim, and to retaliate against your attorney for zealously protecting your rights, to discourage her from filing Motions in future claims. Legislation has been proposed to change the voluntary tender rule, so that an attorneys' fee is based upon the entire award if an advance is made after litigation is started.

Chapter 10

The Workers' Compensation Settlement Process

Your attorney cannot begin the process of negotiating a settlement of your claim until the reports of all of the medical experts who performed permanency evaluations have been received. Thereafter, your attorney and the attorney for the insurance carrier will begin to discuss the nature and extent of your injuries.

What Occurs During a "Pre-Trial Conference," And Do I Need to Appear in Court for It?

Once all of the expert reports have been received, your attorney will attend a "pre-trial conference" in the Workers' Compensation Court with the insurance carrier's attorney. You should not appear in Court unless instructed to do so by your attorney. The conferences are usually held in the chambers of the Judge of Compensation. Only attorneys participate in the pre-trial conference, although some insurance carriers also send claims adjusters to join in the discussions.

At the conference, the parties will discuss all of the issues in dispute, including any gaps in temporary disability payments which were not previously resolved by a motion, as well as any unpaid medical bills or liens. Your attorney will review the history of medical treatment you received with the carrier's attorney, and point out the objective evidence that you sustained a permanent injury. If you suffered from a pre-existing medical condition, the attorneys will also argue about the credit the insurance carrier should receive for the prior injury. Multiple conferences may be required to review all of the outstanding issues, or obtain additional information regarding questions which may arise during a conference. After all of the relevant information has been received and discussed by the parties, the Judge of Compensation will then adjourn your case to enable the insurance carrier's attorney to obtain settlement authority from his client, the workers' compensation carrier.

Following the pre-trial conference, the insurance carrier's attorney will generally write a letter to the claims adjuster, setting forth his opinion regarding the settlement value of your claim, and requesting authorization to extend a settlement offer to resolve the claim. Your attorney will contact you once an offer has been received to discuss whether you should accept the offer or make a counter-offer.

What is a Fair Settlement Value for My Permanent Partial Disability Claim?

Most claims for partial permanent disability benefits settle somewhere between the estimates provided by the competing medical experts. The dollar value of the claim will depend on several factors, including:

- Your average weekly wage at the time of the accident.
- The amount of lost time from work.
- The results of objective medical testing.
- The nature and amount of treatment provided, and whether that treatment was authorized through workers' compensation.
- Any permanent work restrictions as a result of the accident, which prevent you from continuing in the same line of work, or require your employer to provide you with ongoing accommodations to do your job.
- Your level of impairment at both work and home.
- Any recreational activities you are unable to enjoy as a result of your injuries.
- A comparison between your pre-accident disability level and current disability level if you had a pre-existing injury.

- The nature and extent of medical treatment you underwent. Generally, if you had surgery the value of the permanency claim increases.

If the medical testing failed to reveal objective evidence of an injury and you only received minimal medical treatment, you will most likely receive a token settlement offer, since the insurance carrier knows that your case could be dismissed at a Trial. The settlement award should reflect the degree to which your injury has limited your ability to work and engage in your usual activities. Please see the "Permanent Disability" chapter for information on how the dollar amount of the award is calculated.

You must remember that when there is a dispute over a claim, and either side may prevail at Trial, a fair settlement represents a compromise between the highest amount you could be awarded, and possibility of an outright dismissal of the claim.

What Is a Reasonable Time to Wait for A Settlement Offer?

There are a multitude of reasons why a settlement of your claim could be delayed. If the experts were not provided with all of your medical records at the time of your permanency examination, the case may be adjourned in order to obtain supplemental reports from the experts. If you failed to provide the experts with a history of a prior accident, your case will be delayed to obtain those records. Even when all of the records have been provided and the expert reports have been completed, the insurance carrier's attorney usually needs at least 6 weeks to obtain settlement authority from the carrier to resolve your claim, from the time a settlement demand has been made by your attorney.

If you were employed by a municipality or public school district, it will take even longer to obtain settlement authority since the employer's attorney must generally meet with an entire board in order to obtain authorization for a settlement. Additional time will also be required if the workers' compensation insurance policy provides the insured (your employer) with the right to reject a settlement proposal. Human nature suggests that if your employer harbors animosity towards you it may take more time and effort for the carrier's attorney to convince them that a settlement offer should be extended as opposed to forcing a Trial on your claim.

Is There Any Way to Force the Insurance Carrier to Make a Settlement Offer?

Neither party may be forced into a settlement, although some Judges are adept at pressuring one side or the other to "make a deal." If the parties cannot come to an agreement on their own, they may ask the Judge of Compensation to review the medical reports and provide her opinion on the value of the claim. The Judge may advise the insurance carrier's attorney that she believes the settlement offer is too low. If so, the insurance carrier's attorney will generally request an adjournment to consult with the carrier about whether to increase the offer based upon the Judge's recommendation. On the other hand, the Judge may advise your attorney that your expectations are too high, and that the offer is fair or even too generous. If the Judge finds the settlement proposal to be fair, the insurance carrier is unlikely to increase the offer short of a dramatic change in circumstances.

You may also reject the settlement proposal recommended by the Judge of Compensation if you believe it is unfair. However, keep in mind that the Judge is only likely to change his opinion if your testimony is compelling enough to persuade him that his original evaluation of your claim was incorrect. The vanity of some Judges prevents them from ever admitting that their original settlement analysis was flawed. Such a jurist will reflexively award the same amount at Trial, or could even "punish" the party which rejected their recommendation, by awarding more money if the insurance carrier refused to follow her recommendation or less money if the injured worker rejected her settlement proposal. Although the Judge could certainly be persuaded at Trial that the opinion she provided at the Pre-Trial Conference was incorrect after listening to your testimony, many Judges reflexively stick to their original estimates of disability to encourage more settlements.

Why Do I Need Appear in Court if I Reached an Agreement With the Insurance Carrier to Settle My Claim?

Unlike a Superior Court claim, in which the plaintiff usually just signs a Release Agreement to memorialize a settlement, a Court Appearance is required to process a workers' compensation settlement. If the parties attempt to enter into a private settlement, without the approval of the Court, it cannot be enforced by the Division of Workers' Compensation. The insurance carrier may thus require you to appear in Court before it agrees to pay any settlement award.

If you moved out of state, or for other good cause shown, the Judge of Compensation may permit you to sign an Affidavit in lieu of a making a Court appearance. Unless you are truly unable to make the trip to Court though, most judges will require you to testify in person before approving of any settlement.

Once a settlement has been reached, you will be instructed to appear in Court on the next hearing date for your case. The purpose of the hearing is to: (1) to confirm "on the record" that you understand the settlement offer and wish to accept it; (2) for the Judge make a ruling that the settlement award is fair; and (3) set a baseline for the limitations you suffer due to the injury, in the event it is necessary to reopen your claim.

How Should I Prepare For the Settlement Hearing?

Depending upon the type of settlement which was negotiated, you may not need to speak much at the Hearing, aside from assenting to the terms of the agreement. If the settlement includes the right to

"reopen" your claim, you will also need to testify about the nature of your pain and explain your limitations. You should thus make a list of your complaints in the days leading up the Hearing, to help you recall the manner in which your injuries have affected your everyday living.

You must dress appropriately for your day in Court. While there is no need for you to come to Court dressed in a business suit, you must have a neat and clean presentation in order to show respect for the institution. I would advise against wearing shorts, sweatpants, short skirts, revealing tops for woman, flip-flops, baseball hats, or any clothing which looks like you just rolled out of bed. There are Judges who will refuse to process a settlement if a claimant is dressed inappropriately. One Judge directed a claimant to the local Walmart to purchase a new outfit, when she arrived in Court in shorts and a low-cut top. Use your common sense in your choice of a wardrobe to avoid that uncomfortable scenario.

What Happens On The Day Of My Settlement Hearing Process?

You must check in with the security guard who will be stationed at the entrance of the Division of Workers' Compensation. Have a seat in the waiting area and your attorney will meet you when she is finished checking in with the Judge. Do not be alarmed if your attorney does not come out to meet you immediately. She is most likely in the Judge's chambers, awaiting her turn for the Judge to review your settlement paperwork, which is done the morning of the Hearing. Your attorney will thereafter present you with the Order Approving Settlement, which sets forth the amount of the settlement award, and the deductions which are set by the Judge for costs and fees. You should compute the net amount you will receive with your attorney, after the deduction of all costs and fees. Your attorney should then go over the questions you will be asked during the Hearing, to obtain the Court's approval of the settlement.

Since many cases are scheduled every day before each Judge of Compensation, you may need to wait through several other Hearings before your case is called. Each Judge has a different style for handling settlement hearings. Your attorney should make you aware of the procedures followed by the particular Judge assigned to your case. Most Judges will take the settlements involving the largest awards last. Some Judges like to explain the implications of a settlement to you themselves, while others will cede that responsibility to your attorney. To help prepare you for the hearing process and familiarize yourself with the Judge's style, you may wish to wait in the Courtroom to listen to other settlements being processed.

Before you begin to testify (answer questions under oath in the presence of the Judge), you will be sworn in by the court reporter. You may use the religious book of your preference or merely affirm to tell the truth.

What Is a Section 20 Settlement Award?

The term "section 20" refers to the portion of the Workers' Compensation Act (NJSA 34:15-20) which outlines the basis for entering into a "lump sum" settlement agreement between the injured worker and the employer. A settlement reached under section 20 forever ends the right of the worker to return to the Court for additional benefits. This type of settlement is only permitted if the accident was denied by the employer, if there is a dispute regarding causal relationship between the accident and injuries, or if it is questionable that the injury was permanent in nature. Since an award under NJSA 34:15-20 is not considered a payment of "compensation," it may be paid in a lump sum, rather than on a weekly basis.

What Are the Drawbacks of Settling A Claim Under Section 20?

While you may prefer to receive your entire net award up-front, you are giving up significant rights in the future in exchange for such a settlement. Some Judges are reluctant to approve section 20 awards, since they completely terminate the injured workers' right to receive future medical treatment or benefits related to the accident, through workers' compensation. If you have private health insurance though, you may consider it a blessing that you do not need to deal with obtaining the approval of a workers' compensation carrier to receive future medical treatment. Moreover, if there is a new accident or injury, a section 20 settlement does not foreclose the possibility of filing of a new claim.

What Are the Terms of a Non-Section 20 Settlement Agreement?

If the insurance carrier agrees to a settlement of your claim under NJSA 34:15-22 of the Workers' Compensation Act, you may reopen your case if you need additional medical treatment or if your symptoms significantly worsen within two years of the date of your last workers' compensation benefit, including authorized medical treatment. Accordingly, the only right you give up by settling your claim at a specific disability level is your right to a Trial, at which time the Judge would hear your testimony, as well as the testimony of the medical experts, to make a determination regarding your level of permanent disability. Orders Approving Settlement generally include language indicating that the Respondent has paid or will pay all reasonable and customary charges for outstanding bills related to authorized medical treatment. The Order will also set forth the degree of permanent disability which the parties agree you suffered as a result of the accident. As outlined in Chapter 9, the percentage of permanent disability awarded corresponds to a specific dollar amount of weekly benefits, based upon the year of the accident, your wages, and extent of the injury sustained to each body part.

Why Will I Only Be Receiving Part of the Weekly Permanent Disability Benefits Up Front?

Unlike a "lump sum" award under Section 20, which is not considered to be a payment of compensation, all compensation awards in New Jersey are payable on a weekly basis, since their purpose is to replace the injured worker's income. As outlined in Chapter 9, the percentage of permanent disability awarded corresponds to the number of weeks of benefits to be paid, at a rate of no more than 70% of your average wage. The second page of the Order Approving Settlement ("OAS") sets forth the number of weeks and weekly rate you will be receiving in the settlement. See, Appendix G for sample OAS. After the settlement is processed, the insurance carrier will pay the accrued benefits to you upfront, less your share of costs and fees.

The term "accrued benefits" refers to the number of weeks which have passed since the date you last received either temporary or permanent disability benefits from the workers' compensation carrier. For example, if you received temporary disability benefits until March 1, 2016, and the insurance carrier cuts your first check for partial permanent disability benefits on March 1, 2017, you will be receiving approximately 52 weeks of benefits up front at your permanent weekly rate, less your share of costs and fees. If the benefits have not all accrued, the remaining weeks will be paid at your permanent disability rate until the settlement award has been completely paid out.

What Statements Must I Make at the Hearing to Ensure that the Court Approves of the Settlement?

If you are receiving a "section 20" or "lump sum" settlement award, your testimony will be very brief. Your attorney will review the settlement figures with you when you are on the witness stand, and ask you to confirm that you understand that by accepting this settlement your case will be closed forever, with no opportunity to seek additional payments from the insurance carrier or employer for medical bills or any other benefits. If any medical bills remain in dispute, you must pay them out of the proceeds of your settlement, or make a separate agreement with that provider. You must simply affirm that you understand and agree to these terms. If you waiver, the Judge may not approve of the settlement, and instead set your case down for a Trial.

No matter your age, the Court will also require you to testify about your eligibility for Medicare at the settlement hearing. Federal law provides that Medicare's interests must be taken into consideration whenever a personal injury or workers' compensation case is resolved, to ensure that the parties are not inappropriately diverting the cost of medical treatment to Medicare in order to make deal. If you are not a Medicare recipient, the inquiry will end there. By contrast, if you are enrolled in Medicare, your attorney will ask you whether any of the medical treatment you received related to the work injury was paid by Medicare, and must present documentation from Medicare confirming that it did not pay any medical bills related to your injury. If Medicare did pay for some medical treatment which may have been related to the work injury, the carrier must obtain a printout of the "conditional payments" made by Medicare, which must be either paid by the carrier or paid out of the proceeds of your settlement award.

Why Must I Testify About My Injuries If My Case Has Been Settled?

Additional testimony is necessary if your case is being settled pursuant to NJSA 34:15-22, with a right to reopen your claim. Beyond affirming that you agree to the terms of the settlement, you will need to explain in Court how the work injuries have affected your life. To finalize the settlement, the Judge of Compensation must find that you fully understand the terms and that the settlement fairly compensates you for your injuries. Keep in mind that although your case has already been tentatively settled, pending the approval of the Court, if you fail to place complaints on the record to justify the payment of an award, the attorney for the insurance carrier could revoke the offer, although this scenario is highly unusual. Accordingly, if you are unable to enunciate any complaints regarding your injuries, the negotiated settlement agreement could fall apart during the Hearing.

How Many Details Must I Share with the Court Concerning the Nature and Extent of My Disability at the Settlement Hearing?

Since you may return to Court if your condition significantly deteriorates or if you need additional medical treatment related to your work injuries, it is important to place some bright lines on the record regarding your limitations due to the accident. For instance, it is not sufficient to merely indicate that you suffer from pain in your lower back. You should describe the pain – is a burning or stabbing pain, or merely an ache? Where precisely do you experience the pain? Is the pain in your mid-back, or predominantly on one side? Does the pain radiate into either one of your legs? How far down each leg? Please see Chapter 12 for an explanation of how your testimony during a settlement Hearing or a Trial will affect your right to receive additional benefits in the event your claim is reopened.

When Will I Start Receiving My Partial Permanent Disability Checks?

At the conclusion of the settlement hearing your attorney will provide you with a copy of the Order Approving

Settlement ("OAS"). You should keep the OAS in a safe place for future reference. The Workers' Compensation Act provides that the insurance carrier must issue the first check for all net accrued benefits within 60 days of the day the Order was entered by the Court. However, most carriers will process the settlement award within 4-6 weeks. Thereafter, depending upon the specific carrier involved, the remaining weekly benefits will be paid out every 2-4 weeks, until the net award is paid in full.

What Effect Will A Workers' Compensation Partial Total Disability Settlement Have on My Social Security Benefits?

Federal law provides that before your full retirement age, an individual cannot be paid more than 80% of his average cumulative earnings, known as the "80% ACE" rule. If you receive an award of partial total disability benefits, your social security benefits may thus be reduced if your combined benefits exceed your 80% ACE. The offset which the Social Security Administration ("SSA") takes for partial permanent workers' compensation benefits is only applied for the specific dates through which you receive those benefits. Thus, if your workers' compensation award is all accrued and represents payment for the period prior to the date you began to receive social security benefits, than the SSA will not take any offset. The offset will end after you reach full retirement age, which varies depending on your year of birth, under the guidelines of the SSA.

What Effect Will a "Lump Sum" Settlement Have on My Social Security Benefits?

The same 80% ACE rule applies even if you receive a lump sum settlement as opposed to weekly partial permanent disability benefits. In order to more accurately reflect the reality of a lump sum payment and avoid having your social security benefits being wiped out by a large offset from a lump sum settlement, you should ask your attorney to provide you with a written breakdown of the gross "section 20" settlement, on a monthly basis, stretched over your remaining lifetime. For example, if you are a social security recipient and received a section 20 award of $25,000, your attorney may prepare an addendum to the OAS with Dismissal, outlining the monthly equivalent of the award, for you to provide to the Social Security Administration, i.e.:

Gross Settlement:	$25,000.00
Less costs/fees:	($5000.00)
Net Settlement:	$20,000.00

Lifetime Expectancy: 15 years: 180 months

Monthly Net Settlement: $111.11

While the SSA is not bound by the findings of the New Jersey Compensation Court, or the analysis of your attorney, if the calculation makes sense, the federal government will generally accept that amount as the offset.

CHAPTER 11

TRIAL PRACTICE IN THE DIVISION OF WORKERS' COMPENSATION

You will be disappointed if you expect to see the level of courtroom drama depicted on the big screen in the Division of Workers' Compensation. While there are always a few moments during any trial which include a surprise question or unanticipated answer, explosive testimony is rare in the Division.

How Is the Value of My Claim Effected by The Judge of Compensation Who Is Assigned to Hear My Case?

Unlike a Superior Court case in New Jersey, which would be decided by a jury of 6-12 people, workers' compensation cases involve a "bench trial," in which the Judge of Compensation decides both questions of fact and law. All judges are appointed by the Governor, often based on political ties rather than expertise.

Judges are human beings, with their own set of biases, likes, and dislikes. You should ask your attorney of the inclinations of the Judge assigned to your case. Is the Judge naturally sympathetic to injured workers? Was the Judge a former insurance defense attorney or an attorney for a Union? Is the Judge more worried about providing a windfall to an undeserving petitioner, than he is about ensuring that an injured worker is adequately compensated? Some Judges see fraud around every corner, while others are more leary about the tactics of insurance carriers. There are a few Judges who are compassionate, and several who believe that most claimants are trying to milk the system. I wish that I could report that the value of a claim in one county in New Jersey was the same as a value of a claim in another county. Unfortunately, while the same chart of disabilities applies in every case, where your compensation award lands on that chart is disproportionately impacted by which Judge is assigned to hear your case. Accordingly, your attorney may recommend that you reject a settlement offer and hold out for a higher award at Trial if you are lucky enough to have your case assigned to a more generous jurist. On the other hand, if your case is listed with a Judge who is more concerned with protecting insurance carriers from overpayments, your attorney is more likely to recommend a settlement offer to avoid the risk of a dismissal or lower award at Trial.

How Should I Begin Preparing for a Trial?

In the weeks leading up to the Trial you should think about the ways in which the injury has affected your everyday activities, at work and at home. Hopefully you have learned methods of compensating for your injury, which enable you to live a normal life and forget about your injury. However, you must be prepared to explain the details of how your daily movements and activities have been changed due to the injury. For instance, you might explain that while you are still able to go up and down stairs, you must now take one step at a time and hold the railing due to your injury. Even if your injuries do not prevent you from performing an activity, you should note if the activity causes you pain or it takes you longer to perform. It would be helpful if you paid close attention to your daily activities while you are awaiting Trial, writing down the specific ways in which your life has changed due to the work injury.

Your attorney should obviously review the case with you prior to the Trial, and discuss all the issues which will be presented to the Court. Most attorneys prepare their clients for testifying immediately prior to the settlement hearing, while waiting in Court. Unfortunately, your time before the Judge of Compensation is often limited, so only relevant information should be presented to the Court. Do not be alarmed if your attorney cuts you off during preparation for your testimony, to keep you on track. She is not being rude. She is trying to focus your testimony on the issues which are important to the Court to win your case. If you have a tendency to ramble on, you must have the discipline to stay on topic when answering questions about your injury. On the other hand, if you are a quiet, reserved person, you may have difficulty talking about yourself. It is therefore critical that you practice explaining your injuries so that you do not freeze up in Court. Speak with a friend or family member to help you remember all of the ways in which your injury affects you, and practice your testimony by discussing your limitations with them and in front of a mirror.

What Is the Procedure on the Day My Case Is Scheduled for a Trial?

Several cases may be scheduled for Trial on the same day, at either 9am or 1:30pm. When you arrive at the Division of Compensation you should wait for your attorney in the area outside of the courtrooms. Do not be alarmed if your attorney does not appear to greet you immediately. Get comfortable and acquaint yourself with the building by locating the restroom and walking off your nerves. Your attorney will check in with you after she speaks with the Judge and the insurance carrier's attorney. Court is in session between 9am – 12:30pm and 1:30pm - 4:30pm. Most Judges hold settlement conferences first and begin processing settlements mid-morning. Trials usually do not get reached until early afternoon.

Your attorney will review the issues with you again as you are waiting for the Judge to reach your case. Do not be afraid to bring up any facts you are unsure of now with your attorney. Please do not wait until you are on the stand to raise an issue for the first time! Discuss any issues of concern with your attorney prior to taking the witness stand. Although the Judge may have reviewed your medical records prior to the Trial, you should assume that the Judge is a blank slate on which you and your attorney will be writing your story.

Before testifying, you will be sworn in by the court reporter. You may use the religious book of your preference or merely affirm to tell the truth. Your testimony will begin with answering questions from your own lawyer – referred to as "direct testimony." Thereafter, the insurance carrier's attorney will have the opportunity to "cross examine" you.

Direct Examination: Answering Questions by Your Own Attorney in Court

The purpose of your testimony in Court is to lay out all the disputed aspects of your claim in the most favorable light. Your testimony should follow a logical pattern, so that the Judge can follow the relevant facts and make a decision. Your attorney will create an outline for you to tell your story with the questions she asks you on the record, in front of the Judge. Only you may tell your story though – your attorney cannot testify for you by asking "leading questions," to which you answer yes or no.

Your attorney will not spend a lot of time eliciting facts which have been stipulated as true by the insurance carrier. For example, if your employer admits that an accident occurred, then it will not be necessary for you to testify about the fine details surrounding the accident. You will only need to provide a general description of how the accident happened, and the manner in which your body was impacted by the trauma. For instance, if you fell 12 feet from a roof, you need not provide the Court with details about why you were on the roof and what sort of material you were using that day. It is more important for you to explain the details of the trauma, i.e.: that you struck a fence on the way down, breaking it, and then landed on concrete, feeling immediate pain in your back, neck, and shoulder. On the other hand, if the accident was denied by your employer, then your attorney will ask you to elaborate on the details leading up to the accident, such as how it occurred, and who was present at the time you were hurt. You must indicate if you are unsure of a particular fact, or do not know the answer to a question. Otherwise, your credibility will be significantly undermined if your statement turns out to be untrue.

Your attorney's job is to help you illustrate to the Court how your injuries are affecting your life. She will guide you through a set of questions designed to elicit the most relevant and compelling information to persuade the Judge regarding the facts at issue in your case. Listen to the questions asked by your attorney and try not to answer far beyond the scope of the question. That does not mean that you should provide short, yes or no responses when answering the questions of your own lawyer. Remember – only you can tell your story with guidance from your attorney.

What to Expect During Cross Examination

You should approach the cross-examination questions of the insurance carrier attorney much differently than direct examination. The other attorney will attempt to poke holes in your testimony, to either catch you in a lie or an exaggeration. Every defense attorney has a different style. The most effective cross examiners often start off with friendly questions, so that you will let down your guard. You should be courteous and truthful when answering all questions. However, <u>do not fall into the trap of answering yes to every question just to be agreeable to the friendly cross-examiner.</u> The defense attorney is trying to paint his own picture for the Court, so you must vigilantly listen to his questions and deny any facts which you are unsure about, or indicate if your memory is failing you. On the other hand, you will appear to hiding something if you indicate that "you do not recall" in response to every single question. In short – pay attention closely to the questions and answer honestly. Do not forget that Judges are human beings, who hear stories like yours every day. If the Judge feels that you are being evasive or he does not like your attitude, he may rule against you or limit your award.

A fertile ground for cross-examination is the issue of prior accidents. Please do not make the mistake of denying a prior accident because you feel it is irrelevant. The insurance carrier will have a list of every single prior work injury, fender-bender, or insurance claim you ever made during your lifetime. A prior accident may very well be irrelevant to your workers' compensation case. But you cannot make it disappear by denying it, or playing games on the stand. If a prior injury occurred but was minimal, just admit it, explain how quickly you recovered from it, and what limitations you suffered from it, if any. If you received a settlement from a prior accident you should keep in mind that the insurance carrier's attorney may have the transcript from your testimony in that case. Your attorney should have reviewed this prior transcript with you in detail, to make sure that you do not contradict yourself.

Keep in mind that your attorney cannot come to your rescue during cross-examination by yelling "objection" every time you are asked a tough question on the stand. Courtroom dramas on television are rarely accurate. After the insurance carrier's attorney finishes his questions, your own attorney will have an opportunity on "re-direct" to clarify any misrepresentations which arose during cross-examinations. If you misspoke during cross-examination, now is the time for you to correct the record.

What Happens in the Trial After I Testify?

Trials in the Division of Workers' Compensation are not continuous in that multiple witnesses do not testify immediately after one another. Generally, only one witness testifies every day the case is listed for Trial, since the Court must address multiple cases on a daily basis. After each witness testifies, the case will be adjourned at least "one cycle," which is three weeks. Accordingly, a Trial may take more than six months to be completed, depending upon the number of witnesses scheduled to testify.

After your testimony has been completed, your attorney will call any lay witnesses (non-experts) to the stand if necessary to establish a particular factual element of your case. For example, if the accident was denied by your employer, a co-worker who was present when the accident occurred may be subpoenaed to testify. If family members are able to articulate how the injuries impact your life it would be helpful if least one of them could testify on your behalf. Keep in mind however, that the Court frowns upon duplicative testimony and will not appreciate hearing from multiple witnesses who do not add any new facts to the record.

The workers' compensation carrier's attorney may also call lay witnesses to contradict or undermine your testimony. If your employer disputes your injury, do not be surprised to see your supervisor or one of your co-workers testify that they never witnessed any accident, or that your injuries are not as substantial as you claim. You should be present during such testimony, to look these witnesses in the eye and make it more uncomfortable for them to lie. It is also critical for you to listen to their testimony to assist your attorney in preparing cross-examination of such lay witnesses. You may also be called back to the stand to explain why their testimony was incorrect.

Once all fact witnesses are finished testifying, your attorney will schedule the medical experts to appear on your behalf. These are the experts who evaluated you for the purpose of estimating your permanent disability as a result of the accident. Treating physicians rarely appear in Court, both because of their busy schedules and the high cost of paying for their appearance at Trial. The medical experts who will be called to the stand are experienced in providing testimony before the Workers' Compensation Court, and understand the New Jersey disability schedule. Your attorney will review the objective medical evidence of injury with each expert, and ask them to explain their estimate of disability to the Court, and why it is causally related to the work accident. The other attorney will go through the same process with the insurance carrier's medical experts, trying to persuade the Court that the injuries had a minimal impact, if any, on your functional abilities and/or were unrelated to the work accident.

There are generally no closing statements made by attorneys in the Division of Workers' Compensation. After all witnesses have testified, the Court will unceremoniously close the record, and then take some time to review the transcripts of the testimony before rendering a decision. Both parties should submit Trial briefs to summarize the testimony and try to persuade the Court to rule on behalf of their clients. Thereafter, it could take weeks or even months for the Judge to write an opinion on your case. Your attorney has little control over when the Court will issue a written opinion, although the Chief Judge of the Division may pressure the errant Judge who lags far behind in issuing rulings.

What is the Process After the Court Issues an Opinion on My Case?

The Judge of Compensation may summon both attorneys back to Court to read his decision into the record. A

Judge may also prepare a written decision which will be provided to one of the attorneys, with a directive to prepare an Order for Judgment consistent with his ruling. If the Judge rules in your favor, the insurance carrier must begin payment of accrued benefits pursuant to the judgment within 60 days of the date of the Order, unless an appeal is filed and a stay is granted.

What If I Disagree With the Judge's Decision Following a Trial?

Both parties have 45 days from the date the final Order is signed by the Judge to file an appeal. If the insurance carrier disagrees with the Court's decision their attorney they may file an appeal to the Appellate Division of the Superior Court of New Jersey, and request that the Court enter a "stay" of the judgment, which allows the carrier to postpone payment of the award until the appeal is heard. You may also wish to file an appeal. However, your attorney is not required to file an appeal on your behalf, and may refuse to do so if she believes that there is little chance of success on the appeal. Of course, you may retain the services of another attorney to file the appeal.

The Appellate Division will only overturn a decision of the Division of Workers' Compensation if the Judge applied the law incorrectly, or if a factual finding could not have reasonably been reached based upon the credible evidence produced at Trial. In other words, it is very difficult to overturn the decision of a Judge of Compensation, if the decision was based upon his interpretation of the facts, such as the degree of your disability. The Appellate Division gives great deference to the expertise of the Judge of Compensation. An appeal is unlikely to be successful if the Judge's decision solely hinged on his evaluation of the credibility of the parties. This standard again illustrates the importance of which Judge of Compensation is assigned to hear your case.

CHAPTER 12

REOPENER CLAIMS

Settlements or judgments entered in the Division of Workers' Compensation may include the right to "reopen" the claim, depending upon the type of award. As explained in Chapter 10, only a lump sum settlement under "section 20" of the Workers' Compensation Act is final and cannot be revived to obtain additional benefits. If you received a workers' compensation award in the past and cannot recall whether it included a right to reopen, you should contact your attorney or look at the Court Order you received at the time of settlement. If the paperwork you received at the settlement hearing is entitled "Order Approving Settlement with Dismissal NJSA 34:15-20," then you cannot reopen your case to receive additional medical treatment or benefits through workers' compensation. See, Appendix I.

What is the Deadline for Reopening a Workers' Compensation Claim?

If you received judgement or settlement which includes a right to reopen the claim you must file an "Application for Review or Modification of Award" within two years. See,

Appendix J. The two year deadline starts to run as of the date you received your last workers' compensation benefit, including authorized medical care. Thus, it is often a "moving" deadline, since you may have additional time to file if the workers' compensation carrier subsequently authorizes you for more medical treatment, or if your settlement benefits for partial permanent disability benefits continue to be paid out for a period after the Order is entered. The following examples illustrate this point:

(1) <u>All of the weekly benefits due under the OAS are accrued and payable immediately after the Order is entered.</u>

You will then be receiving all of the weekly benefits up front, less costs and fees, within 60 days of the entry of the Order. The deadline for reopening this claim is 2 years from the date your one and only check is received.

(2) <u>Not all of the benefits were accrued under the OAS, so you continued to receive checks for partial permanent disability benefits every 2-4 weeks.</u>

In this scenario, you will receive one check for all past due benefits, and thereafter will be entitled to weekly benefits, until the award has been paid in full. The deadline for reopening this claim is 2 years from the date your <u>last</u> check is received. Thus, if you are receiving weekly permanency benefits for a three year period, you will have approximately 5 years to file an application to reopen the claim from the date the OAS was first entered.

(3) You received checks for partial permanent disability benefits every 2-4 weeks after entry of the OAS and you were authorized to return to active medical treatment.

If you returned to active medical treatment after the entry of the OAS, the deadline for filing a reopener application may be pushed back even farther. Remember, the cut-off date for filing is two years from the date you received any type of workers' compensation benefits, including authorized medical treatment. The medical records and bills will provide proof of the last date of treatment. Note that the deadline is based upon the actual date of treatment, rather than the date the medical bills are paid by the carrier.

In all of the above examples, it is advisable to keep a copy of the last check you received, with the check stub and the post-marked envelope, to prove the date permanent disability benefits were last paid. To ensure that the medical treatment you received was authorized by workers' compensation, it is advisable to obtain a copy of your doctor's billing records, to confirm that payment was issued by the workers' compensation carrier.

I Continue To Suffer From The Same Pain Years After A Work Accident And I Am No Longer Receiving Benefits. Can I Apply For An Increased Permanent Disability Rating?

You are not entitled to receive additional permanent disability benefits because you continue to suffer from the same pain and limitations for which you received your compensation award. You were previously paid for the complaints you were experiencing at the time your original settlement award was entered. If there is no change in your complaints or limitations, and you have not received any significant medical treatment, it is unlikely that the Court will award you additional permanency benefits. However, you are certainly not prohibited from filing an Application to Modify Your Award. It would be up to the Court to decide whether or not there is objective medical evidence sufficient to prove that your permanent disability level has increased. If it is questionable whether disability has gotten worse, the

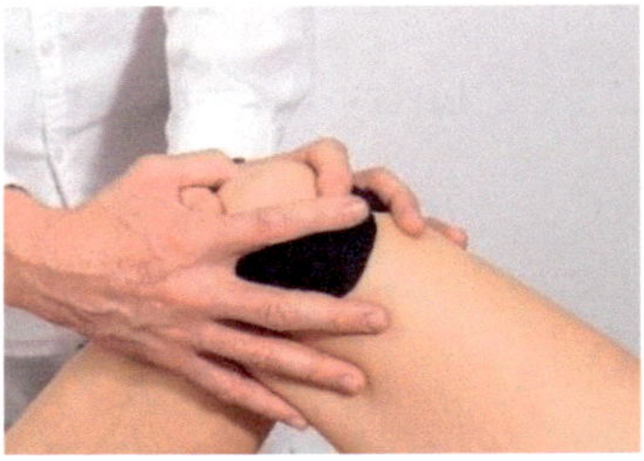

carrier may offer you a lump sum settlement in exchange for closing your claim forever. Please note however, that the attorney who handled your original claim is not obligated to file an application to reopen the claim if she does not believe it is economically worthwhile to do so.

What Happens If My Condition Gets Worst After I Settle My Workers' Compensation Case?

You should file an "Application for Review or Modification of Award" if your condition significantly deteriorates and your permanent disability level increases. Even if you do not believe that medical treatment can cure you, it is advisable for you to return to the doctor, preferably the authorized workers' compensation physician, to document your condition. If the previously authorized physician believes that you need additional medical treatment which relates back to the original work accident, the workers' compensation carrier should pay for this treatment.

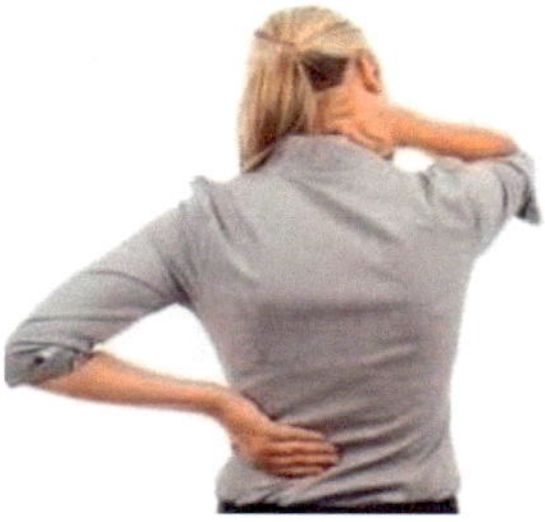

What Should I Do If I Need Additional Medical Treatment After My Claim Is Settled And The Workers' Compensation Carrier Will Not Respond To Me?

Unless you receive a "Section 20" lump sum award, you will be advised at the time of the settlement hearing that you have the right to receive medical treatment related to the accident in the future. Unfortunately, many carriers ignore requests to return to treatment. You should therefore document all of the attempts you make to obtain authorization from the carrier for additional treatment. Initially, you should call the insurance carrier with your claim number in hand and ask to be connected to the claims adjuster currently assigned to your case. Do not be surprised if you are only able to reach his voicemail, and he never returns your call. Keep a written, chronological log of your efforts to reach the adjuster and call your attorney. Either you or your attorney should send a certified letter to the workers' compensation carrier, formally requesting authorization for additional medical treatment, and warning that you will seek treatment with the provider of your choice if you are not directed to a particular doctor.

If your request is still ignored by the carrier, you should contact the physician who primarily treated you after the work accident to request an appointment through your health insurance. Some physicians will not even schedule an appointment unless it is preauthorized through workers' compensation. However, others are only too happy to bill your health insurance if the treatment involves an "old" work injury for which the workers' compensation claims file is now closed.

If the doctor believes that you need additional medical treatment related to the accident, be sure to obtain a copy of his office note and provide it to your attorney. That office note may be used to file a Motion for Medical Treatment with the Court, to force the workers' compensation carrier to pay for the recommended treatment. If the Motion is granted, your health insurance carrier has the right to be reimbursed by the workers' compensation carrier for any benefits paid on your behalf.

If your medical bills are paid by health insurance, your health insurance may assert a lien on any future settlement you receive through workers' compensation and has the right to directly seek reimbursement from the workers' compensation carrier. The likelihood of a health insurance lien being asserted diminishes as more time passes between the original accident date and the medical treatment.

Medicare/Medicaid recipients may also obtain medical treatment outside of workers' compensation. However, federal law provides that treatment covered by Medicare must be reimbursed through workers' compensation. Similarly, New Jersey law requires Medicaid recipients to reimburse the state for any benefits paid for a work related injury out of the proceeds of any monetary award received from workers' compensation. Accordingly, if you are a Medicare/Medicaid recipient, it is even more important for you to first request treatment through workers' compensation. See, Chapter 6 for additional information regarding Medicare.

Am I Entitled to Receive Additional Temporary Disability Benefits When My Case is Reopened?

If you resume active medical treatment, and you believe that you cannot work due to your injuries, then you should request an "out of work" note from the doctor, even if you do not currently have a job. However, there are several scenarios which occur after a settlement or judgment is entered, which make it increasingly difficult for claimants to obtain temporary disability benefits:

(1) You are working with a different employer and feel increasing pain when you work.

The workers' compensation carrier will inevitably argue that your subsequent employment is exacerbating your injury, and will use it as an excuse to deny temporary disability benefits if you are taken out of work again when you return to active medical treatment. Unless you were involved in a new specific accident, the mere fact that your symptoms flared up while you were employed elsewhere is not a basis to terminate the obligation of the workers' compensation carrier to provide you with additional benefits. However, if there was a specific, discrete incident in which you reinjured yourself at your new job, which may be classified as an accident, you should report it and file a new claim. Let your doctor sort out whether your symptoms relate back to the original work accident, or the new incident. If your inability to return to work relates back to the original work accident, you are entitled to again receive temporary disability benefits on that claim. You should provide your attorney with a copy of your last paystub prior to being taken out of work.

(2) I am out of work already and receiving unemployment benefits.

Many claimants make the mistake of mentioning to their doctor that that are out of work at their first visit to the doctor, who then fails to comment upon temporary disability. To be eligible for unemployment benefits you must be "ready, willing, and able" to work. So if you are physically unable to work, your temporary disability benefits should resume, and your unemployment benefits should stop.

If your physician recommends additional treatment and you honestly do not believe that you could perform a job in your chosen profession if one was offered to you, then you should request an "out of work" note from the doctor. Your attorney should then forward the out of work note to the workers' compensation carrier, together with proof that you are currently collecting unemployment benefits. If the carrier fails to begin payment of benefits, a Motion for Medical and Temporary Disability Benefits should be filed. Once temporary disability benefits are paid, you must reimburse the Division of Unemployment if there is any overlap in the dates you were paid workers' compensation and unemployment benefits. See, Chapter 8 for additional information regarding the interplay between workers' compensation and unemployment benefits.

What is the Process for Obtaining Additional Permanent Disability Benefits?

Even if you receive additional medical treatment after the initial settlement of your claim, there may not be a change in your overall permanent disability level. To determine whether your disability level has increased you must be reevaluated by medical experts familiar with the New Jersey compensation schedule – preferably the same experts who examined you for the first permanency award you received. You will be set up for examinations with your own experts as well as the insurance carrier's experts to determine whether they believe that your disability level has increased since the date of your last examination. See, Chapter 9 for a more detailed discussion regarding permanency examinations.

How Does the Court Evaluate the Level of Permanent Disability on a Reopened Case?

Each medical expert will review a copy of medical records of the treatment you received since the entry of the last settlement or judgment you received in the Division of Workers' Compensation. Based upon the results of the physical examination, the medical records, and your complaints regarding the injury, each expert will generate a narrative report, setting forth their opinion regarding your current permanent disability level. The Judge of Compensation will analyze the value of your reopened claim by comparing the increase in disability, if any, found by each expert.

One difficulty faced by injured workers in reopener claims is caused by the inflated permanent disability ratings estimated by Petitioners' experts in the original case. The Court will compare the "increase" in the disability ratings found by each expert, rather than the overall estimate of disability. Thus, if the Petitioner's expert previously evaluated your disability at 75% partial total and you are still working at the time you attend reopener evaluations, the expert does not have much room to increase his permanent disability rating.

Unless you underwent significant additional medical treatment, such as surgery, most insurance carrier experts will not find a substantial increase in permanent disability. It is typical for insurance carrier experts to remind the Court that additional medical treatment does not necessarily equate to an increase in permanent disability, especially given that the purpose of the medical treatment was presumably to increase function.

If the insurance carrier expert finds no increase in your permanent disability level, the carrier may only offer you a minimal lump sum settlement under "section 20," in exchange for a final dismissal of your claim. At a Trial, your attorney would need to present objective medical evidence, such as a change in your MRI or EMG findings, to prove that your disability level has increased.

CHAPTER 13

TOTAL DISABILITY CLAIMS

Injured workers who are totally disabled as a result of a work injury in New Jersey certainly do not live out the remainder of their lives in the lap of luxury. Their weekly benefits are capped at 70% of the average wages they were being paid at the time of the accident, with no cost of living increases. Unfortunately, many total disability claimants live in poverty, even though their benefits continue past the date of usual retirement, until death. So if you are able to return to work in any capacity after your injury, it may be preferable to accept a partial total award rather than fighting to be declared totally disabled.

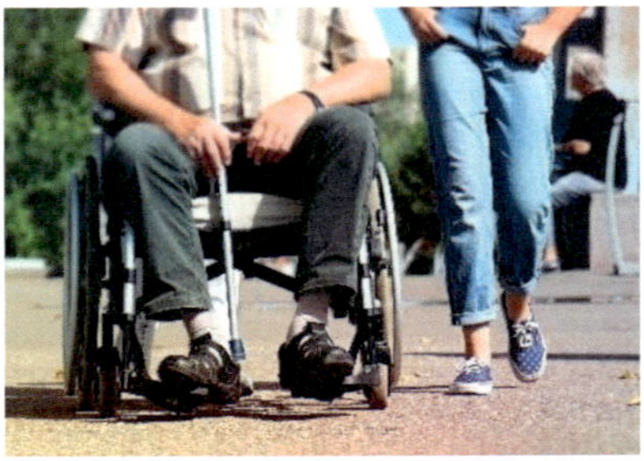

Under What Circumstances Would An Injured Worker Be Awarded Total Permanent Disability?

If you are unable to return to work in any capacity you may be entitled to receive an award of total disability under the Workers' Compensation Act. You must be deemed permanently unemployable in all industries – not just in your chosen profession. Please note that you are not automatically entitled to receive workers' compensation total disability benefits just because you were declared disabled by the Social Security Administration.

What Does a Total Disability Award Entitle Me to Receive?

A Petitioner who is declared totally, permanently disabled will receive 70% of his average weekly wages, up to the state maximum rate (the same rate paid for temporary disability) from the date he was declared totally disabled to the date of his death. Total disability benefits do not end at retirement age. However, after 450 weeks of permanent total disability benefits have been paid, you will be required to attend a medical evaluation to confirm that you are still totally disabled.

How Do My Social Security Benefits Effect My Workers' Compensation Total Disability Settlement?

You cannot receive more than 80% of your average cumulative earnings ("ACE") between a combination of workers' compensation and social security benefits. Before being declared totally disabled, the social security administration will take an offset for any benefits over the 80% ACE. After the date you are declared totally disabled the offset will reverse, meaning that the workers' compensation carrier will receive the offset for any benefits in excess of the 80% ACE.

What Is the Second Injury Fund and Why Should I Apply for These Benefits?

The Second Injury Fund ["SIF"] was created in New Jersey to encourage employers to hire workers with disabilities. Due to the lifetime benefits which would be owed to a totally disabled employee, many employers became fearful of hiring individuals with pre-existing injuries. The SIF was thus established to allay the fears of employers by promising to pay a portion of total disability benefits for employees who became disabled due to a combination of the last accident and pre-existing injuries.

Your attorney may recommend applying for SIF benefits if one or more of the medical experts believe that you are totally, permanently disabled due to a combination of medical conditions. Procedurally, the first step to obtaining these benefits is to file a Second Injury Fund Verified Petition. See, Verified Petition at Appendix K. The workers' compensation carrier will be more amenable to a total disability award if the SIF is paying a portion of the lifetime benefits.

Under What Circumstances Is My Spouse Eligible To Receive Continued Benefits After My Death?

Total disability benefits end with the death of the Petitioner. However, if the Petitioner's death is directly related to the work-related injury, then the Petitioner's dependents are entitled to receive "dependency" benefits of up to 70% of his average wages. The spouse and minor children are automatically considered dependents of the injured worker. Of course, the insurance carrier may contend that the death is related to causes other than the work injury, and deny further benefits to the Petitioner's family. If so, a Dependency Claim Petition must be filed in order to force the carrier to pay continued benefits.

CHAPTER 14

FREQUENTLY ASKED QUESTIONS REGARDING WORKERS' COMPENSATION

What is the Deadline for Filing a Workers' Compensation Claim?

A formal Claim Petition must be filed within two years of the date you last received medical treatment authorized by the workers' compensation carrier. If no benefits were provided through workers' compensation, the two year deadline starts from the date of the accident. Please see Chapter 5, Step 9, for further details.

Am I Required To Use All My Sick And Vacation Time Before I Am Entitled To Receive Workers' Compensation Benefits?

No. Workers' compensation temporary disability benefits begin after you have been out of work for 7 consecutive days. Once that 7-day waiting period is over, temporary benefits are payable from the first day, but you cannot receive both workers' compensation and sick leave benefits. If your employer paid you sick leave benefits or vacation time before workers' compensation kicks in, the carrier will normally reimburse the employer for the amount you should have been paid temporary disability benefits for the period you were paid sick/vacation time. Thereafter, those sick/vacation days should be restored to you.

Do Workers' Compensation Claims Cover Pain And Suffering?

No, they do not. The New Jersey Workers' Compensation Act was passed as a compromise in which workers gave up their right to sue for pain and suffering in exchange for the access to quick medical care and disability benefits without the need to prove negligence. You may only collect damages for pain and suffering if your injuries were caused by the negligence or wrongdoing of a third party (an individual or company other than your employer or co-workers). The Division of Workers' Compensation does not have jurisdiction to hear such third party claims.

Is My Employer Required to Pay For My Health Insurance Benefits While I Am Out Of Work?

No, many companies require injured workers to pay their share of the health insurance premium, even when they are out on workers' compensation. Some larger employers will assume responsibility for paying the employees' share of the premium, but they are not required to do so. Check with the human resources department if you are unsure of your employer's policy. Unfortunately, the Division of Workers' Compensation does not have any jurisdiction over the issue of health insurance.

Can My Employer Fire Me While I Am Receiving Workers' Compensation Benefits?

Yes; an employer may fire you while you are receiving workers' compensation benefits, as long as you are not terminated in retaliation for filing a workers' compensation claim. Your workers' compensation claim will not protect you from being fired for other reasons, such as violating company policy. In addition, if the entire company is down-sizing, or you work for a small company which needs to fill your position in order to stay in business, the employer may legally terminate you. See, Chapter 15 for further information regarding employment law claims.

I Am Afraid That My Employer Will Fire Me If I File a Workers' Compensation Claim. Wouldn't The Safer Course Of Action Be To Just Use My Health Insurance To Pay For Medical Treatment?

No; you are not protecting your job by failing to assert your rights under the Workers' Compensation Act. On the contrary, you are putting your job in greater jeopardy if you fail to report a work injury through workers' compensation. It is illegal for an employer to retaliate against you for filing a workers' compensation claim. Moreover, health insurance generally denies coverage for any medical treatment which is clearly related to a work injury. You will be committing insurance fraud if you lie about the cause of your injuries to your doctor.

If your injury is serious, your failure to report the work injury could have long-term implications, including the loss of income once your sick time runs out, and loss of health insurance if your employer eventually terminates you due to your inability to perform your job.

Although retaliation certainly does occur in the workplace, do not make the mistake of believing that you will be protecting your job by declining to file a workers' compensation claim. If an employee fails to report a work injury due to fear of retaliation, but is later terminated, that employee may be left without recourse to any benefits. For example, this same employee may advise his doctor that an injury occurred at home to obtain health insurance coverage and stay in the good graces of his employer. If he is unable to work full duty for a significant period of time the employer may grow tired of accommodating him, and once enough time has passed, feel safe enough to terminate the employee. With the termination, the employee's health benefits end. Since the work accident was never documented though, the employee will find it difficult to successfully pursue a workers' compensation claim.

By contrast, if the work injury is documented and medical care provided by the workers' compensation carrier, a reasonable employer will think twice before terminating that employee. Especially if you believe that your employer is looking for an excuse to fire you, the safest course of action is to file a workers' compensation claim right away. Many employers are apprehensive about terminating an employee who has filed a workers' compensation claim, since they are fearful of being accused of retaliation.

What If My Employer Does Not Have Workers' Compensation Insurance?

An employer which fails to secure workers' compensation insurance coverage in New Jersey is potentially liable for criminal and civil penalties. The employer may be charged with a crime in the 4th degree and fined up to $5,000 for the first 10 days, and up to $5,000 for each additional 10-day period. These penalties can't be discharged in bankruptcy.

Corporate officers may also be held individually liable. Accordingly, it is crucial for New Jersey businesses to acquire workers' compensation insurance for their protection as well as for the protection of their employees.

If your employer fails to carry workers' compensation insurance you may apply for benefits through the New Jersey Uninsured Employers' Fund ("UEF"). The UEF provides both medical and temporary disability benefits. However, the procedural hurdles necessary to obtain those benefits are substantial. In addition, the UEF does not pay permanent disability benefits. To avoid the long process of obtaining benefits from the UEF, depending upon your injuries, it may be preferable to accept a "lump sum" settlement directly from an uninsured employer.

How Long Does It Take To Settle a Workers' Compensation Claim?

As a rule of thumb, most cases take 9 to 12 months to settle from the date you are released from medical treatment. Your attorney cannot begin to negotiate a settlement of your claim until you have been discharged from active medical care and attended all expert examinations. So if you receive five years of active medical treatment, you should not be surprised if it takes six years for a settlement to be reached in your case, or to <u>begin</u> the Trial process.

CHAPTER 15

ISSUES OUTSIDE OF THE WORKERS' COMPENSATION SYSTEM WHICH AFFECT INJURED WORKERS

There are several areas of the law which may touch the lives of injured workers, but are not covered by the New Jersey Workers' Compensation Act. The Division of Workers' Compensation does not have any jurisdiction to decide issues which arise under these areas of the law, although decisions you make surrounding these issues may affect your workers' compensation benefits.

Am I Eligible To Receive Social Security Retirement Benefits?

Depending on your age, you may already be eligible to receive your full social security retirement benefit. The full retirement age is has been gradually raised – it is currently either 66 or 67, depending upon the year you were born. You may start receiving social security retirement benefits as early as age 62, although you will receive a reduced amount.

What Do I Need To Know About Social Security Disability If I Am Hurt At Work?

As a rule of thumb, if it appears that you will be out of work for at least a year due to your injuries, you should apply for Social Security Disability Insurance Benefits ("SSD"). You must have earned enough work credits, and paid social security taxes, over the past 10 years to qualify.

You cannot collect more than 80% of your pre-accident income, so applying for SSD while you are receiving workers' compensation benefits will not result in a windfall. However, if you are seriously injured, it is important to get the SSD benefits in place, so that you are receiving some income if the workers' compensation benefits are abruptly stopped. Remember, temporary disability benefits are supposed to be <u>temporary</u> in nature, so they will end once your treatment ends, even if you are not medically able to return to the same line of work. If you are awarded SSD and then recover from your injuries in the future, you may try to return to work for a trial period without the risk of losing SSD in the event that your injuries prevent you from continuing to work on a long-term basis.

Can I Apply for a Private Pension If I Am Receiving Workers' Compensation Benefits?

Yes, you may take advantage of any pension offered by your employer, but keep in mind that your pension benefits may cause unintended consequences to your workers' compensation benefits. It is generally not a good idea to apply for a pension if you are still receiving temporary disability benefits from the workers' compensation carrier. If you do so, the insurance carrier will argue that you intentionally removed yourself from the workforce and are therefore ineligible to receive lost wage benefits. Practically speaking though, if you have made the personal decision to retire early, you may not financially have any choice but to start the bureaucratic process of applying for your pension to avoid being left without an income when the workers' compensation physician releases you to return to work or discharges you from treatment.

Should a Public Employee Apply For an Ordinary or Accidental Disability Pension Following a Work Accident?

New Jersey State employees usually have more generous pension benefits than their counterparts in private industry. Employees who have worked for the State for at least 10 years and are unable to return to the same line of work as a result of a disabling condition may apply for either an accidental or ordinary disability pension. You may apply for a pension yourself, or with the assistance of an attorney. The application for disability retirement benefits must be submitted online. See, Fact Sheet #15, attached at Appendix L.

If you were employed by the State, you should apply for an accidental disability pension if you were injured as a "direct result of a traumatic event" which permanently prevents you from doing the same job, even if you may be able to work in a different field in the future. Keep in mind though, that the definition of a traumatic event for purposes of a disability pension is much narrower than the definition of an accident under the Worker's Compensation Act. For example, a traumatic event must be caused by an external force (i.e.: being struck by a truck), as opposed to the more broad classification of an accident, which includes injuries caused by movements of an employee (i.e.: a muscle strain caused by lifting).

Accidental disability pensions pay two-thirds of an employee's salary, and your application must be submitted within five years of the date of last employment. If you are granted accidental disability benefits, there will be a "dollar for dollar" offset for any workers' compensation award you receive, which discourages many attorneys from pursuing workers' compensation claims on behalf of recipients of accidental disability pensions. However, given the uncertainty in the overburdened New Jersey pension system, it is advisable for State employees to also file a workers' compensation claim while the pension application is pending.

If a State worker is unable to return to work due a non-occupational condition or a combination of work and non-work injuries, he may still be eligible for the less generous "ordinary" disability pension, which pays approximately 40% of average wages. There is also a "dollar for dollar" offset on the workers' compensation award for any pension benefits paid by the State which are attributable to the work injury. Accordingly, although recipients of an ordinary disability pension may still be entitled to receive a workers' compensation award, that award may be reduced substantially by the pension credit. If you were granted a pension due to multiple health conditions, and not just the work injury, your attorney may argue that the State is only entitled to a partial offset for the pension benefits on your workers' compensation award. It is therefore critical for you to provide a copy of your pension application to your workers' compensation attorney.

May I Apply For Unemployment Benefits If My Job Is No Longer Available By The Time I Am Medically Released to Return to Work?

Absolutely, but be careful not to apply for unemployment if you are still entitled to receive workers' compensation. For instance, if you are still receiving medical treatment though workers' compensation and you are released to return to work light duty, your temporary disability benefits should continue if your employer terminates you because no light duty work is available. However, if you are released from medical treatment with permanent light duty restrictions, and your prior job is not available, then you should apply for unemployment benefits. For a more in depth discussion regarding the interplay between unemployment and workers' compensation please see Chapter 8.

Under What Circumstances May An Employee Sue a Third-Party For Injuries Incurred On The Job?

You cannot sue your employer or co-workers for causing the accident in which you were injured. However, if the accident was caused by the negligence of a third party -- someone other than your employer or a coworker --then

you may file a lawsuit against that third party outside of the workers' compensation system. An employee may pursue both a workers' compensation claim and a third party claim at the same time. Keep in mind though, that you may not recover duplicate benefits for the same injury. If you obtain compensation for your injuries and lost wages from a third party, you must then pay back all of the benefits you received through workers' compensation, less the workers' compensation carrier's share of the attorney's fee and a maximum of $750 towards the costs of the lawsuit. Even though you cannot have a "double recovery," it is still important to investigate the possibility of a third party claim, since damages for such a claim may be more generous than those offered through the Workers' Compensation Act. You may collect damages for "pain and suffering," if you file a third party claim in the Superior Court of New Jersey, which are not recoverable in a workers' compensation claim. Moreover, a jury would not be limited by a schedule of disabilities in rendering a third party award to you.

What Recourse Do I Have If My Employer Retaliates Against Me Because I Filed a Workers' Compensation Claim?

The Workers' Compensation Act prohibits retaliation against an employee for filing a claim or seeking workers' compensation benefits. However, these claims may be difficult to prove unless there is direct evidence that you were terminated or demoted due to the filing of a worker's compensation claim. There are subtle ways that the employer may show their displeasure over you filing a claim, short of termination. If your supervisor is being openly hostile to you after a work injury, ask your attorney to forward your employer a friendly "reminder" letter, pointing that it is illegal to retaliate against you for seeking workers' compensation benefits, and indicating that you are eager to return to work and/or full duty as soon as you are physically able to do so. If your employer cannot be dissuaded from terminating you as a direct result of seeking workers' compensation benefits, retaliation claims may be filed either in the Department of Labor or the Superior Court of New Jersey.

Can I Force My Employer To Create a Position For Me Once I Have Been Released to Permanent Light Duty?

The Workers' Compensation Court does not have jurisdiction to decide issues regarding continued employment. However, your employment may be protected under federal law, including the Americans With Disabilities Act (the "ADA") and the Family and Medical Leave Act ("FMLA"). New Jersey State law may also be implicated under the Law Against Discrimination ("LAD").

The ADA applies to employers with 15 or more employees and prevents your employer from discriminating against you based upon a disability, or a perceived disability. The ADA and LAD do not require your employer to create a separate light duty job for you in order to continue your employment. However, your employer must provide you with a "reasonable accommodation" if one is needed to allow you to perform your job. For example, if you are able to accomplish most of your job duties, but cannot lift the occasional package which weighs over 50 pounds, your employer may be obligated to offer you assistance to accommodate your disability. On the other hand, if your injuries prevent you from performing the "essential functions" of your job, then your employer may terminate you. In short, if you just need a bit of help to keep your job, and offering that assistance does not negatively impact the business, your employer may be forced to keep your job open.

Please note that your workers' compensation attorney's representation will be limited to issues arising under the Workers' Compensation Act, unless you sign a separate retainer agreement to cover another issue. You should request a referral to an attorney who specializes in employment law issues if you believe that you were discriminated against due to your disability.

CHAPTER 16

LEGAL REPRESENTATION IN THE DIVISION OF WORKERS' COMPENSATION

If you have read this manual, it should be abundantly clear that there will be legal ramifications to decisions made in the aftermath of a work injury, which will impact your medical and financial well-being in the future. The insurance carriers have an army of lawyers, doctors, and nurses at their disposal, whose goal is to minimize the amount of benefits paid on your claim. Shouldn't you at least have one person with knowledge of the workers' compensation system on your side?

Why Do I Need A Lawyer If The Insurance Carrier Is Paying My Medical Bills And Sending Me A Check Every Week?

Many workers' compensation claims begin rather uneventfully, with the employer correctly reporting the claim and the insurance carrier assigning a doctor to provide medical treatment. Unfortunately, if you blindly follow the directives of the insurance carrier without first hearing legal advice you are more likely to be discharged prematurely from medical treatment. It is also quite common for insurance carriers to pay temporary disability benefits at the incorrect rate, which may be rectified by a competent attorney. Once you are discharged from medical treatment and returned to work it is highly doubtful that you will be fully compensated for your permanent injuries unless you are represented by an experienced workers' compensation attorney. See, Chapter 9 on Permanent Disability.

What Is The Cost Of Hiring An Attorney In a Workers' Compensation Claim?

No attorney should ever charge you a retainer for representing you in a workers' compensation claim. If your claim has been denied, your attorney may ask you to obtain a copy of your medical records, including records regarding prior injuries. New Jersey law provides that physicians must provide copies of their medical records, at a charge of no more than $1.00 per page, up to a maximum of $100 per record. If your claim is viable, many attorneys will agree to pay these costs for you, to be reimbursed at the time of settlement.

The Workers' Compensation Act provides for a maximum attorneys' fee of 20% of the award. Please note that an attorney will not receive 20% of your temporary disability benefits. Rather, at the close of your case, when a settlement or judgment is entered on your behalf, the Court may award your attorney up to 20% of the permanent disability benefits or lump sum you are awarded. If you have the right to reopen your claim, the Court will generally order the insurance carrier to pay 60% of the attorney's total fee, with the remainder to be paid out of the proceeds of your settlement funds. On the other hand, if you receive a "lump sum" settlement, all of the 20% attorney's fee will be deducted from your award. See, Chapter 10 regarding settlements.

What Documents Should I Bring To a Meeting With a Workers' Compensation Lawyer?

If possible, the following documents should be obtained and brought to your first appointment with a workers' compensation attorney in order to successfully pursue a claim:

(1) Accident Report, if any.

(2) Paystub showing an "average" weekly wage prior to the accident.

(3) If your wages vary every week, bring your payroll records for the six month period prior to the accident. If your wage varies depending upon the

season, then you should also bring a W2 form, showing your annual wage.

(4) If you had more than one job at the time of the accident, bring a copy of your paystubs from the second job.

(5) Medical records in your possession following the accident, as well as a list of the names/addresses of all of your physicians.

(6) Medical records of any prior injury to the same part of your body. If you don't have the records, bring a list of the names/addresses of all of your prior physicians.

(7) If the accident has not been admitted by your employer, try to obtain witness statements from your co-workers, or at least collect their names and contact information for your attorney.

(8) For occupational claims, a job description from your employer, with a list of all job duties. If you do not have a formal job description, then make a list of your daily work activities.

(9) A copy of any prior workers' compensation awards. If you did not retain a copy of the Court Order, then provide the name of your prior attorney.

(10) Any correspondence you received from the workers' compensation carrier containing your claim number and the name of the adjuster assigned to your case.

Although your attorney may obtain many of these documents through the discovery process or from your physicians, it is helpful to obtain this information in advance, to expedite the claims process.

Why Would It Be a Mistake To Hire The General Practice Attorney Who Handles Everything From Traffic Tickets to Divorces To Take My Workers' Compensation Case?

There are attorneys out there who dabble in workers' compensation law. These "jacks of all trades" are easily flummoxed by issues which are addressed on a daily basis by attorneys who regularly handle these claims. The New Jersey Division of Workers' Compensation is very much a close circle of attorneys who often work together. If you hire an attorney who does not regularly appear in workers' compensation court, your case is more likely to get sidetracked, as the attorney may be unfamiliar with the normal practices of the Judge assigned to your case, the style of his legal adversary, and which medical doctors may be trusted to render a fair opinion. Such attorneys are spotted immediately by Judges and experienced practitioners, and their clients unfortunately end up suffering the consequences of their lack of knowledge and poor technique.

May I Change Attorneys, And If So, What Are The Implications To My Case?

Yes, you may change your attorney at any time. However, the further into the process you are, the more difficult it will be to switch attorneys. The attorneys' fee remains at 20%, even if multiple attorneys work on your case. At the close of your case, the Court would split the fee among the attorneys, based upon the work performed by each one. Obviously, your case will become less attractive for a new attorney to take your case since he must share his fee with another lawyer. In addition, many attorneys shy away from taking over cases started by other lawyers. For this reason and others, it is important to retain the right attorney as soon as possible.

If you are unhappy with your current legal representation you may certainly consult with a new attorney. Most lawyers will insist upon speaking with your current attorney to determine the status of your claim and whether or not you are a difficult client. A competent attorney will run for the hills if you have unreasonable expectations, are overly demanding, or fail to answer questions directly.

Just remember that an attorney is also interviewing you, to determine whether your case is worth his time and effort.

So if you are contacting a new attorney to evaluate your case, be prepared to recite a brief summary of the medical treatment you have received, the benefits you have been provided or denied by the workers' compensation carrier, and an explanation of why you are unhappy with your current attorney. You should pick up a copy of your entire file from your current attorney, if possible, to make it as easy as possible for a new attorney to take over your case. The difficulty you may experience in changing legal representation highlights the importance of retaining the right attorney from the start of your claim.

CHAPTER 17

REPRESENTATION BY PEZZANO MICKEY & BORNSTEIN

We do not like to brag, but we are good at what we do. As a firm, we take pride in helping members of our community to get their lives back together following an accident or injury. We are not "ambulance chasers" though – and we will decline any case which we do not believe has merit.

How Long Have The Attorneys At The Firm Been Practicing Law, And What Are Their Backgrounds?

Lisa Pezzano Mickey has been handling workers' compensation cases since 1991, shortly after she graduated from George Washington Law School. She began her career working for a non-profit organization, where she defended workers' compensation claims. Thereafter, she spent nine years as an associate with an insurance defense firm, representing

employers and insurance carriers in the Division of Workers' Compensation. In that capacity, she was able to learn the tricks of the insurance industry, and gained insights into how they evaluate claims. In 2001, she opened her own firm focusing on workers' compensation claims on behalf of injured workers. Ms. Mickey has given lectures to other attorneys regarding workers' compensation issues. She is a vice president and on the executive board of the N.J. Council of Safety & Health, a group of attorneys and doctors who fight to reform the New Jersey workers' compensation system.

As the mother of two children with roots in Central New Jersey, she is passionate about protecting the rights of her clients. She resides in Hunterdon County, New Jersey with her husband and two children.

Wendy S. Bornstein was born and raised in New Jersey. She is a 1983 graduate of Seton Hall Law School. Before starting her own law practice in 1990, she spent seven years representing nearly every insurance carrier in the State of New Jersey, defending personal injury claims. That experience has given her the unique ability to understand how insurance adjusters think, and what they need to settle a claim for the maximum amount. She is certified by the New Jersey Supreme Court as a Civil Trial Attorney, and is a former arbitrator for civil cases in the Superior Court of

New Jersey. She has served as a lecturer for continuing legal education in the field of personal injury law, and is the author of "The Five Deadly Sins That Can Wreck Your New Jersey Injury Claim." Wendy lives in Hillsborough with her twin daughters and their golden doodle.

When a client has both a workers' compensation claim and a third party negligence claim, Ms. Bornstein and Ms. Mickey work together to obtain the optimal results for their clients.

What Sets Pezzano Mickey & Bornstein Apart In Handling Workers' Compensation Cases?

PERSONAL ATTENTION

At larger law firms, your file may be passed around from one attorney to another, which could leave you feeling more like a file number than a client. We will handle your case personally from start to finish, ensuring that there are no loose ends. We do not handle every type of law under the sun. We don't want to; we don't need to. Each year we accept a limited number of cases involving accidents and injuries. Being picky about the cases we take, and having competent staff to delegate clerical tasks to, enables us to spend more time on your legal issues.

STRAIGHT TALK

We promise to give you our honest assessment of the likelihood of success in your case, as well as the limits of what a workers' compensation claim can accomplish. We will walk you through every step of the claims process before we begin, and answer all of your questions along the way.

It does not serve people well for them to incorrectly operate under the illusion that their cases will make them "millionaires" because they heard that an old lady was awarded a lot of money for spilling a cup of hot coffee (in actuality, the woman went through multiple surgeries for severe burns caused by scalding coffee which the restaurant chain knew was 30 degrees too hot). Such awards are impossible in the NJ Division of Compensation. We will "tell it like it is," rather than telling you what you would like to hear, so that you will be able to make plans accordingly.

RESPECTFUL / RETURN CALLS

We hear that there are lawyers out there who fail to show common courtesy to their clients by neglecting to return phone calls. At Pezzano Mickey & Bornstein, your calls will always be returned within 24 hours, and we will provide you with a complete status of your case at any time. Almost as important, you will not get "attitude" from our attorneys or staff when we have a conversation. We know that you have not been through this before and understand that you may be nervous. We will not make you feel uncomfortable for asking questions and certainly will not talk down to you.

TEAM APPROACH

We believe in empowering people to help themselves, so we will arm you with the knowledge you need to avoid making expensive mistakes. We will aggressively represent you in and out of Court and give you advice as to whether you should settle your case or go to trial. Together, as a team, we will decide on the best tactics for your case.

MODERN TECHNOLOGY

Although we are a small law firm, we utilize modern technology to organize the smallest details of your case. Your medical records will be scanned and electronically stored on our secure server, where they may be accessed at the click of a button. Since we handle so many cases in the Division of Workers' Compensation, we have an account with the Division to file Claim Petitions electronically, possibly the same day as your consultation.

FRIENDLY STAFF

We are proud of our friendly and helpful staff, who have been trained to show you every courtesy. Unlike many firms, whose receptionists may be curt and cold, you will be greeted by a pleasant member of our team, who genuinely care about our clients. If your attorney is in Court and is not immediately available, our knowledgeable paralegals are a valuable source of information in their own right. Forgot something that the attorney advised you? Lost the phone number of the insurance carrier? Don't recall the date of your next appointment? Our approachable staff will help you handle these details with a smile and <u>no attitude.</u>

WE WILL TELL YOU IF YOU ARE BETTER OFF WITH ANOTHER ATTORNEY OR NO ATTORNEY AT ALL!

If you call us and we cannot help you ourselves, we will do our best to point you in the right direction, to a professional who may help achieve your goals. We are not too proud to let you know if you are better off consulting with a different attorney, and will even help you to find the right attorney for you. Sometimes, the best advice you can get when you are thinking about taking legal action is that you do not have a claim that can be won, or it is simply not worth the time and cost of pursuing a particular claim. If that is true, we will tell you. But if we accept your case, you can be assured that you will receive zealous representation.

IN COURT EVERY DAY

There is an art to representing workers' compensation clients that comes from years of experience. We are in Court every single day. We know the judges, the insurance carriers, and the doctors involved in the small world of New Jersey workers' compensation. We treat every client as an individual, with different needs, and have no patience for insurance carriers who seek to denigrate them. We will use every available legal argument to persuade insurance carriers to do the right thing. If the carrier cannot be persuaded, we will not hesitate to seek court intervention because we understand that the cruelest form of denial is delay.

WE BUILD RELATIONSHIPS

Every person has their strengths and weaknesses, including judges, lawyers, and doctors. We use our network of contacts to research the background of the individuals who play a prominent role in our client's claims, to determine the best strategy for their cases. We have many repeat clients, who trust us to represent them again years after their initial cases have closed, because we do not just build cases – we build relationships.

Appendix

A. Claim Petition

B. Motion for Medical and Temporary Disability Benefits.

C. Application for State Temporary Disability Insurance Benefits

D. Certification of Contested Workers' Compensation Claim form

E. List of DVRS field offices

F. Rate Charts for 2012 – 2018)

G. Order Approving Settlement ("OAS")

H. Application for Review or Modification of Award

I. Order Approving Settlement with Dismissal ("Section 20")

J. Second Injury Fund Verified Petition

K. Fact Sheet #15, Disability Retirement Benefits, a publication of the N.J. Division of Pension and Benefits.

Pezzano Mickey & Bornstein
Phillipsburg * Flemington * Bridgewater
908-332-5552
www.pmblawfirm.com

A. Claim Petition

State of New Jersey Department of Labor and Workforce Development Division of Workers' Compensation PO Box 381 Trenton, New Jersey 08625-0381 WC-365 8/26/2015	**EMPLOYEE CLAIM PETITION** ☐ NEW FILING ☐ AMENDED FILING	Case No.: Vicinage: **please enter above only if filing an Amended Claim**

PETITIONER

SOCIAL SECURITY NUMBER ☐ SSN Not Available	
NAME:	
ADDRESS:	
DATE OF BIRTH:	SEX:
☐ A guardian or other representative is filing on behalf of the petitioner. See Supplemental Page for details.	

ATTORNEY FOR PETITIONER

TAX IDENTIFICATION NUMBER	
NAME:	
ADDRESS	
TELEPHONE NUMBER:	FAX NUMBER:

VS

EMPLOYER

NAME:
IF EMPLOYER IS KNOWN BY DIFFERENT NAME, PLEASE INDICATE HERE:
ADDRESS:
INDICATE THE STATUS OF THE EMPLOYER: ☐INSURED ☐UNINSURED ☐SELF-INSURED (PRIVATE) ☐SELF-INSURED (GOVT AGENCY)
☐ If uninsured, individual corporate officers, or others, are also named as respondent(s). See Supplemental Page for details.

INSURANCE CARRIER or SELF-INSURED ENTITY

NAME:		
ADDRESS		
CARRIER CLAIM NUMBER		
PERIOD OF COVERAGE:	FROM:	TO:
☐ See Supplemental Page for additional carriers		

TO THE DIVISION OF WORKERS' COMPENSATION - INJURY AND EMPLOYMENT DETAILS:

Date of Accident or Last Exposure:	Occupational Disease: ☐ YES ☐ NO	If Occupational Disease Give Periods of Exposure:
Where Injury Occurred (incl. town and county):		How Injury Occurred:
DESCRIBE EXTENT AND CHARACTER OF INJURY: If there has been amputation or disability to any member or impairment of any physical function, explain fully:		

Date Stopped Work:	Date Returned to Work:	Date Injury Reported:	Injury Reported To Whom:	Occupation and Type of Work:

Gross Wages $	Wage Period:	Rate of Temp. Compensation: $	Weeks of Temp. Disability paid:	Temporary Disability Paid: $	Permanent Disability Paid: $
Employer Furnished Medical Aid: ☐ YES ☐ NO					

☐ **Demand is hereby made for answers to standard occupational disease interrogatories. [N.J.A.C. 12:235-3.8(f)]**

☐ **Demand is hereby made for all records of medical treatment, examinations and diagnostic studies. [N.J.A.C. 12:235-3.8 (c)]**

Are you Medicare eligible or a Medicare beneficiary? ☐ **YES** ☐ **NO**

Were you eligible for Medicaid benefits at the time of the work injury? ☐ **YES** ☐ **NO**

Did you become eligible for Medicaid benefits after the work injury? ☐ **YES** ☐ **NO**

What other facts are there that you believe important:

Summary of Changes (*Complete only if filing an Amended pleading*):

Petitioner therefore requests that the Division of Workers' Compensation determine the amount of compensation due Petitioner from said Respondent, pursuant to R.S. 34:15-7 et seq., and that Petitioner may be awarded Petitioner's costs in this proceeding, and such other or further relief as may be proper.

____
Petitioner

STATE OF NEW JERSEY
COUNTY OF ______________________

Subscribed and sworn or affirmed
to before me this _______ day of _________________ , 20_____

____

Please be advised that information collected from the filing of this claim petition may be used by the Division of Workers' Compensation for record keeping, record access/distribution, and case scheduling purposes. Petitions filed with the Division are public documents and may be inspected and copied except where prohibited by Section 34:15-128 of the Workers' Compensation Statute.

The Privacy Act, 5 U.S.C. §552a, the Social Security Act, 42 U.S.C. § 405, and N.J.S.A. 34:15-1 et seq. authorize the Division of Workers' Compensation to request that the Petitioner supply the Division with his or her Social Security Number for record keeping purposes and cross-matches with the Social Security Administration, Workforce New Jersey, Temporary Disability Insurance and any other proper public purpose.

State of New Jersey Department of Labor and Workforce Development Division of Workers' Compensation PO Box 381 Trenton, New Jersey 08625-0381 WC-365.1 5/7/2015	**EMPLOYEE CLAIM PETITION SUPPLEMENTAL PAGE**	Case No.: Vicinage:

GUARDIAN OR REPRESENTATIVE

NAME:

ADDRESS:

RELATIONSHIP TO PETITIONER:

ADDITIONAL CARRIERS

NAME:	NAME:
ADDRESS:	ADDRESS:
CARRIER CLAIM NUMBER:	CARRIER CLAIM NUMBER:
PERIOD OF COVERAGE: FROM: TO:	PERIOD OF COVERAGE: FROM: TO:

NAME:	NAME:
ADDRESS:	ADDRESS:
CARRIER CLAIM NUMBER:	CARRIER CLAIM NUMBER:
PERIOD OF COVERAGE: FROM: TO:	PERIOD OF COVERAGE: FROM: TO:

INDIVIDUAL CORPORATE OFFICERS/PARTNERS/LLC MEMBERS

NAME:	NAME:
ADDRESS:	ADDRESS:

NAME:	NAME:
ADDRESS:	ADDRESS:

B. Motion for Medical and Temporary Disability Benefits

State of New Jersey Department of Labor and Workforce Development DIVISION OF WORKERS' COMPENSATION WC-101i PDF (r-3-07)	**NOTICE OF MOTION FOR TEMPORARY AND/OR MEDICAL BENEFITS (N.J.A.C. 12:235-3.2)**	CASE NO'S.: VICINAGE:

PETITIONER

SOCIAL SECURITY NUMBER	DOB
NAME:	
ADDRESS:	

ATTORNEY FOR PETITIONER

☐ SSN ☐ FEDERAL EMPLOYER NUMBER ☐ NJ REG NUMBER
NAME
ADDRESS:
TELEPHONE NUMBER (AREA CODE):

vs

RESPONDENT

NAME:
ADDRESS:

INSURANCE CARRIER

NAME ☐ SELF-INSURED ☐ NOT-COVERED
CLAIM NUMBER
ADDRESS:

TO: ____
(Respondent's Attorney)

____
(Address)

This Motion is supported by affidavit(s) and/or certification(s) made in the personal knowledge of the:

☐ **Petitioner and/or** ☐ **Petitioner's Attorney**

Petitioner alleges that:

A. Temporary Disability Benefits

☐ Petitioner is currently totally temporarily disabled and entitled to temporary disability benefits from ________________ and continuing at the rate of $ ____________ per week. Respondent provided benefits from ________________ through __________________ at the rate of $ ____________ per week.

B. Medicals

☐ **As set forth in the attached medical report(s)* of** ______________________________

Petitioner is currently in need of:

☐ **Medical treatment** ______________________________

☐ **Diagnostic studies** ______________________________ **; and/or**

☐ **Referral to a specialist(s)** ______________________________

* Medical report(s) must state the medical diagnosis. If the petitioner, having received treatment, cannot secure a report of the medical provider authorized by the respondent, this may be set forth in the affidavit in lieu of the physician's report.

State of New Jersey Department of Labor and Workforce Development DIVISION OF WORKERS' COMPENSATION WC-101i PDF (r-3-07)	**NOTICE OF MOTION FOR TEMPORARY AND/OR MEDICAL BENEFITS (N.J.A.C. 12:235-3.2) page 2**	CASE NO'S.: VICINAGE:

C. Other Information Attached or Enclosed if available **(see attached)** ☐

Itemized bill (s) and report(s) of treating physician(s) and/or institutions for which services petitioner is seeking payment (list here or attach).

D. Other Evidence in Support of Motion **(see attached)** ☐

(list here or attach)

Dated: ______________________ ______________________________________

Attorney for Petitioner

C. Application for State Temporary Disability Insurance Benefits

DS-1 Part A

New Jersey – Temporary Disability Insurance Application

You are responsible for having your healthcare provider and employer complete Parts B & C of this application. *Print clearly and answer ALL questions or your benefits may be delayed.* WDS-1 (1/17)

1 Name: Last First Middle DSDSDS 2 Date of Birth ___|___|___

Internal Code: DSDSDS 3 Social Security Number

4 Home Address (Street, Apt #, City, State, ZIP Code) 5 County

6 Mailing Address – *if different from home address* (Street, Apt #, City, State, ZIP Code) 7 ☐ Male ☐ Female 8 Occupation

9 Are you a citizen of the United States? ☐ Yes ☐ No 10 Alien Reg. No. 11 Work Authorization

If **NO**, answer #10 & 11 and give country of origin: ____________ from ________ to ________

	Month	Day	Year
12 What was the last day that you actually worked before your disability began?			
13 Reason for separation: ☐ Illness/Accident/Maternity ☐ Terminated ☐ Quit			
14 What was the **first day you were unable to work and under medical care** due to this disability? (Include Saturday, Sunday or holiday.)			
15 If you have **recovered or returned to work from this disability, give the date** (Do not use dates in the future)			

16 Date(s) of emergency room care or hospitalization: from ___|___|___ to ___|___|___
If dates are provided, please attach proof (eg. discharge papers) Month Day Year Month Day Year

17 Describe your disability (How, when, where it happened)____________________

18 Was this injury or illness caused by your job? (**This question must be answered.**) ☐ Yes or ☐ No

If Yes, date of work-related injury or illness: ___|___|___
Was your employer notified that your injury was caused by your job? ☐ Yes ☐ No

19 Physician's Name ____________ Address ____________ Phone ( ) ________

20 Other Benefits – During the period of disability covered by this claim, have you:
a Received any sick or vacation pay? ☐ Yes ☐ No
b Worked any days, including self-employment? ☐ Yes ☐ No
If Yes, specify employer____________ and dates worked, from ___|___|___ to___|___|___

21 Since your last day of work, have you received, claimed or applied for:
a Federal Social Security Disability benefits? ☐ Yes ☐ No
If yes, enter start/application date ___|___|___
If you received a Social Security award letter, attach a copy.
b Pension benefits from most recent employer? ☐ Yes ☐ No
c Temporary Disability benefits from another state? ☐ Yes ☐ No
d Unemployment Insurance benefits? ☐ Yes ☐ No

22 Certification and Signature: I was unable to work during the period for which I am claiming benefits. I certify that I have read and understand my benefit rights and responsibilities. I am aware that if I provide any information in this application that I know to be false, or if I knowingly fail to disclose a material fact, I may be subject to penalties, which may include criminal prosecution. You are hereby authorized to verify my Social Security Account Number, and obtain any medical, employment and Social Security benefit information necessary to determine my eligibility for benefits.

Sign Here ____________________ **Date**___|___|___

Witness signature if claimant writes an "X" ____________________

Phone ( ) ________ Alternate Phone ( ) ________ E-Mail ____________

You may designate a representative to obtain claim information for you if you cannot call us yourself. The law permits us to give claim information only to you or your representative.

23 Representative Name ____________________ Date of Birth___|___|___

Note: The NJ Temporary Disability Benefits program is not a "covered entity" under the Federal Health Information Portability and Accountability Act (HIPAA). All medical records of the Division, except to the extent necessary for the proper administration of the Temporary Disability Benefits Law, are confidential and are not open to public inspection. The Division protects all records that may reveal the identity of the claimant, or the nature or cause of the disability and the records may only be used in proceedings arising under the law. 1

Claimant's Name ______________________ WDS-1 (1/17)

Claimant's Address ______________________

Claimant's Phone ( ) ______________________

Social Security Number

___ ___ ___ - ___ ___ - ___ ___ ___ ___

PART A-1 CLAIMANT'S EMPLOYMENT INFORMATION

Instructions: Beginning with your last employer, list all of your employers for full-time, part-time, per diem work, etc. that you worked for over the past year. Any missing employment will delay your claim.

1a Name and address of your most recent employer:

(Street) (City) (State) (ZIP)

Period of employment: from ___ | ___ | ___ to ___ | ___ | ___
month day year month day year

Phone ______ Work Location ______ City State

Occupation ______ ☐ Full time ☐ Part time Union ______

Check the days of the week you normally work ☐ Sun ☐ Mon ☐ Tue ☐ Wed ☐ Thur ☐ Fri ☐ Sat

1b Employer Name and address:

(Street) (City) (State) (ZIP)

Period of employment: from ___ | ___ | ___ to ___ | ___ | ___
month day year month day year

Phone ______ Work Location ______ City State

Occupation ______ ☐ Full time ☐ Part time Union ______

Check the days of the week you normally work ☐ Sun ☐ Mon ☐ Tue ☐ Wed ☐ Thur ☐ Fri ☐ Sat

1c Employer Name and address:

(Street) (City) (State) (ZIP)

Period of employment: from ___ | ___ | ___ to ___ | ___ | ___
month day year month day year

Phone ______ Work Location ______ City State

Occupation ______ ☐ Full time ☐ Part time Union ______

Check the days of the week you normally work ☐ Sun ☐ Mon ☐ Tue ☐ Wed ☐ Thur ☐ Fri ☐ Sat

1d Employer Name and address:

(Street) (City) (State) (ZIP)

Period of employment: from ___ | ___ | ___ to ___ | ___ | ___
month day year month day year

Phone ______ Work Location ______ City State

Occupation ______ ☐ Full time ☐ Part time Union ______

Check the days of the week you normally work ☐ Sun ☐ Mon ☐ Tue ☐ Wed ☐ Thur ☐ Fri ☐ Sat

If you are submitting this claim more than 30 days after your first day of disability, please give your reason:

____

____

____

____

____

If more space is needed, attach an additional sheet of paper. Be sure your name and Social Security number appears on all pages.

IMPORTANT TAX INFORMATION

If you choose to have federal income tax withheld from your disability benefits, you should complete a W-4S. List the specific dollar amount you would like withheld weekly from your benefits. Do not give a % amount.

2

WDS-1 (1/17)

Claimant's Name ______________________________

Claimant's Address ______________________________

Claimant's Phone (   ) ______________________________

Social Security Number

___ ___ ___ - ___ ___ - ___ ___ ___ ___

PART B **MEDICAL CERTIFICATE** – Have your healthcare provider complete Part B.

N.J.S.A 12:18-1.6 prohibits charging a fee to complete this form.

1 Patient has been under my care for this disability **FROM** ____|____|____ (first date of treatment) **TO** ____|____|____ (most recent treatment) ______ (frequency)

2 Date the patient was unable to perform regular work due to this disability ____|____|____ (Month / Day / Year)
(Doctor's signature date must be on or after this date unless this is a pregnancy claim)

3 Estimated recovery date (approximate date patient will be able to return to work) ____|____|____ (Month / Day / Year)

4 If now recovered, on what date was the patient first able to work? ____|____|____ (Month / Day / Year)

5 Diagnosis (what is the disabling condition) ______________________________

______________________________ **ICD Code** ______________

6 Do you believe this patient is mentally capable of handling their own affairs, including the use of benefits? ☐ Yes ☐ No

7a If pregnancy, provide estimated date of delivery: ____|____|____ (Month / Day / Year)

b Complications, if any ______________________________

c If pregnancy terminated, enter the date: ____|____|____ (Month / Day / Year)

And identify the reason: ☐ Birth ☐ C-Section ☐ Miscarriage ☐ Abortion

8 Date(s) of emergency room care or hospitalization: from ____|____|____ (Month / Day / Year) to ____|____|____ (Month / Day / Year)

9 Type of surgery ______________ Date of Surgery ____|____|____ (Month / Day / Year) Anticipated Surgery Date ____|____|____ (Month / Day / Year)

Is surgery for cosmetic purposes only? ☐ Yes ☐ No

10 Was this disability ☐ Due to an accident at work ☐ Due to the nature of the work ☐ Not related to their work

11a Was this patient referred to you? ☐ Yes ☐ No If Yes, name of referring doctor ______________

Referring doctor's phone (   ) ______________ **11b** Name of any specialist treating the patient ______________

12 I certify that the above statements, in my opinion, truly describe the patient's disability and the estimated duration thereof

______________ Print Doctor's Name ______________ License No. and State* ______________ Specialty

______________ Street Address Phone (   ) ______________

City State ZIP Code Fax (   ) ______________

______________ **Signature of Doctor** ____|____ **Date Signed** ☐ Check, if Resident

Must be signed on or after the date in Question 2, unless a pregnancy claim.

***If completed by a Physician's Assistant (PA-C), provide the license number of the supervising doctor.** 3

Claimant's Name ____________________ Phone (   ) ____________ WDS-1 (1/17) Social Security Number ___ ___ ___-___ ___-___ ___ ___ ___

Claimant's Address ______________________________

PART C

EMPLOYER STATEMENT – Have your employer or company representative complete Part C.

2 EMPLOYER STATUS

Your Federal Employer Identification Number (FEIN) ______________

3 PRIVATE PLAN COVERAGE

a Do you have a New Jersey approved Private Plan? ☐ Yes ☐ No

b If Yes, is the claimant covered under this plan? ☐ Yes ☐ No

4 Check the days of the week that the claimant normally works.

☐ Sun ☐ Mon ☐ Tues ☐ Wed ☐ Thurs ☐ Fri ☐ Sat ☐ Varies

5 LAST ACTUAL DAY WORKED before this disability

(Do not use a payroll week ending date) ____|____|____ (Month Day Year)

a Reason for separation from work ______________

b Is separation ☐ Temporary? ☐ Permanent?

c Has claimant returned to work? ☐ Yes ☐ No

If Yes, give date ____|____|____

d If the work was intermittent, list dates ______________

6 CONTINUED PAY

a Have you paid or do you expect to pay the claimant for any period after the last day of work? ☐ Yes ☐ No

b If Yes, give dates from: ____|____|____ to: ____|____|____ (Month Day Year Month Day Year)

c Amount per week $__________ (if amount varies attach a list of dates/amounts)

d Total amount paid for entire given period $__________

e Check the number that best describes the monies paid in item c.

☐ 1. Paid time off (vacation, sick, personal, etc.)

☐ 2. Difference between regular wkly wages and disability benefits to be received

☐ 3. Supplemental benefits (unallocated payout will have no impact)

☐ 4. Severance pay With notice ☐ In lieu of notice ☐

☐ 5. Pension (attach pension approval letter)

Note: Items 1, 4, and 5 may reduce benefits to the claimant.

7 GOVERNMENT EMPLOYERS

a Payroll Number (For N.J. state employees) ______________

b If claimant has applied for or received donated leave, attach dates and amounts.

8 WORKERS' COMPENSATION LIABILITY

a Did the claimant's disability happen in connection with their work or while on your premises, or was the disability due in any way to their occupation? ☐ Yes ☐ No

b If Yes, have you filed or do you intend to file a Workers' Compensation claim on behalf of this claimant? ☐ Yes ☐ No

c If Yes, list Workers' Compensation Insurance carrier below:

Name ______________ Phone (   ) ______________

Address ______________

Policy # ______________ Claim # ______________

I CERTIFY THE INFORMATION GIVEN ABOVE IS CORRECT

Firm Name ______________ Phone (   ) ______________

Address ______________ Fax (   ) ______________

City ______________ State ________ ZIP Code ______________

Name/Title ______________

9 BASE WEEKS / BASE YEAR WAGES

A base week is a calendar week in which the N.J. employee had gross earnings of $168 or more.

a Total number of **Base Weeks** ________

b Total **Gross Wages** in Base Year $ ________

(52 weeks prior to first day of disability)

10 Weekly Wage (base hrs x rate) $________

Hourly Rate $______/hr

11 Weekly Wages

Provide claimant's GROSS earnings in New Jersey employment and period ending dates.

Note: If the weeks listed below, include overtime, bonuses, etc., attach an explanation and separate the regular wages earned.

Description of Calendar Week	Week Ending Date	Gross Wages
Week Disability Began	/ /	$
Week before Disability	/ /	$
2nd Week Before Disability	/ /	$
3rd Week Before Disability	/ /	$
4th Week Before Disability	/ /	$
5th Week Before Disability	/ /	$
6th Week Before Disability	/ /	$
7th Week Before Disability	/ /	$
8th Week Before Disability	/ /	$
9th Week Before Disability	/ /	$
10th Week Before Disability	/ /	$
TOTAL GROSS WAGES FOR ABOVE WEEKS		$

Are you exempt from FICA tax? ☐ Yes ☐ No

Signature ______________

Do not sign/date before the last day worked

Date (required) ____|____|____

4

— *KEEP THIS PAGE FOR YOUR RECORDS — DO NOT RETURN* —

How to complete the Claim for Disability Benefits *(form DS-1)*

▷ You (the claimant) must complete the first 2 pages of the application (parts A and A1).

▷ ***You*** are responsible for having your doctor complete part B and for having your last employer complete part C.

▷ If you worked for more than one employer during the past year, you may copy part C for your other employer(s) to complete. This will help us process your claim more quickly.

▷ If your doctor and employer(s) submit their parts separately, please complete and return parts A and A1 as soon as possible. If you cannot submit all parts together, we can process your claim quicker if we receive parts A and A1 first.

For quicker processing

▷ It is very important that you provide information that is accurate and true. Missing, incorrect, or illegible information will delay payment of your benefits. Print clearly.

▷ Write your name and Social Security number on each part of your claim and on all attachments.

▷ Give exact dates when dates are requested.

▷ If you need help completing the form, call 609-292-7060. You may need to hold to speak to an agent.

Submitting your application

1. Whenever possible, send all parts of your claim together. Sending separate pages will delay your claim. **Sending duplicate copies will also delay your claim.** Send additional copies *ONLY* if information has changed.
2. If you fax your claim, be sure to fax all 4 pages together (but not these instructions).
3. Send all parts (parts A, A1, B, and C) and any attachments to:

   mail: Division of Temporary Disability Insurance / P.O. Box 387 / Trenton, NJ 08625-0387

   fax: 609-984-4138

Claimant's Rights and Responsibilities

To file a claim for temporary disability benefits

It is your responsibility to file this claim *immediately after* you stop working due to your disability. If you file a claim before your last day of work, your benefits will be delayed.

By law, you must file a claim within 30 days after the start of your disability. If you file later, benefits may be denied or reduced. If you file more than 30 days after you disability started, give the reason why on the bottom of part A1.

Other income

You must tell us about any other income you are receiving. This includes sick pay, wages, pension, workers compensation benefits, Social Security Disability benefits, or disability benefits from your employer or union.

Continued medical certification

If you are eligible for TDI benefits, we will periodically send you a request for continued medical certification (form P30) to verify that you are still disabled and under a doctor's care. Return the form promptly to guarantee continuous benefits.

Online information

about temporary disability benefits: *nj.gov/labor*

Return to work

When you recover or return to work, report this date immediately to the Division of Temporary Disability Insurance to avoid overpayment.

Income tax withholding

If you want federal income tax (F.I.T.) deductions withheld from your disability benefits, attach form W-4S (Request for Federal Income Tax Withholding From Sick Pay) to your claim. You can get this form from your employer or the Internal Revenue Service (*irs.gov/pub/irs-access/fw4s_accessible.pdf*).

Help with your claim

Customer Service 609-292-7060

D. Certification of Contested Workers' Compensation Claim form

New Jersey Department of Labor
And Workforce Development
Private Plan Compliance Section

CLAIM PETITION NUMBER

CERTIFICATION OF CONTESTED WORKERS' COMPENSATION CLAIM

______________________ (Claimant)

[ ] Social Security Number

VS.

______________________ (Employer)

______________________ (Employer Address)

______________________ (Workers' Compensation Insurer)

______________________ (Workers' Compensation Insurer Address)

______________________ **(Workers' Compensation Insurer Telephone #)**

______________________ (Attorney for Claimant)

______________________ (Attorney's Address)

______________________ (Attorney's Telephone Number)

AGREEMENT

In consideration of the payment of temporary disability benefits from the Private Plan insurer, ____________________, for a disability beginning ____________________, which I consider as having been attributable to my work, I do hereby agree to pursue my claim within the time specified and to obtain a determination as to eligibility under the Workers' Compensation Law. I further agree to reimburse fully the Private Plan insurer for such advances if I receive any Workers' Compensation award or settlement for such disability or if I should not pursue my claim in the time specified under the Workers' Compensation Law. If I have not yet done so, I also agree to:

1. File a Private Plan temporary disability claim. (Private Plan claim forms may be obtained from your employer or the Private Plan insurer.)

2. File an "Employee's Claim Petition" with the Division of Workers' Compensation. For information concerning this petition consult the Division of Workers' Compensation, PO Box 381, Trenton, New Jersey 08625-0381, Telephone: (609) 292-2515, or an attorney licensed to practice in New Jersey.

______________________ Date

______________________ Claimant's Signature

______________________ Claimant's Address

TO BE COMPLETED BY THE DIVISION OF TEMPORARY DISABILITY INSURANCE

To the Private Plan insurer:
This is to certify that the petitioner's claim for benefits under the Workers' Compensation Law is contested and that an "Employee's Claim Petition" has been filed. Benefits may therefore be released by you subject to the right of subrogation held by you under Section 43:21-30 of the New Jersey Temporary Disability Benefits Law.

______________________ Date

______________________ Authorized Representative, Div. Temporary Disability Insurance

DP-221 (R-7-04)

(SEE INSTRUCTIONS ON REVERSE)

New Jersey Department of Labor & Workforce Development
Division of Temporary Disability Insurance
Private Plan Compliance Section
PO Box 957
Trenton, NJ 08625-0957
Telephone (609) 292-2715
FAX (609) 292-2537

EXPLANATION OF CONTESTED WORKERS' COMPENSATION CLAIMS

If your disability is work-related, but your workers' compensation claim is contested and you are not receiving workers' compensation benefits, you may apply for non work-related Private Plan temporary disability benefits. You must take the following actions:

- You should obtain an attorney to pursue your workers' compensation claim. Your attorney must file the appropriate forms, such as the Employee's Claim Petition, with the New Jersey Division of Workers' Compensation (see address on front of this form).
- You must complete this Form DP-221, Certification of Contested Workers' Compensation Claim (see instructions below).
- You must submit a temporary disability claim to your employer's Private Plan temporary disability insurer, who must determine whether you are eligible for benefits under the New Jersey Temporary Disability Benefits Law and the employer's Private Plan.

Please note that you must take all of the above three actions in order to receive temporary disability benefits.

After receiving your completed Form DP-221 and verifying that the case is contested, the Private Plan Compliance Section will notify the Private Plan temporary disability insurer that benefits must be paid to you. After benefits are paid, that insurer may file a lien so that they can be reimbursed when workers' compensation benefits are later awarded to you.

If your disability is not work-related, Form DP-221 cannot be used. If this is your situation, contact the Private Plan Compliance Section at the above address so that we can determine what action is needed on your claim.

INSTRUCTIONS FOR COMPLETING FORM DP-221

All information must be supplied.

In the section entitled "Agreement", on the first line enter the name of the Private Plan insurer who will be paying temporary disability benefits to you (do not enter the name of the workers' compensation insurer). In the "Agreement" on the second line enter the date your workers' compensation disability started (do not enter the date your workers' compensation payments ended).

This completed Form DP-221 should be returned to the Division of Temporary Disability Insurance, Private Plan Compliance Section, PO Box 957, Trenton, NJ 08625-0957.

E. List of DVRS Field Offices

Atlantic County

2 South Main Street

1st Floor Suite 2

Pleasantville, New Jersey 08232-2728

Phone: 609-813-3933

Fax: 609-813-3959

VP: 609-224-1218

Bergen County

60 State Street

2nd Floor

Hackensack, New Jersey 07601-5471

Phone: 201-996-8970

Fax: 201-996-8880

VP: 973-968-6556

Burlington County

795 Wood lane Road

Suite 201

Westhampton, New Jersey 08060

Phone: 609-518-3948

Option 3

Fax: 609-518 3956

VP: 973-518-3956

Middlesex County

506 Jersey Avenue

P.O. Box 2672

New Brunswick, New Jersey
08901-2672

Phone: 732-937-6300

Fax: 732-934-6358

VP: 732-393-8056

Monmouth County

60 Taylor Avenue North

Neptune, New Jersey 07753-
4844

Phone: 732-775-1799

Fax: 732-775-1666

VP: 732-606-4961

Morris County

13 Emery Avenue

2nd Floor

Randolph, New Jersey
07869-3886

Phone: 862-397-5600

Fax: 973-895-6420

VP: 973-607-2034

Camden County
2600 Mt. Ephraim Avenue
Suite 103
Camden, New Jersey 08104-3290
08753-2225
Phone: 856-614-2500
Fax: 856 614-2538
VP: 856 831-7599

Cape May County
3810 New Jersey Avenue
Wildwood, New Jersey 08260
Phone: 609-523-0330
Fax: 609-523-0212
VP: 609-224-1218

Cumberland County
40 East Broad Street
Suite 204
Bridgeton, New Jersey 08302-2881
08302-2881
Phone: 856-453-3888
Fax: 856-453-3909
VP: 856-497-0075

Essex County
75 Veterans Memorial Drive East
Suite 101
Somerville, New Jersey 08876-2952
Phone: 908-704-3030

Ocean County
1027 Hooper Avenue
Building 6 3rd Floor Suite 1
Toms River, New Jersey

Phone: 732-505-2317
Fax: 732-505-2317
VP: 732-606-4961

Passaic County
200 Memorial Drive
1st Floor
Paterson, New Jersey 07505
Phone: 973-742 -9226
Fax: 973-279-5895
VP: 973-968-6556

Salem County
40 East Broad Street
Suite 204
Bridgeton, New Jersey

Phone: 856-453-3888
Fax: 856-453-3909
VP: 856-497-0075

Somerset County
990 Broad Street
2nd Floor
Newark, New Jersey 07102
Phone: 973-648-3494

Fax: 908-704-3476
VP: 732-393-8056

Gloucester County
215 Crown Point Road
Suite 200
Therefore, New Jersey 08086-2153
07840-1217
Phone: 856-384-3730
VP: 856-497-0075

Hudson County
438 Summit Avenue
6th Floor
07201-2306
Jersey City, New Jersey 07306-3187
Phone: 201-217-7180
Fax: 201-217-7287
VP: 201-942-0085

Hunterdon County
75 Veterans Memorial Drive East
Suite 101
Somerville, New Jersey 08876-2952
07840-1217
Phone: 908-704-3030
Fax: 908-704-3476
VP: 732-393-8056

Mercer County
Office)
Labor Station Plaza
28 Yard Avenue
0398

Fax: 973-648-3902
VP: 862-772-7166

Sussex County
223 West Stiger Street
Suite A
Hackettstown, New Jersey

Phone: 908-852-4110
Fax: 908-813-9745
VP: 908-645-0616

Union County
921 Elizabeth Avenue
Elizabeth, New Jersey

Phone: 908-965-3940
Fax: 908-965-2976
VP: 908-242-3563

Warren County
223 West Stiger Street
Suite A
Hackettstown, New Jersey

Phone: 908-852-4110
Fax: 908-813-9745
VP: 908-645-0616

Administrative (Central

P.O. Box 398
Trenton, New Jersey 08625-

P.O. Box 959
Trenton, New Jersey 08625-0959

Phone: 609-292-2940
Fax: 609-984-3553
VP: 609-498-7011

Phone: 609-292-9339
Fax: 609-292-8347

VP: 609-498-6221

F. Rate Charts for 2012 – 2018

SCHEDULE OF DISABILITIES AND MAXIMUM BENEFITS EXCLUSIVE OF AMPUTATION AND ENUCLEATION

EFFECTIVE 1/1/2012

PER-CENT	HAND 245 WEEKS	ARM 330 WEEKS	FINGERS - SEE FOOTNOTE					LEG 315 WEEKS	FOOT 230 WEEKS	TOES		EYE 200 WEEKS	HEARING		PARTIAL TOTAL BASED ON 600 WEEKS	PER-CENT
			THUMB 75 WEEKS	FIRST 50 WEEKS	SECOND 40 WEEKS	THIRD 30 WEEKS	FOURTH 20 WEEKS			GREAT TOE 40 WEEKS	OTHER TOE 15 WEEKS		1 EAR 60 WEEKS	2 EARS 200 WEEKS		
1	2.4500 529.20	3.3000 712.80	0.7500 162.00	0.5000 108.00	0.4000 86.40	0.3000 64.80	0.2000 43.20	3.1500 680.40	2.3000 496.80	0.4000 86.40	0.1500 32.40	2.0000 432.00	0.6000 129.60	2.0000 432.00	6.0000 1,296.00	1
1 1/2	3.6750 793.80	4.9500 1,069.20	1.1250 243.00	0.7500 162.00	0.6000 129.60	0.4500 97.20	0.3000 64.80	4.7250 1,020.60	3.4500 745.20	0.6000 129.60	0.2250 48.60	3.0000 648.00	0.9000 194.40	3.0000 648.00	9.0000 1,944.00	1 1/2
2	4.9000 1,058.40	6.6000 1,425.60	1.5000 324.00	1.0000 216.00	0.8000 172.80	0.6000 129.60	0.4000 86.40	6.3000 1,360.80	4.6000 993.60	0.8000 172.80	0.3000 64.80	4.0000 864.00	1.2000 259.20	4.0000 864.00	12.0000 2,592.00	2
2 1/2	6.1250 1,323.00	8.2500 1,782.00	1.8750 405.00	1.2500 270.00	1.0000 216.00	0.7500 162.00	0.5000 108.00	7.8750 1,701.00	5.7500 1,242.00	1.0000 216.00	0.3750 81.00	5.0000 1,080.00	1.5000 324.00	5.0000 1,080.00	15.0000 3,240.00	2 1/2
3	7.3500 1,587.60	9.9000 2,138.40	2.2500 486.00	1.5000 324.00	1.2000 259.20	0.9000 194.40	0.6000 129.60	9.4500 2,041.20	6.9000 1,490.40	1.2000 259.20	0.4500 97.20	6.0000 1,296.00	1.8000 388.80	6.0000 1,296.00	18.0000 3,888.00	3
3 1/2	8.5750 1,852.20	11.5500 2,494.80	2.6250 567.00	1.7500 378.00	1.4000 302.40	1.0500 226.80	0.7000 151.20	11.0250 2,381.40	8.0500 1,738.80	1.4000 302.40	0.5250 113.40	7.0000 1,512.00	2.1000 453.60	7.0000 1,512.00	21.0000 4,536.00	3 1/2
4	9.8000 2,116.80	13.2000 2,851.20	3.0000 648.00	2.0000 432.00	1.6000 345.60	1.2000 259.20	0.8000 172.80	12.6000 2,721.60	9.2000 1,987.20	1.6000 345.60	0.6000 129.60	8.0000 1,728.00	2.4000 518.40	8.0000 1,728.00	24.0000 5,184.00	4
5	12.2500 2,646.00	16.5000 3,564.00	3.7500 810.00	2.5000 540.00	2.0000 432.00	1.5000 324.00	1.0000 216.00	15.7500 3,402.00	11.5000 2,484.00	2.0000 432.00	0.7500 162.00	10.0000 2,160.00	3.0000 648.00	10.0000 2,160.00	30.0000 6,480.00	5
7 1/2	18.3750 3,969.00	24.7500 5,346.00	5.6250 1,215.00	3.7500 810.00	3.0000 648.00	2.2500 486.00	1.5000 324.00	23.6250 5,103.00	17.2500 3,726.00	3.0000 648.00	1.1250 243.00	15.0000 3,240.00	4.5000 972.00	15.0000 3,240.00	45.0000 9,720.00	7 1/2
10	24.5000 5,292.00	33.0000 7,128.00	7.5000 1,620.00	5.0000 1,080.00	4.0000 864.00	3.0000 648.00	2.0000 432.00	31.5000 6,804.00	23.0000 4,968.00	4.0000 864.00	1.5000 324.00	20.0000 4,320.00	6.0000 1,296.00	20.0000 4,320.00	60.0000 12,960.00	10
12 1/2	30.6250 6,615.00	41.2500 8,910.00	9.3750 2,025.00	6.2500 1,350.00	5.0000 1,080.00	3.7500 810.00	2.5000 540.00	39.3750 8,505.00	28.7500 6,210.00	5.0000 1,080.00	1.8750 405.00	25.0000 5,400.00	7.5000 1,620.00	25.0000 5,400.00	75.0000 16,200.00	12 1/2
15	36.7500 7,938.00	49.5000 10,692.00	11.2500 2,430.00	7.5000 1,620.00	6.0000 1,296.00	4.5000 972.00	3.0000 648.00	47.2500 10,206.00	34.5000 7,452.00	6.0000 1,296.00	2.2500 486.00	30.0000 6,480.00	9.0000 1,944.00	30.0000 6,480.00	90.0000 19,440.00	15
17 1/2	42.8750 9,261.00	57.7500 12,474.00	13.1250 2,835.00	8.7500 1,890.00	7.0000 1,512.00	5.2500 1,134.00	3.5000 756.00	55.1250 11,907.00	40.2500 8,694.00	7.0000 1,512.00	2.6250 567.00	35.0000 7,560.00	10.5000 2,268.00	35.0000 7,560.00	105.0000 23,964.00	17 1/2
20	49.0000 10,584.00	66.0000 14,256.00	15.0000 3,240.00	10.0000 2,160.00	8.0000 1,728.00	6.0000 1,296.00	4.0000 864.00	63.0000 13,608.00	46.0000 9,936.00	8.0000 1,728.00	3.0000 648.00	40.0000 8,640.00	12.0000 2,592.00	40.0000 8,640.00	120.0000 27,882.00	20
22 1/2	55.1250 11,907.00	74.2500 16,038.00	16.8750 3,645.00	11.2500 2,430.00	9.0000 1,944.00	6.7500 1,458.00	4.5000 972.00	70.8750 15,309.00	51.7500 11,178.00	9.0000 1,944.00	3.3750 729.00	45.0000 9,720.00	13.5000 2,916.00	45.0000 9,720.00	135.0000 32,226.00	22 1/2
25	61.2500 13,230.00	82.5000 17,820.00	18.7500 4,050.00	12.5000 2,700.00	10.0000 2,160.00	7.5000 1,620.00	5.0000 1,080.00	78.7500 17,010.00	57.5000 12,420.00	10.0000 2,160.00	3.7500 810.00	50.0000 10,800.00	15.0000 3,240.00	50.0000 10,800.00	150.0000 36,954.00	25
27 1/2	67.3750 14,553.00	90.7500 20,600.25	20.6250 4,455.00	13.7500 2,970.00	11.0000 2,376.00	8.2500 1,782.00	5.5000 1,188.00	86.6250 18,711.00	63.2500 13,662.00	11.0000 2,376.00	4.1250 891.00	55.0000 11,880.00	16.5000 3,564.00	55.0000 11,880.00	165.0000 42,108.00	27 1/2
30	73.5000 15,876.00	99.0000 22,506.00	22.5000 4,860.00	15.0000 3,240.00	12.0000 2,592.00	9.0000 1,944.00	6.0000 1,296.00	94.5000 21,451.50	69.0000 14,904.00	12.0000 2,592.00	4.5000 972.00	60.0000 12,960.00	18.0000 3,888.00	60.0000 12,960.00	180.0000 47,646.00	30
33 1/3	81.6667 17,640.01	110.0000 25,226.00	25.0000 5,400.00	16.6667 3,600.01	13.3333 2,879.99	10.0000 2,160.00	6.6667 1,440.01	105.0000 23,964.00	76.6667 16,560.01	13.3333 2,879.99	5.0000 1,080.00	66.6667 14,400.01	20.0000 4,320.00	66.6667 14,400.01	200.0000 75,600.00	33 1/3
35	85.7500 18,522.00	115.5000 26,667.00	26.2500 5,670.00	17.5000 3,780.00	14.0000 3,024.00	10.5000 2,268.00	7.0000 1,512.00	110.2500 25,290.75	80.5000 17,388.00	14.0000 3,024.00	5.2500 1,134.00	70.0000 15,120.00	21.0000 4,536.00	70.0000 15,120.00	210.0000 79,380.00	35
37 1/2	91.8750 20,855.63	123.7500 28,935.75	28.1250 6,075.00	18.7500 4,050.00	15.0000 3,240.00	11.2500 2,430.00	7.5000 1,620.00	118.1250 27,375.75	86.2500 18,630.00	15.0000 3,240.00	5.6250 1,215.00	75.0000 16,200.00	22.5000 4,860.00	75.0000 16,200.00	225.0000 97,200.00	37 1/2
40	98.0000 22,268.00	132.0000 31,320.00	30.0000 6,480.00	20.0000 4,320.00	16.0000 3,456.00	12.0000 2,592.00	8.0000 1,728.00	126.0000 29,568.00	92.0000 20,884.00	16.0000 3,456.00	6.0000 1,296.00	80.0000 17,280.00	24.0000 5,184.00	80.0000 17,280.00	240.0000 103,680.00	40
45	110.2500 25,290.75	148.5000 36,468.00	33.7500 7,290.00	22.5000 4,860.00	18.0000 3,888.00	13.5000 2,916.00	9.0000 1,944.00	141.7500 34,305.75	103.5000 23,592.00	18.0000 3,888.00	6.7500 1,458.00	90.0000 19,440.00	27.0000 5,832.00	90.0000 19,440.00	270.0000 131,220.00	45
50	122.5000 28,584.50	165.0000 42,108.00	37.5000 8,100.00	25.0000 5,400.00	20.0000 4,320.00	15.0000 3,240.00	10.0000 2,160.00	157.5000 39,483.00	115.0000 26,532.00	20.0000 4,320.00	7.5000 1,620.00	100.0000 22,744.00	30.0000 6,480.00	100.0000 22,744.00	300.0000 162,000.00	50
55	134.7500 32,150.50	181.5000 58,607.00	41.2500 8,910.00	27.5000 5,940.00	22.0000 4,752.00	16.5000 3,564.00	11.0000 2,376.00	173.2500 45,102.75	126.5000 29,714.00	22.0000 4,752.00	8.2500 1,782.00	110.0000 25,226.00	33.0000 7,128.00	110.0000 25,226.00	330.0000 196,020.00	55
60	147.0000 35,982.00	198.0000 74,844.00	45.0000 9,720.00	30.0000 6,480.00	24.0000 5,184.00	18.0000 3,888.00	12.0000 2,592.00	189.0000 71,442.00	138.0000 33,132.00	24.0000 5,184.00	9.0000 1,944.00	120.0000 27,882.00	36.0000 7,776.00	120.0000 27,882.00	360.0000 233,280.00	60
65	159.2500 40,088.50	214.5000 92,664.00	48.7500 10,530.00	32.5000 7,020.00	26.0000 5,616.00	19.5000 4,212.00	13.0000 2,808.00	204.7500 77,395.50	149.5000 36,792.00	26.0000 5,616.00	9.7500 2,106.00	130.0000 30,736.00	39.0000 8,424.00	130.0000 30,736.00	390.0000 273,780.00	65
66 2/3	163.3333 41,514.65	220.0000 95,040.00	50.0000 10,800.00	33.3333 7,199.99	26.6667 5,760.01	20.0000 4,320.00	13.3333 2,879.99	210.0000 79,380.00	153.3333 38,070.66	26.6667 5,760.01	10.0000 2,160.00	133.3333 31,722.66	40.0000 8,640.00	133.3333 31,722.66	400.0000 302,400.00	66 2/3
70	171.5000 44,460.50	231.0000 99,792.00	52.5000 11,340.00	35.0000 7,560.00	28.0000 6,048.00	21.0000 4,536.00	14.0000 3,024.00	220.5000 95,256.00	161.0000 40,694.00	28.0000 6,048.00	10.5000 2,268.00	140.0000 33,758.00	42.0000 9,072.00	140.0000 33,758.00	420.0000 317,520.00	70
75	183.7500 69,457.50	247.5000 120,285.00	56.2500 12,150.00	37.5000 8,100.00	30.0000 6,480.00	22.5000 4,860.00	15.0000 3,240.00	236.2500 102,060.00	172.5000 44,827.50	30.0000 6,480.00	11.2500 2,430.00	150.0000 36,954.00	45.0000 9,720.00	150.0000 36,954.00	450.0000 364,500.00	75
80	196.0000 74,088.00	264.0000 128,304.00	60.0000 12,960.00	40.0000 8,640.00	32.0000 6,912.00	24.0000 5,184.00	16.0000 3,456.00	252.0000 122,472.00	184.0000 69,552.00	32.0000 6,912.00	12.0000 2,592.00	160.0000 40,348.00	48.0000 10,368.00	160.0000 40,348.00	480.0000 388,800.00	80
85	208.2500 78,718.50	280.5000 151,470.00	63.7500 13,770.00	42.5000 9,180.00	34.0000 7,344.00	25.5000 5,508.00	17.0000 3,672.00	267.7500 130,126.50	195.5000 73,899.00	34.0000 7,344.00	12.7500 2,754.00	170.0000 43,910.00	51.0000 11,016.00	170.0000 43,910.00	510.0000 413,100.00	85
90	220.5000 95,256.00	297.0000 160,380.00	67.5000 14,580.00	45.0000 9,720.00	36.0000 7,776.00	27.0000 5,832.00	18.0000 3,888.00	283.5000 153,090.00	207.0000 78,246.00	36.0000 7,776.00	13.5000 2,916.00	180.0000 47,646.00	54.0000 11,664.00	180.0000 47,646.00	540.0000 437,400.00	90
95	232.7500 100,548.00	313.5000 186,219.00	71.2500 15,390.00	47.5000 10,260.00	38.0000 8,208.00	28.5000 6,156.00	19.0000 4,104.00	299.2500 161,595.00	218.5000 94,392.00	38.0000 8,208.00	14.2500 3,078.00	190.0000 71,820.00	57.0000 12,312.00	190.0000 71,820.00	570.0000 461,700.00	95
100	245.0000 119,070.00	330.0000 196,020.00	75.0000 16,200.00	50.0000 10,800.00	40.0000 8,640.00	30.0000 6,480.00	20.0000 4,320.00	315.0000 187,110.00	230.0000 99,360.00	40.0000 8,640.00	15.0000 3,240.00	200.0000 75,600.00	60.0000 12,960.00	200.0000 75,600.00	600.0000 XXXXXXXX	100

Footnote: Hand or Thumb and First and Second Fingers (on 1 Hand) or 4 Fingers (on 1 Hand)

EXPLANATION: The percent columns on the outside of the chart represent percentage of disability. The remaining columns show this percentage in terms of weeks and total benefits. The top figure in each box represents weeks, and the lower figure is dollar benefits.

NEW JERSEY MANUFACTURERS INSURANCE COMPANY

WCC-231 (10/11) **301 SULLIVAN WAY, WEST TRENTON, N.J. 08628**

WEEKS		90	90	97	103	109	115	121	127	133	139	145	151	157	163	169	175									
			96	102	108	114	120	126	132	138	144	150	156	162	168	174	180									
MAX. DOLLAR AMT.		19,440	21,792	23,220	24,708	26,262	27,882	29,568	31,320	33,132	35,010	36,954	38,964	41,040	43,176	45,378	47,646									
90	20% of SAWW	216																								
91 TO 96	21% of SAWW	227	227																							
97 TO 102	22% of SAWW	227	227	238																						
103 TO 108	23% of SAWW	227	227	238	248																					
109 TO 114	24% of SAWW	227	227	238	248	259																				
115 TO 120	25% of SAWW	227	227	238	248	259	270																			
121 TO 126	26% of SAWW	227	227	238	248	259	270	281																		
127 TO 132	27% of SAWW	227	227	238	248	259	270	281	292																	
133 TO 138	28% of SAWW	227	227	238	248	259	270	281	292	302																
139 TO 144	29% of SAWW	227	227	238	248	259	270	281	292	302	313															
145 TO 150	30% of SAWW	227	227	238	248	259	270	281	292	302	313	324														
151 TO 156	31% of SAWW	227	227	238	248	259	270	281	292	302	313	324	335													
157 TO 162	32% of SAWW	227	227	238	248	259	270	281	292	302	313	324	335	346												
163 TO 168	33% of SAWW	227	227	238	248	259	270	281	292	302	313	324	335	346	356											
169 TO 174	34% of SAWW	227	227	238	248	259	270	281	292	302	313	324	335	346	356	367										
175 TO 180	35% of SAWW	227	227	238	248	259	270	281	292	302	313	324	335	346	356	367	378									
181 TO 210	35% of SAWW	-	-	-	-	-	-	-	-	-	-	-	-	-	-	-	-	378								
211 TO 240	40% of SAWW	-	-	-	-	-	-	-	-	-	-	-	-	-	-	-	-	-	432							
241 TO 270	45% of SAWW	-	-	-	-	-	-	-	-	-	-	-	-	-	-	-	-	-	-	486						
271 TO 300	50% of SAWW	-	-	-	-	-	-	-	-	-	-	-	-	-	-	-	-	-	-	-	540					
301 TO 330	55% of SAWW	-	-	-	-	-	-	-	-	-	-	-	-	-	-	-	-	-	-	-	-	594				
331 TO 360	60% of SAWW	-	-	-	-	-	-	-	-	-	-	-	-	-	-	-	-	-	-	-	-	-	648			
361 TO 390	65% of SAWW	-	-	-	-	-	-	-	-	-	-	-	-	-	-	-	-	-	-	-	-	-	-	702		
391 TO 420	70% of SAWW	-	-	-	-	-	-	-	-	-	-	-	-	-	-	-	-	-	-	-	-	-	-	-	756	
421 TO 600	75% of SAWW	-	-	-	-	-	-	-	-	-	-	-	-	-	-	-	-	-	-	-	-	-	-	-	-	810

SAWW $ 1,079.91
Maximum Rate $810.00
Maximum Rate Chart
Permanent Partial Disability
Compensation Rate - 70% of Wage
Minimum Rate $35.00 per week
Amputation - 30% of Award - Added
no counsel fee
25 Weeks Additional for Enucleation of Eye

1/1/2012
TOTAL PERMANENT DISABILITY- 70% of Wages - Maximum $810.00 - Minimum $216.00 - 450 Weeks, Plus Additional Benefits as Set Forth in R.S. 34:15-12(b)
TEMPORARY DISABILITY - 70% of Wages - Maximum $810.00 - Minimum $216.00 - Maximum 400 Weeks
DEATH BENEFITS - 70% of Wages - 450 Weeks Plus Spouse's Statutory Benefits - Maximum Rate $810.00
FUNERAL ALLOWANCE - Not to Exceed $3,500.00

SCHEDULE OF DISABILITIES AND MAXIMUM BENEFITS EXCLUSIVE OF AMPUTATION AND ENUCLEATION

EFFECTIVE 1/1/2013

			FINGERS - SEE FOOTNOTE							TOES			HEARING			
PER-CENT	HAND 245 WEEKS	ARM 330 WEEKS	THUMB 75 WEEKS	FIRST 50 WEEKS	SECOND 40 WEEKS	THIRD 30 WEEKS	FOURTH 20 WEEKS	LEG 315 WEEKS	FOOT 230 WEEKS	GREAT TOE 40 WEEKS	OTHER TOE 15 WEEKS	EYE 200 WEEKS	1 EAR 60 WEEKS	2 EARS 200 WEEKS	PARTIAL TOTAL BASED ON 600 WEEKS	PER-CENT
1	2.4500 539.00	3.3000 726.00	0.7500 165.00	0.5000 110.00	0.4000 88.00	0.3000 66.00	0.2000 44.00	3.1500 693.00	2.3000 506.00	0.4000 88.00	0.1500 33.00	2.0000 440.00	0.6000 132.00	2.0000 440.00	6.0000 1,320.00	1
1 1/2	3.6750 808.50	4.9500 1,089.00	1.1250 247.50	0.7500 165.00	0.6000 132.00	0.4500 99.00	0.3000 66.00	4.7250 1,039.50	3.4500 759.00	0.6000 132.00	0.2250 49.50	3.0000 660.00	0.9000 198.00	3.0000 660.00	9.0000 1,980.00	1 1/2
2	4.9000 1,078.00	6.6000 1,452.00	1.5000 330.00	1.0000 220.00	0.8000 176.00	0.6000 132.00	0.4000 88.00	6.3000 1,386.00	4.6000 1,012.00	0.8000 176.00	0.3000 66.00	4.0000 880.00	1.2000 264.00	4.0000 880.00	12.0000 2,640.00	2
2 1/2	6.1250 1,347.50	8.2500 1,815.00	1.8750 412.50	1.2500 275.00	1.0000 220.00	0.7500 165.00	0.5000 110.00	7.8750 1,732.50	5.7500 1,265.00	1.0000 220.00	0.3750 82.50	5.0000 1,100.00	1.5000 330.00	5.0000 1,100.00	15.0000 3,300.00	2 1/2
3	7.3500 1,617.00	9.9000 2,178.00	2.2500 495.00	1.5000 330.00	1.2000 264.00	0.9000 198.00	0.6000 132.00	9.4500 2,079.00	6.9000 1,518.00	1.2000 264.00	0.4500 99.00	6.0000 1,320.00	1.8000 396.00	6.0000 1,320.00	18.0000 3,960.00	3
3 1/2	8.5750 1,886.50	11.5500 2,541.00	2.6250 577.50	1.7500 385.00	1.4000 308.00	1.0500 231.00	0.7000 154.00	11.0250 2,425.50	8.0500 1,771.00	1.4000 308.00	0.5250 115.50	7.0000 1,540.00	2.1000 462.00	7.0000 1,540.00	21.0000 4,620.00	3 1/2
4	9.8000 2,156.00	13.2000 2,904.00	3.0000 660.00	2.0000 440.00	1.6000 352.00	1.2000 264.00	0.8000 176.00	12.6000 2,772.00	9.2000 2,024.00	1.6000 352.00	0.6000 132.00	8.0000 1,760.00	2.4000 528.00	8.0000 1,760.00	24.0000 5,280.00	4
5	12.2500 2,695.00	16.5000 3,630.00	3.7500 825.00	2.5000 550.00	2.0000 440.00	1.5000 330.00	1.0000 220.00	15.7500 3,465.00	11.5000 2,530.00	2.0000 440.00	0.7500 165.00	10.0000 2,200.00	3.0000 660.00	10.0000 2,200.00	30.0000 6,600.00	5
7 1/2	18.3750 4,042.50	24.7500 5,445.00	5.6250 1,237.50	3.7500 825.00	3.0000 660.00	2.2500 495.00	1.5000 330.00	23.6250 5,197.50	17.2500 3,795.00	3.0000 660.00	1.1250 247.50	15.0000 3,300.00	4.5000 990.00	15.0000 3,300.00	45.0000 9,900.00	7 1/2
10	24.5000 5,390.00	33.0000 7,260.00	7.5000 1,650.00	5.0000 1,100.00	4.0000 880.00	3.0000 660.00	2.0000 440.00	31.5000 6,930.00	23.0000 5,060.00	4.0000 880.00	1.5000 330.00	20.0000 4,400.00	6.0000 1,320.00	20.0000 4,400.00	60.0000 13,200.00	10
12 1/2	30.6250 6,737.50	41.2500 9,075.00	9.3750 2,062.50	6.2500 1,375.00	5.0000 1,100.00	3.7500 825.00	2.5000 550.00	39.3750 8,662.50	26.7500 6,325.00	5.0000 1,100.00	1.8750 412.50	25.0000 5,500.00	7.5000 1,650.00	25.0000 5,500.00	75.0000 16,500.00	12 1/2
15	36.7500 8,085.00	49.5000 10,890.00	11.2500 2,475.00	7.5000 1,650.00	6.0000 1,320.00	4.5000 990.00	3.0000 660.00	47.2500 10,395.00	34.5000 7,590.00	6.0000 1,320.00	2.2500 495.00	30.0000 6,600.00	9.0000 1,980.00	30.0000 6,600.00	90.0000 19,800.00	15
17 1/2	42.8750 9,432.50	57.7500 12,705.00	13.1250 2,887.50	8.7500 1,925.00	7.0000 1,540.00	5.2500 1,155.00	3.5000 770.00	55.1250 12,127.50	40.2500 8,855.00	7.0000 1,540.00	2.6250 577.50	35.0000 7,700.00	10.5000 2,310.00	35.0000 7,700.00	105.0000 24,387.00	17 1/2
20	49.0000 10,780.00	66.0000 14,520.00	15.0000 3,300.00	10.0000 2,200.00	8.0000 1,760.00	6.0000 1,320.00	4.0000 880.00	63.0000 13,860.00	46.0000 10,120.00	8.0000 1,760.00	3.0000 660.00	40.0000 8,800.00	12.0000 2,640.00	40.0000 8,800.00	120.0000 28,380.00	20
22 1/2	55.1250 12,127.50	74.2500 16,335.00	16.8750 3,712.50	11.2500 2,475.00	9.0000 1,980.00	6.7500 1,485.00	4.5000 990.00	70.8750 15,592.50	51.7500 11,385.00	9.0000 1,980.00	3.3750 742.50	45.0000 9,900.00	13.5000 2,970.00	45.0000 9,900.00	135.0000 32,811.00	22 1/2
25	61.2500 13,475.00	82.5000 18,150.00	18.7500 4,125.00	12.5000 2,750.00	10.0000 2,200.00	7.5000 1,650.00	5.0000 1,100.00	78.7500 17,325.00	57.5000 12,650.00	10.0000 2,200.00	3.7500 825.00	50.0000 11,000.00	15.0000 3,300.00	50.0000 11,000.00	150.0000 37,644.00	25
27 1/2	67.3750 14,822.50	90.7500 20,963.25	20.6250 4,537.50	13.7500 3,025.00	11.0000 2,420.00	8.2500 1,815.00	5.5000 1,210.00	86.6250 19,057.50	63.2500 13,915.00	11.0000 2,420.00	4.1250 907.50	55.0000 12,100.00	16.5000 3,630.00	55.0000 12,100.00	165.0000 42,906.00	27 1/2
30	73.5000 16,170.00	99.0000 22,902.00	22.5000 4,950.00	15.0000 3,300.00	12.0000 2,640.00	9.0000 1,980.00	6.0000 1,320.00	94.5000 21,829.50	69.0000 15,180.00	12.0000 2,640.00	4.5000 990.00	60.0000 13,200.00	18.0000 3,960.00	60.0000 13,200.00	180.0000 48,564.00	30
33 1/3	81.6667 17,966.67	110.0000 25,674.00	25.0000 5,500.00	16.6667 3,666.67	13.3333 2,933.33	10.0000 2,200.00	6.6667 1,466.67	105.0000 24,387.00	76.6667 16,866.67	13.3333 2,933.33	5.0000 1,100.00	66.6667 14,666.67	20.0000 4,400.00	66.6667 14,666.67	200.0000 77,200.00	33 1/3
35	85.7500 18,865.00	115.5000 27,142.50	26.2500 5,775.00	17.5000 3,850.00	14.0000 3,080.00	10.5000 2,310.00	7.0000 1,540.00	110.2500 25,740.00	80.5000 17,710.00	14.0000 3,080.00	5.2500 1,155.00	70.0000 15,400.00	21.0000 4,620.00	70.0000 15,400.00	210.0000 81,060.00	35
37 1/2	91.8750 21,223.13	123.7500 29,452.50	28.1250 6,187.50	18.7500 4,125.00	15.0000 3,300.00	11.2500 2,475.00	7.5000 1,650.00	118.1250 27,864.38	86.2500 18,975.00	15.0000 3,300.00	5.6250 1,237.50	75.0000 16,500.00	22.5000 4,950.00	75.0000 16,500.00	225.0000 99,225.00	37 1/2
40	98.0000 22,660.00	132.0000 31,884.00	30.0000 6,600.00	20.0000 4,400.00	16.0000 3,520.00	12.0000 2,640.00	8.0000 1,760.00	126.0000 30,096.00	92.0000 21,252.00	16.0000 3,520.00	6.0000 1,320.00	80.0000 17,600.00	24.0000 5,280.00	80.0000 17,600.00	240.0000 105,840.00	40
45	110.2500 25,740.00	148.5000 37,147.50	33.7500 7,425.00	22.5000 4,950.00	18.0000 3,960.00	13.5000 2,970.00	9.0000 1,980.00	141.7500 34,938.00	103.5000 24,007.50	18.0000 3,960.00	6.7500 1,485.00	90.0000 19,800.00	27.0000 5,940.00	90.0000 19,800.00	270.0000 133,920.00	45
50	122.5000 29,095.00	165.0000 42,906.00	37.5000 8,250.00	25.0000 5,500.00	20.0000 4,400.00	15.0000 3,300.00	10.0000 2,200.00	157.5000 40,225.50	115.0000 27,005.00	20.0000 4,400.00	7.5000 1,650.00	100.0000 23,144.00	30.0000 6,600.00	100.0000 23,144.00	300.0000 165,300.00	50
55	134.7500 32,733.75	181.5000 70,059.00	41.2500 9,075.00	27.5000 6,050.00	22.0000 4,840.00	16.5000 3,630.00	11.0000 2,420.00	173.2500 45,966.75	126.5000 30,245.00	22.0000 4,840.00	8.2500 1,815.00	110.0000 25,674.00	33.0000 7,260.00	110.0000 25,674.00	330.0000 199,980.00	55
60	147.0000 36,651.00	198.0000 76,428.00	45.0000 9,900.00	30.0000 6,600.00	24.0000 5,280.00	18.0000 3,960.00	12.0000 2,640.00	189.0000 72,954.00	138.0000 33,738.00	24.0000 5,280.00	9.0000 1,980.00	120.0000 28,380.00	36.0000 7,920.00	120.0000 28,380.00	360.0000 237,960.00	60
65	159.2500 40,843.25	214.5000 94,594.50	48.7500 10,725.00	32.5000 7,150.00	26.0000 5,720.00	19.5000 4,290.00	13.0000 2,860.00	204.7500 79,033.50	149.5000 37,478.50	26.0000 5,720.00	9.7500 2,145.00	130.0000 31,288.00	39.0000 8,580.00	130.0000 31,288.00	390.0000 279,240.00	65
66 2/3	163.3333 42,299.32	220.0000 97,020.00	50.0000 11,000.00	33.3333 7,333.33	26.6667 5,866.67	20.0000 4,400.00	13.3333 2,933.33	210.0000 81,060.00	153.3333 38,783.99	26.6667 5,866.67	10.0000 2,200.00	133.3333 32,295.99	40.0000 8,800.00	133.3333 32,295.99	400.0000 308,400.00	66 2/3
70	171.5000 45,310.50	231.0000 101,871.00	52.5000 11,550.00	35.0000 7,700.00	28.0000 6,160.00	21.0000 4,620.00	14.0000 3,080.00	220.5000 97,240.50	161.0000 41,461.00	28.0000 6,160.00	10.5000 2,310.00	140.0000 34,378.00	42.0000 9,240.00	140.0000 34,378.00	420.0000 323,820.00	70
75	183.7500 70,927.50	247.5000 122,760.00	56.2500 12,375.00	37.5000 8,250.00	30.0000 6,600.00	22.5000 4,950.00	15.0000 3,300.00	236.2500 104,186.25	172.5000 45,685.50	30.0000 6,600.00	11.2500 2,475.00	150.0000 37,644.00	45.0000 9,900.00	150.0000 37,644.00	450.0000 371,700.00	75
80	196.0000 75,656.00	264.0000 130,944.00	60.0000 13,200.00	40.0000 8,800.00	32.0000 7,040.00	24.0000 5,280.00	16.0000 3,520.00	252.0000 124,992.00	184.0000 71,024.00	32.0000 7,040.00	12.0000 2,640.00	160.0000 41,108.00	48.0000 10,560.00	160.0000 41,108.00	480.0000 396,480.00	80
85	208.2500 80,384.50	280.5000 154,555.50	63.7500 14,025.00	42.5000 9,350.00	34.0000 7,480.00	25.5000 5,610.00	17.0000 3,740.00	267.7500 132,804.00	195.5000 75,463.00	34.0000 7,480.00	12.7500 2,805.00	170.0000 44,748.00	51.0000 11,220.00	170.0000 44,748.00	510.0000 421,260.00	85
90	220.5000 97,240.50	297.0000 163,647.00	67.5000 14,850.00	45.0000 9,900.00	36.0000 7,920.00	27.0000 5,940.00	18.0000 3,960.00	283.5000 156,208.50	207.0000 79,902.00	36.0000 7,920.00	13.5000 2,970.00	180.0000 48,564.00	54.0000 11,880.00	180.0000 48,564.00	540.0000 446,040.00	90
95	232.7500 102,642.75	313.5000 189,981.00	71.2500 15,675.00	47.5000 10,450.00	38.0000 8,360.00	28.5000 6,270.00	19.0000 4,180.00	299.2500 164,886.75	218.5000 96,358.50	38.0000 8,360.00	14.2500 3,135.00	190.0000 73,340.00	57.0000 12,540.00	190.0000 73,340.00	570.0000 470,820.00	95
100	245.0000 121,520.00	330.0000 199,980.00	75.0000 16,500.00	50.0000 11,000.00	40.0000 8,800.00	30.0000 6,600.00	20.0000 4,400.00	315.0000 190,890.00	230.0000 101,430.00	40.0000 8,800.00	15.0000 3,300.00	200.0000 77,200.00	60.0000 13,200.00	200.0000 77,200.00	600.0000 XXXXXXXX	100

Footnote: Hand or Thumb and First and Second Fingers (on 1 Hand) or 4 Fingers (on 1 Hand)

EXPLANATION: The percent columns on the outside of the chart represent percentage of disability. The remaining columns show this percentage in terms of weeks and total benefits. The top figure in each box represents weeks, and the lower figure is dollar benefits.

NEW JERSEY MANUFACTURERS INSURANCE COMPANY
301 SULLIVAN WAY, WEST TRENTON, N.J. 08628

WCC-231 (10/12)

WEEKS		90	90	97	103	109	115	121	127	133	139	145	151	157	163	169	175									
			96	102	108	114	120	126	132	138	144	150	156	162	168	174	180									
MAX. DOLLAR AMT.		19,800	22,176	23,628	25,146	26,730	28,380	30,096	31,884	33,738	35,658	37,644	39,696	41,814	43,998	46,248	48,564									
90	20% of SAWW	220																								
91 TO 96	21% of SAWW	231	231																							
97 TO 102	22% of SAWW	231	231	242																						
103 TO 108	23% of SAWW	231	231	242	253																					
109 TO 114	24% of SAWW	231	231	242	253	264																				
115 TO 120	25% of SAWW	231	231	242	253	264	275																			
121 TO 126	26% of SAWW	231	231	242	253	264	275	286																		
127 TO 132	27% of SAWW	231	231	242	253	264	275	286	298																	
133 TO 138	28% of SAWW	231	231	242	253	264	275	286	298	309																
139 TO 144	29% of SAWW	231	231	242	253	264	275	286	298	309	320															
145 TO 150	30% of SAWW	231	231	242	253	264	275	286	298	309	320	331														
151 TO 156	31% of SAWW	231	231	242	253	264	275	286	298	309	320	331	342													
157 TO 162	32% of SAWW	231	231	242	253	264	275	286	298	309	320	331	342	353												
163 TO 168	33% of SAWW	231	231	242	253	264	275	286	298	309	320	331	342	353	364											
169 TO 174	34% of SAWW	231	231	242	253	264	275	286	298	309	320	331	342	353	364	375										
175 TO 180	35% of SAWW	231	231	242	253	264	275	286	298	309	320	331	342	353	364	375	386									
181 TO 210	35% of SAWW	-	-	-	-	-	-	-	-	-	-	-	-	-	-	-	-	386								
211 TO 240	40% of SAWW	-	-	-	-	-	-	-	-	-	-	-	-	-	-	-	-	-	441							
241 TO 270	45% of SAWW	-	-	-	-	-	-	-	-	-	-	-	-	-	-	-	-	-	-	496						
271 TO 300	50% of SAWW	-	-	-	-	-	-	-	-	-	-	-	-	-	-	-	-	-	-	-	551					
301 TO 330	55% of SAWW	-	-	-	-	-	-	-	-	-	-	-	-	-	-	-	-	-	-	-	-	606				
331 TO 360	60% of SAWW	-	-	-	-	-	-	-	-	-	-	-	-	-	-	-	-	-	-	-	-	-	661			
361 TO 390	65% of SAWW	-	-	-	-	-	-	-	-	-	-	-	-	-	-	-	-	-	-	-	-	-	-	716		
391 TO 420	70% of SAWW	-	-	-	-	-	-	-	-	-	-	-	-	-	-	-	-	-	-	-	-	-	-	-	771	
421 TO 600	75% of SAWW	-	-	-	-	-	-	-	-	-	-	-	-	-	-	-	-	-	-	-	-	-	-	-	-	826

SAWW $ 1,101.89
Maximum Rate $826.00
Maximum Rate Chart
Permanent Partial Disability
Compensation Rate - 70% of Wage
Minimum Rate $35.00 per week
Amputation - 30% of Award - Added
no counsel fee
25 Weeks Additional for Enucleation of Eye

1/1/2013
TOTAL PERMANENT DISABILITY- 70% of Wages - Maximum $826.00 - Minimum $220.00 - 450 Weeks, Plus Additional Benefits as Set Forth in R.S. 34:15-12(b)
TEMPORARY DISABILITY - 70% of Wages - Maximum $826.00 - Minimum $220.00 - Maximum 400 Weeks
DEATH BENEFITS - 70% of Wages - 450 Weeks Plus Spouse's Statutory Benefits - Maximum Rate $826.00
FUNERAL ALLOWANCE - Not to Exceed $3,500.00

SCHEDULE OF DISABILITIES AND MAXIMUM BENEFITS EXCLUSIVE OF AMPUTATION AND ENUCLEATION

EFFECTIVE 1/1/2014

PER-CENT	HAND 245 WEEKS	ARM 330 WEEKS	FINGERS - SEE FOOTNOTE					LEG 315 WEEKS	FOOT 230 WEEKS	TOES		EYE 200 WEEKS	HEARING		PARTIAL TOTAL BASED ON 600 WEEKS	PER-CENT
			THUMB 75 WEEKS	FIRST 50 WEEKS	SECOND 40 WEEKS	THIRD 30 WEEKS	FOURTH 20 WEEKS			GREAT TOE 40 WEEKS	OTHER TOE 15 WEEKS		1 EAR 60 WEEKS	2 EARS 200 WEEKS		
1	2.4500 551.25	3.3000 742.50	0.7500 168.75	0.5000 112.50	0.4000 90.00	0.3000 67.50	0.2000 45.00	3.1500 708.75	2.3000 517.50	0.4000 90.00	0.1500 33.75	2.0000 450.00	0.6000 135.00	2.0000 450.00	6.0000 1,350.00	1
1 1/2	3.6750 826.88	4.9500 1,113.75	1.1250 253.13	0.7500 168.75	0.6000 135.00	0.4500 101.25	0.3000 67.50	4.7250 1,063.13	3.4500 776.25	0.6000 135.00	0.2250 50.63	3.0000 675.00	0.9000 202.50	3.0000 675.00	9.0000 2,025.00	1 1/2
2	4.9000 1,102.50	6.6000 1,485.00	1.5000 337.50	1.0000 225.00	0.8000 180.00	0.6000 135.00	0.4000 90.00	6.3000 1,417.50	4.6000 1,035.00	0.8000 180.00	0.3000 67.50	4.0000 900.00	1.2000 270.00	4.0000 900.00	12.0000 2,700.00	2
2 1/2	6.1250 1,378.13	8.2500 1,856.25	1.8750 421.88	1.2500 281.25	1.0000 225.00	0.7500 168.75	0.5000 112.50	7.8750 1,771.88	5.7500 1,293.75	1.0000 225.00	0.3750 84.38	5.0000 1,125.00	1.5000 337.50	5.0000 1,125.00	15.0000 3,375.00	2 1/2
3	7.3500 1,653.75	9.9000 2,227.50	2.2500 506.25	1.5000 337.50	1.2000 270.00	0.9000 202.50	0.6000 135.00	9.4500 2,126.25	6.9000 1,552.50	1.2000 270.00	0.4500 101.25	6.0000 1,350.00	1.8000 405.00	6.0000 1,350.00	18.0000 4,050.00	3
3 1/2	8.5750 1,929.38	11.5500 2,598.75	2.6250 590.63	1.7500 393.75	1.4000 315.00	1.0500 236.25	0.7000 157.50	11.0250 2,480.63	8.0500 1,811.25	1.4000 315.00	0.5250 118.13	7.0000 1,575.00	2.1000 472.50	7.0000 1,575.00	21.0000 4,725.00	3 1/2
4	9.8000 2,205.00	13.2000 2,970.00	3.0000 675.00	2.0000 450.00	1.6000 360.00	1.2000 270.00	0.8000 180.00	12.6000 2,835.00	9.2000 2,070.00	1.6000 360.00	0.6000 135.00	8.0000 1,800.00	2.4000 540.00	8.0000 1,800.00	24.0000 5,400.00	4
5	12.2500 2,756.25	16.5000 3,712.50	3.7500 843.75	2.5000 562.50	2.0000 450.00	1.5000 337.50	1.0000 225.00	15.7500 3,543.75	11.5000 2,587.50	2.0000 450.00	0.7500 168.75	10.0000 2,250.00	3.0000 675.00	10.0000 2,250.00	30.0000 6,750.00	5
7 1/2	18.3750 4,134.38	24.7500 5,568.75	5.6250 1,265.63	3.7500 843.75	3.0000 675.00	2.2500 506.25	1.5000 337.50	23.6250 5,315.63	17.2500 3,881.25	3.0000 675.00	1.1250 253.13	15.0000 3,375.00	4.5000 1,012.50	15.0000 3,375.00	45.0000 10,125.00	7 1/2
10	24.5000 5,512.50	33.0000 7,425.00	7.5000 1,687.50	5.0000 1,125.00	4.0000 900.00	3.0000 675.00	2.0000 450.00	31.5000 7,087.50	23.0000 5,175.00	4.0000 900.00	1.5000 337.50	20.0000 4,500.00	6.0000 1,350.00	20.0000 4,500.00	60.0000 13,500.00	10
12 1/2	30.6250 6,890.63	41.2500 9,281.25	9.3750 2,109.38	6.2500 1,406.25	5.0000 1,125.00	3.7500 843.75	2.5000 562.50	39.3750 8,859.38	28.7500 6,468.75	5.0000 1,125.00	1.8750 421.88	25.0000 5,625.00	7.5000 1,687.50	25.0000 5,625.00	75.0000 16,875.00	12 1/2
15	36.7500 8,268.75	49.5000 11,137.50	11.2500 2,531.25	7.5000 1,687.50	6.0000 1,350.00	4.5000 1,012.50	3.0000 675.00	47.2500 10,631.25	34.5000 7,762.50	6.0000 1,350.00	2.2500 506.25	30.0000 6,750.00	9.0000 2,025.00	30.0000 6,750.00	90.0000 20,250.00	15
17 1/2	42.8750 9,646.88	57.7500 12,993.75	13.1250 2,953.13	8.7500 1,968.75	7.0000 1,575.00	5.2500 1,181.25	3.5000 787.50	55.1250 12,403.13	40.2500 9,056.25	7.0000 1,575.00	2.6250 590.63	35.0000 7,875.00	10.5000 2,362.50	35.0000 7,875.00	105.0000 24,912.00	17 1/2
20	49.0000 11,025.00	66.0000 14,850.00	15.0000 3,375.00	10.0000 2,250.00	8.0000 1,800.00	6.0000 1,350.00	4.0000 900.00	63.0000 14,175.00	46.0000 10,350.00	8.0000 1,800.00	3.0000 675.00	40.0000 9,000.00	12.0000 2,700.00	40.0000 9,000.00	120.0000 28,992.00	20
22 1/2	55.1250 12,403.13	74.2500 16,706.25	16.8750 3,796.88	11.2500 2,531.25	9.0000 2,025.00	6.7500 1,518.75	4.5000 1,012.50	70.8750 15,946.88	51.7500 11,643.75	9.0000 2,025.00	3.3750 759.38	45.0000 10,125.00	13.5000 3,037.50	45.0000 10,125.00	135.0000 33,507.00	22 1/2
25	61.2500 13,781.25	82.5000 18,562.50	18.7500 4,218.75	12.5000 2,812.50	10.0000 2,250.00	7.5000 1,687.50	5.0000 1,125.00	78.7500 17,718.75	57.5000 12,937.50	10.0000 2,250.00	3.7500 843.75	50.0000 11,250.00	15.0000 3,375.00	50.0000 11,250.00	150.0000 38,430.00	25
27 1/2	67.3750 15,159.38	90.7500 21,417.00	20.6250 4,640.63	13.7500 3,093.75	11.0000 2,475.00	8.2500 1,856.25	5.5000 1,237.50	86.6250 19,490.63	63.2500 14,231.25	11.0000 2,475.00	4.1250 928.13	55.0000 12,375.00	16.5000 3,712.50	55.0000 12,375.00	165.0000 43,791.00	27 1/2
30	73.5000 16,537.50	99.0000 23,397.00	22.5000 5,062.50	15.0000 3,375.00	12.0000 2,700.00	9.0000 2,025.00	6.0000 1,350.00	94.5000 22,302.00	69.0000 15,525.00	12.0000 2,700.00	4.5000 1,012.50	60.0000 13,500.00	18.0000 4,050.00	60.0000 13,500.00	180.0000 49,554.00	30
33 1/3	81.6667 18,375.01	110.0000 26,226.00	25.0000 5,625.00	16.6667 3,750.01	13.3333 2,999.99	10.0000 2,250.00	6.6667 1,500.01	105.0000 24,912.00	76.6667 17,250.01	13.3333 2,999.99	5.0000 1,125.00	66.6667 15,000.01	20.0000 4,500.00	66.6667 15,000.01	200.0000 78,600.00	33 1/3
35	85.7500 19,293.75	115.5000 27,727.50	26.2500 5,906.25	17.5000 3,937.50	14.0000 3,150.00	10.5000 2,362.50	7.0000 1,575.00	110.2500 26,293.50	80.5000 18,112.50	14.0000 3,150.00	5.2500 1,181.25	70.0000 15,750.00	21.0000 4,725.00	70.0000 15,750.00	210.0000 82,530.00	35
37 1/2	91.8750 21,682.50	123.7500 30,087.00	28.1250 6,328.13	18.7500 4,218.75	15.0000 3,375.00	11.2500 2,531.25	7.5000 1,687.50	118.1250 28,465.13	86.2500 19,406.25	15.0000 3,375.00	5.6250 1,265.63	75.0000 16,875.00	22.5000 5,062.50	75.0000 16,875.00	225.0000 101,250.00	37 1/2
40	98.0000 23,150.00	132.0000 32,562.00	30.0000 6,750.00	20.0000 4,500.00	16.0000 3,600.00	12.0000 2,700.00	8.0000 1,800.00	126.0000 30,744.00	92.0000 21,712.00	16.0000 3,600.00	6.0000 1,350.00	80.0000 18,000.00	24.0000 5,400.00	80.0000 18,000.00	240.0000 108,000.00	40
45	110.2500 26,293.50	148.5000 37,924.50	33.7500 7,593.75	22.5000 5,062.50	18.0000 4,050.00	13.5000 3,037.50	9.0000 2,025.00	141.7500 35,674.50	103.5000 24,525.00	18.0000 4,050.00	6.7500 1,518.75	90.0000 20,250.00	27.0000 6,075.00	90.0000 20,250.00	270.0000 136,620.00	45
50	122.5000 29,722.00	165.0000 43,791.00	37.5000 8,437.50	25.0000 5,625.00	20.0000 4,500.00	15.0000 3,375.00	10.0000 2,250.00	157.5000 41,058.00	115.0000 27,587.00	20.0000 4,500.00	7.5000 1,687.50	100.0000 23,644.00	30.0000 6,750.00	100.0000 23,644.00	300.0000 168,600.00	50
55	134.7500 33,428.25	181.5000 71,320.50	41.2500 9,281.25	27.5000 6,187.50	22.0000 4,950.00	16.5000 3,712.50	11.0000 2,475.00	173.2500 46,908.50	126.5000 30,895.50	22.0000 4,950.00	8.2500 1,856.25	110.0000 26,226.00	33.0000 7,425.00	110.0000 26,226.00	330.0000 203,940.00	55
60	147.0000 37,419.00	198.0000 77,814.00	45.0000 10,125.00	30.0000 6,750.00	24.0000 5,400.00	18.0000 4,050.00	12.0000 2,700.00	189.0000 74,277.00	138.0000 34,452.00	24.0000 5,400.00	9.0000 2,025.00	120.0000 28,992.00	36.0000 8,100.00	120.0000 28,992.00	360.0000 242,640.00	60
65	159.2500 41,688.00	214.5000 96,525.00	48.7500 10,968.75	32.5000 7,312.50	26.0000 5,850.00	19.5000 4,387.50	13.0000 2,925.00	204.7500 80,466.75	149.5000 38,261.50	26.0000 5,850.00	9.7500 2,193.75	130.0000 31,956.00	39.0000 8,775.00	130.0000 31,956.00	390.0000 284,700.00	65
66 2/3	163.3333 43,172.65	220.0000 99,000.00	50.0000 11,250.00	33.3333 7,499.99	26.6667 6,000.01	20.0000 4,500.00	13.3333 2,999.99	210.0000 82,530.00	153.3333 38,589.99	26.6667 6,000.01	10.0000 2,250.00	133.3333 32,981.99	40.0000 9,000.00	133.3333 32,981.99	400.0000 314,800.00	66 2/3
70	171.5000 46,241.00	231.0000 103,950.00	52.5000 11,812.50	35.0000 7,875.00	28.0000 6,300.00	21.0000 4,725.00	14.0000 3,150.00	220.5000 99,225.00	161.0000 42,318.00	28.0000 6,300.00	10.5000 2,362.50	140.0000 35,104.00	42.0000 9,450.00	140.0000 35,104.00	420.0000 330,540.00	70
75	183.7500 72,213.75	247.5000 125,235.00	56.2500 12,656.25	37.5000 8,437.50	30.0000 6,750.00	22.5000 5,062.50	15.0000 3,375.00	236.2500 106,312.50	172.5000 46,623.00	30.0000 6,750.00	11.2500 2,531.25	150.0000 38,430.00	45.0000 10,125.00	150.0000 38,430.00	450.0000 379,350.00	75
80	196.0000 77,028.00	264.0000 133,584.00	60.0000 13,500.00	40.0000 9,000.00	32.0000 7,200.00	24.0000 5,400.00	16.0000 3,600.00	252.0000 127,512.00	184.0000 72,312.00	32.0000 7,200.00	12.0000 2,700.00	160.0000 41,958.00	48.0000 10,800.00	160.0000 41,958.00	480.0000 404,640.00	80
85	208.2500 81,842.25	280.5000 157,641.00	63.7500 14,343.75	42.5000 9,562.50	34.0000 7,650.00	25.5000 5,737.50	17.0000 3,825.00	267.7500 135,481.50	195.5000 76,831.50	34.0000 7,650.00	12.7500 2,868.75	170.0000 45,668.00	51.0000 11,475.00	170.0000 45,668.00	510.0000 429,930.00	85
90	220.5000 99,225.00	297.0000 166,914.00	67.5000 15,187.50	45.0000 10,125.00	36.0000 8,100.00	27.0000 6,075.00	18.0000 4,050.00	283.5000 159,327.00	207.0000 81,351.00	36.0000 8,100.00	13.5000 3,037.50	180.0000 49,554.00	54.0000 12,150.00	180.0000 49,554.00	540.0000 455,220.00	90
95	232.7500 104,737.50	313.5000 193,743.00	71.2500 16,031.25	47.5000 10,687.50	38.0000 8,550.00	28.5000 6,412.50	19.0000 4,275.00	299.2500 168,178.50	218.5000 98,325.00	38.0000 8,550.00	14.2500 3,206.25	190.0000 74,670.00	57.0000 12,825.00	190.0000 74,670.00	570.0000 490,510.00	95
100	245.0000 123,970.00	330.0000 203,940.00	75.0000 16,875.00	50.0000 11,250.00	40.0000 9,000.00	30.0000 6,750.00	20.0000 4,500.00	315.0000 194,670.00	230.0000 103,500.00	40.0000 9,000.00	15.0000 3,375.00	200.0000 78,600.00	60.0000 13,500.00	200.0000 78,600.00	600.0000 XXXXXXXX	100

Footnote: **Hand or Thumb and First and Second Fingers (on 1 Hand) or 4 Fingers (on 1 Hand)**

EXPLANATION: The percent columns on the outside of the chart represent percentage of disability. The remaining columns show this percentage in terms of weeks and total benefits. The top figure in each box represents weeks, and the lower figure is dollar benefits.

NEW JERSEY MANUFACTURERS INSURANCE COMPANY
301 SULLIVAN WAY, WEST TRENTON, N.J. 08628

WCC-231 (10/13)

WEEKS		90	90	97	103	109	115	121	127	133	139	145	151	157	163	169	175									
			96	102	108	114	120	126	132	138	144	150	156	162	168	174	180									
MAX. DOLLAR AMT.		19,440	21,792	23,220	24,708	26,262	27,882	29,568	31,320	33,132	35,010	36,954	38,964	41,040	43,176	45,378	47,646									
90	20% of SAWW	225																								
91 TO 96	21% of SAWW	236	236																							
97 TO 102	22% of SAWW	236	236	247																						
103 TO 108	23% of SAWW	236	236	247	258																					
109 TO 114	24% of SAWW	236	236	247	258	270																				
115 TO 120	25% of SAWW	236	236	247	258	270	281																			
121 TO 126	26% of SAWW	236	236	247	258	270	281	292																		
127 TO 132	27% of SAWW	236	236	247	258	270	281	292	303																	
133 TO 138	28% of SAWW	236	236	247	258	270	281	292	303	315																
139 TO 144	29% of SAWW	236	236	247	258	270	281	292	303	315	326															
145 TO 150	30% of SAWW	236	236	247	258	270	281	292	303	315	326	337														
151 TO 156	31% of SAWW	236	236	247	258	270	281	292	303	315	326	337	348													
157 TO 162	32% of SAWW	236	236	247	258	270	281	292	303	315	326	337	348	360												
163 TO 168	33% of SAWW	236	236	247	258	270	281	292	303	315	326	337	348	360	371											
169 TO 174	34% of SAWW	236	236	247	258	270	281	292	303	315	326	337	348	360	371	382										
175 TO 180	35% of SAWW	236	236	247	258	270	281	292	303	315	326	337	348	360	371	382	393									
181 TO 210	35% of SAWW	-	-	-	-	-	-	-	-	-	-	-	-	-	-	-	-	393								
211 TO 240	40% of SAWW	-	-	-	-	-	-	-	-	-	-	-	-	-	-	-	-	-	450							
241 TO 270	45% of SAWW	-	-	-	-	-	-	-	-	-	-	-	-	-	-	-	-	-	-	506						
271 TO 300	50% of SAWW	-	-	-	-	-	-	-	-	-	-	-	-	-	-	-	-	-	-	-	562					
301 TO 330	55% of SAWW	-	-	-	-	-	-	-	-	-	-	-	-	-	-	-	-	-	-	-	-	618				
331 TO 360	60% of SAWW	-	-	-	-	-	-	-	-	-	-	-	-	-	-	-	-	-	-	-	-	-	674			
361 TO 390	65% of SAWW	-	-	-	-	-	-	-	-	-	-	-	-	-	-	-	-	-	-	-	-	-	-	730		
391 TO 420	70% of SAWW	-	-	-	-	-	-	-	-	-	-	-	-	-	-	-	-	-	-	-	-	-	-	-	787	
421 TO 600	75% of SAWW	-	-	-	-	-	-	-	-	-	-	-	-	-	-	-	-	-	-	-	-	-	-	-	-	843

SAWW $ 1,123.80
Maximum Rate $843.00
Maximum Rate Chart
Permanent Partial Disability
Compensation Rate - 70% of Wage
Minimum Rate $35.00 per week
Amputation - 30% of Award - Added
no counsel fee
25 Weeks Additional for Enucleation
of Eye

1/1/2014
TOTAL PERMANENT DISABILITY- 70% of Wages - Maximum $843.00 - Minimum $225.00 - 450 Weeks, Plus Additional Benefits as Set Forth in R.S. 34:15-12(b)
TEMPORARY DISABILITY - 70% of Wages - Maximum $843.00 - Minimum $225.00 - Maximum 400 Weeks
DEATH BENEFITS - 70% of Wages - 450 Weeks Plus Spouse's Statutory Benefits - Maximum Rate $843.00
FUNERAL ALLOWANCE - Not to Exceed $3,500.00

SCHEDULE OF DISABILITIES AND MAXIMUM BENEFITS EXCLUSIVE OF AMPUTATION AND ENUCLEATION

EFFECTIVE 1/1/2015

PER-CENT	HAND 245 WEEKS	ARM 330 WEEKS	FINGERS - SEE FOOTNOTE					LEG 315 WEEKS	FOOT 230 WEEKS	TOES		EYE 200 WEEKS	HEARING		PARTIAL TOTAL BASED ON 600 WEEKS	PER-CENT
			THUMB 75 WEEKS	FIRST 50 WEEKS	SECOND 40 WEEKS	THIRD 30 WEEKS	FOURTH 20 WEEKS			GREAT TOE 40 WEEKS	OTHER TOE 15 WEEKS		1 EAR 60 WEEKS	2 EARS 200 WEEKS		
1	2.4500 558.60	3.3000 752.40	0.7500 171.00	0.5000 114.00	0.4000 91.20	0.3000 68.40	0.2000 45.60	3.1500 718.20	2.3000 524.40	0.4000 91.20	0.1500 34.20	2.0000 456.00	0.6000 136.80	2.0000 456.00	6.0000 1,368.00	1
1 1/2	3.6750 837.90	4.9500 1,128.60	1.1250 256.50	0.7500 171.00	0.6000 136.80	0.4500 102.60	0.3000 68.40	4.7250 1,077.30	3.4500 786.60	0.6000 136.80	0.2250 51.30	3.0000 684.00	0.9000 205.20	3.0000 684.00	9.0000 2,052.00	1 1/2
2	4.9000 1,117.20	6.6000 1,504.80	1.5000 342.00	1.0000 228.00	0.8000 182.40	0.6000 136.80	0.4000 91.20	6.3000 1,436.40	4.6000 1,048.80	0.8000 182.40	0.3000 68.40	4.0000 912.00	1.2000 273.60	4.0000 912.00	12.0000 2,736.00	2
2 1/2	6.1250 1,396.50	8.2500 1,881.00	1.8750 427.50	1.2500 285.00	1.0000 228.00	0.7500 171.00	0.5000 114.00	7.8750 1,795.50	5.7500 1,311.00	1.0000 228.00	0.3750 85.50	5.0000 1,140.00	1.5000 342.00	5.0000 1,140.00	15.0000 3,420.00	2 1/2
3	7.3500 1,675.80	9.9000 2,257.20	2.2500 513.00	1.5000 342.00	1.2000 273.60	0.9000 205.20	0.6000 136.80	9.4500 2,154.60	6.9000 1,573.20	1.2000 273.60	0.4500 102.60	6.0000 1,368.00	1.8000 410.40	6.0000 1,368.00	18.0000 4,104.00	3
3 1/2	8.5750 1,955.10	11.5500 2,633.40	2.6250 598.50	1.7500 399.00	1.4000 319.20	1.0500 239.40	0.7000 159.60	11.0250 2,513.70	8.0500 1,835.40	1.4000 319.20	0.5250 119.70	7.0000 1,596.00	2.1000 478.80	7.0000 1,596.00	21.0000 4,788.00	3 1/2
4	9.8000 2,234.40	13.2000 3,009.60	3.0000 684.00	2.0000 456.00	1.6000 364.80	1.2000 273.60	0.8000 182.40	12.6000 2,872.80	9.2000 2,097.60	1.6000 364.80	0.6000 136.80	8.0000 1,824.00	2.4000 547.20	8.0000 1,824.00	24.0000 5,472.00	4
5	12.2500 2,793.00	16.5000 3,762.00	3.7500 855.00	2.5000 570.00	2.0000 456.00	1.5000 342.00	1.0000 228.00	15.7500 3,591.00	11.5000 2,622.00	2.0000 456.00	0.7500 171.00	10.0000 2,280.00	3.0000 684.00	10.0000 2,280.00	30.0000 6,840.00	5
7 1/2	18.3750 4,189.50	24.7500 5,643.00	5.6250 1,282.50	3.7500 855.00	3.0000 684.00	2.2500 513.00	1.5000 342.00	23.6250 5,386.50	17.2500 3,933.00	3.0000 684.00	1.1250 256.50	15.0000 3,420.00	4.5000 1,026.00	15.0000 3,420.00	45.0000 10,260.00	7 1/2
10	24.5000 5,586.00	33.0000 7,524.00	7.5000 1,710.00	5.0000 1,140.00	4.0000 912.00	3.0000 684.00	2.0000 456.00	31.5000 7,182.00	23.0000 5,244.00	4.0000 912.00	1.5000 342.00	20.0000 4,560.00	6.0000 1,368.00	20.0000 4,560.00	60.0000 13,680.00	10
12 1/2	30.6250 6,982.50	41.2500 9,405.00	9.3750 2,137.50	6.2500 1,425.00	5.0000 1,140.00	3.7500 855.00	2.5000 570.00	39.3750 8,977.50	28.7500 6,555.00	5.0000 1,140.00	1.8750 427.50	25.0000 5,700.00	7.5000 1,710.00	25.0000 5,700.00	75.0000 17,100.00	12 1/2
15	36.7500 8,379.00	49.5000 11,286.00	11.2500 2,565.00	7.5000 1,710.00	6.0000 1,368.00	4.5000 1,026.00	3.0000 684.00	47.2500 10,773.00	34.5000 7,866.00	6.0000 1,368.00	2.2500 513.00	30.0000 6,840.00	9.0000 2,052.00	30.0000 6,840.00	90.0000 20,520.00	15
17 1/2	42.8750 9,775.50	57.7500 13,167.00	13.1250 2,992.50	8.7500 1,995.00	7.0000 1,596.00	5.2500 1,197.00	3.5000 798.00	55.1250 12,568.50	40.2500 9,177.00	7.0000 1,596.00	2.6250 598.50	35.0000 7,980.00	10.5000 2,394.00	35.0000 7,980.00	105.0000 25,236.00	17 1/2
20	49.0000 11,172.00	66.0000 15,048.00	15.0000 3,420.00	10.0000 2,280.00	8.0000 1,824.00	6.0000 1,368.00	4.0000 912.00	63.0000 14,364.00	46.0000 10,488.00	8.0000 1,824.00	3.0000 684.00	40.0000 9,120.00	12.0000 2,736.00	40.0000 9,120.00	120.0000 29,376.00	20
22 1/2	55.1250 12,568.50	74.2500 16,929.00	16.8750 3,847.50	11.2500 2,565.00	9.0000 2,052.00	6.7500 1,539.00	4.5000 1,026.00	70.8750 16,159.50	51.7500 11,799.00	9.0000 2,052.00	3.3750 769.50	45.0000 10,260.00	13.5000 3,078.00	45.0000 10,260.00	135.0000 33,957.00	22 1/2
25	61.2500 13,965.00	82.5000 18,810.00	18.7500 4,275.00	12.5000 2,850.00	10.0000 2,280.00	7.5000 1,710.00	5.0000 1,140.00	78.7500 17,955.00	57.5000 13,110.00	10.0000 2,280.00	3.7500 855.00	50.0000 11,400.00	15.0000 3,420.00	50.0000 11,400.00	150.0000 38,952.00	25
27 1/2	67.3750 15,361.50	90.7500 21,669.35	20.6250 4,702.50	13.7500 3,135.00	11.0000 2,508.00	8.2500 1,881.00	5.5000 1,254.00	86.6250 19,750.50	63.2500 14,421.00	11.0000 2,508.00	4.1250 940.50	55.0000 12,540.00	16.5000 3,762.00	55.0000 12,540.00	165.0000 44,388.00	27 1/2
30	73.5000 16,758.00	99.0000 23,697.00	22.5000 5,130.00	15.0000 3,420.00	12.0000 2,736.00	9.0000 2,052.00	6.0000 1,368.00	94.5000 22,595.50	69.0000 15,732.00	12.0000 2,736.00	4.5000 1,026.00	60.0000 13,680.00	18.0000 4,104.00	60.0000 13,680.00	180.0000 50,238.00	30
33 1/3	81.6667 18,620.01	110.0000 26,570.00	25.0000 5,700.00	16.6667 3,800.01	13.3333 3,039.99	10.0000 2,280.00	6.6667 1,520.01	105.0000 25,236.00	76.6667 17,480.01	13.3333 3,039.99	5.0000 1,140.00	66.6667 15,200.01	20.0000 4,560.00	66.6667 15,200.01	200.0000 78,800.00	33 1/3
35	85.7500 19,551.00	115.5000 28,093.50	26.2500 5,985.00	17.5000 3,990.00	14.0000 3,192.00	10.5000 2,394.00	7.0000 1,596.00	110.2500 26,638.50	80.5000 18,354.00	14.0000 3,192.00	5.2500 1,197.00	70.0000 15,960.00	21.0000 4,788.00	70.0000 15,960.00	210.0000 83,790.00	35
37 1/2	91.8750 21,958.13	123.7500 30,486.00	28.1250 6,412.50	18.7500 4,275.00	15.0000 3,420.00	11.2500 2,565.00	7.5000 1,710.00	118.1250 28,841.63	86.2500 19,665.00	15.0000 3,420.00	5.6250 1,282.50	75.0000 17,100.00	22.5000 5,130.00	75.0000 17,100.00	225.0000 102,600.00	37 1/2
40	98.0000 23,446.00	132.0000 33,000.00	30.0000 6,840.00	20.0000 4,560.00	16.0000 3,648.00	12.0000 2,736.00	8.0000 1,824.00	126.0000 31,152.00	92.0000 21,988.00	16.0000 3,648.00	6.0000 1,368.00	80.0000 18,240.00	24.0000 5,472.00	80.0000 18,240.00	240.0000 109,440.00	40
45	110.2500 26,638.50	148.5000 38,430.00	33.7500 7,695.00	22.5000 5,130.00	18.0000 4,104.00	13.5000 3,078.00	9.0000 2,052.00	141.7500 36,155.25	103.5000 24,843.00	18.0000 4,104.00	6.7500 1,539.00	90.0000 20,520.00	27.0000 6,156.00	90.0000 20,520.00	270.0000 138,510.00	45
50	122.5000 30,116.00	165.0000 44,288.00	37.5000 8,550.00	25.0000 5,700.00	20.0000 4,560.00	15.0000 3,420.00	10.0000 2,280.00	157.5000 41,617.50	115.0000 27,051.00	20.0000 4,560.00	7.5000 1,710.00	100.0000 23,948.00	30.0000 6,840.00	100.0000 23,948.00	300.0000 171,000.00	50
55	134.7500 33,877.25	181.5000 72,418.50	41.2500 9,405.00	27.5000 6,270.00	22.0000 5,016.00	16.5000 3,762.00	11.0000 2,508.00	173.2500 47,553.00	126.5000 31,306.00	22.0000 5,016.00	8.2500 1,881.00	110.0000 26,570.00	33.0000 7,524.00	110.0000 26,570.00	330.0000 206,910.00	55
60	147.0000 37,928.00	198.0000 79,002.00	45.0000 10,260.00	30.0000 6,840.00	24.0000 5,472.00	18.0000 4,104.00	12.0000 2,736.00	189.0000 75,411.00	138.0000 34,914.00	24.0000 5,472.00	9.0000 2,052.00	120.0000 29,376.00	36.0000 8,208.00	120.0000 29,376.00	360.0000 246,240.00	60
65	159.2500 42,256.25	214.5000 87,812.00	48.7500 11,115.00	32.5000 7,410.00	26.0000 5,928.00	19.5000 4,446.00	13.0000 2,964.00	204.7500 81,695.25	149.5000 38,701.00	26.0000 5,928.00	9.7500 2,223.00	130.0000 32,384.00	39.0000 8,892.00	130.0000 32,384.00	390.0000 288,990.00	65
66 2/3	163.3333 43,761.32	220.0000 100,320.00	50.0000 11,400.00	33.3333 7,599.99	26.6667 6,080.01	20.0000 4,560.00	13.3333 3,039.99	210.0000 83,790.00	153.3333 40,128.65	26.6667 6,080.01	10.0000 2,280.00	133.3333 33,425.32	40.0000 9,120.00	133.3333 33,425.32	400.0000 319,200.00	66 2/3
70	171.5000 46,874.90	231.0000 105,336.00	52.5000 11,970.00	35.0000 7,980.00	28.0000 6,384.00	21.0000 4,788.00	14.0000 3,192.00	220.5000 100,548.00	161.0000 42,895.00	28.0000 6,384.00	10.5000 2,394.00	140.0000 35,576.00	42.0000 9,576.00	140.0000 35,576.00	420.0000 335,160.00	70
75	183.7500 73,316.25	247.5000 125,967.50	56.2500 12,825.00	37.5000 8,550.00	30.0000 6,840.00	22.5000 5,130.00	15.0000 3,420.00	236.2500 107,730.00	172.5000 47,262.00	30.0000 6,840.00	11.2500 2,565.00	150.0000 38,952.00	45.0000 10,260.00	150.0000 38,952.00	450.0000 384,750.00	75
80	196.0000 78,204.00	264.0000 135,432.00	60.0000 13,680.00	40.0000 9,120.00	32.0000 7,296.00	24.0000 5,472.00	16.0000 3,648.00	252.0000 129,276.00	184.0000 73,416.00	32.0000 7,296.00	12.0000 2,736.00	160.0000 42,530.00	48.0000 10,944.00	160.0000 42,630.00	480.0000 410,400.00	80
85	208.2500 93,091.75	280.5000 169,565.00	63.7500 14,535.00	42.5000 9,690.00	34.0000 7,752.00	25.5000 5,814.00	17.0000 3,876.00	267.7500 137,355.75	195.5000 78,004.50	34.0000 7,752.00	12.7500 2,907.00	170.0000 46,292.00	51.0000 11,628.00	170.0000 46,292.00	510.0000 436,050.00	85
90	220.5000 100,548.00	297.0000 169,290.00	67.5000 15,390.00	45.0000 10,260.00	36.0000 8,208.00	27.0000 6,156.00	18.0000 4,104.00	283.5000 161,595.00	207.0000 82,593.00	36.0000 8,208.00	13.5000 3,078.00	180.0000 50,238.00	54.0000 12,312.00	180.0000 50,238.00	540.0000 461,700.00	90
95	232.7500 106,134.00	313.5000 186,564.50	71.2500 16,245.00	47.5000 10,830.00	38.0000 8,664.00	28.5000 6,498.00	19.0000 4,332.00	299.2500 170,572.50	218.5000 99,636.00	38.0000 8,664.00	14.2500 3,249.00	190.0000 75,810.00	57.0000 12,996.00	190.0000 75,810.00	570.0000 487,350.00	95
100	245.0000 125,685.00	330.0000 206,910.00	75.0000 17,100.00	50.0000 11,400.00	40.0000 9,120.00	30.0000 6,840.00	20.0000 4,560.00	315.0000 197,505.00	230.0000 104,880.00	40.0000 9,120.00	15.0000 3,420.00	200.0000 79,800.00	60.0000 13,680.00	200.0000 79,800.00	600.0000 XXXXXXX	100

Footnote: Hand or Thumb and First and Second Fingers (on 1 Hand) or 4 Fingers (on 1 Hand)

EXPLANATION: The percent columns on the outside of the chart represent percentage of disability. The remaining columns show this percentage in terms of weeks and total benefits. The top figure in each box represents weeks, and the lower figure is dollar benefits.

NEW JERSEY MANUFACTURERS INSURANCE COMPANY
301 SULLIVAN WAY, WEST TRENTON, N.J. 08628

WCC-231 (09/14)

WEEKS		90	90	97	103	109	115	121	127	133	139	145	151	157	163	169	175									
			96	102	108	114	120	126	132	138	144	150	156	162	168	174	180									
MAX. DOLLAR AMT.		20,520	22,944	24,450	26,022	27,666	29,376	31,152	33,000	34,914	36,900	38,952	41,070	43,260	45,516	47,844	50,238									
90	20% of SAWW	228																								
91 TO 96	21% of SAWW	239	239																							
97 TO 102	22% of SAWW	239	239	251																						
103 TO 108	23% of SAWW	239	239	251	262																					
109 TO 114	24% of SAWW	239	239	251	262	274																				
115 TO 120	25% of SAWW	239	239	251	262	274	285																			
121 TO 126	26% of SAWW	239	239	251	262	274	285	296																		
127 TO 132	27% of SAWW	239	239	251	262	274	285	296	308																	
133 TO 138	28% of SAWW	239	239	251	262	274	285	296	308	319																
139 TO 144	29% of SAWW	239	239	251	262	274	285	296	308	319	331															
145 TO 150	30% of SAWW	239	239	251	262	274	285	296	308	319	331	342														
151 TO 156	31% of SAWW	239	239	251	262	274	285	296	308	319	331	342	353													
157 TO 162	32% of SAWW	239	239	251	262	274	285	296	308	319	331	342	353	365												
163 TO 168	33% of SAWW	239	239	251	262	274	285	296	308	319	331	342	353	365	376											
169 TO 174	34% of SAWW	239	239	251	262	274	285	296	308	319	331	342	353	365	376	388										
175 TO 180	35% of SAWW	239	239	251	262	274	285	296	308	319	331	342	353	365	376	388	399									
181 TO 210	35% of SAWW	-	-	-	-	-	-	-	-	-	-	-	-	-	-	-	-	399								
211 TO 240	40% of SAWW	-	-	-	-	-	-	-	-	-	-	-	-	-	-	-	-	-	456							
241 TO 270	45% of SAWW	-	-	-	-	-	-	-	-	-	-	-	-	-	-	-	-	-	-	513						
271 TO 300	50% of SAWW	-	-	-	-	-	-	-	-	-	-	-	-	-	-	-	-	-	-	-	570					
301 TO 330	55% of SAWW	-	-	-	-	-	-	-	-	-	-	-	-	-	-	-	-	-	-	-	-	627				
331 TO 360	60% of SAWW	-	-	-	-	-	-	-	-	-	-	-	-	-	-	-	-	-	-	-	-	-	684			
361 TO 390	65% of SAWW	-	-	-	-	-	-	-	-	-	-	-	-	-	-	-	-	-	-	-	-	-	-	741		
391 TO 420	70% of SAWW	-	-	-	-	-	-	-	-	-	-	-	-	-	-	-	-	-	-	-	-	-	-	-	798	
421 TO 600	75% of SAWW	-	-	-	-	-	-	-	-	-	-	-	-	-	-	-	-	-	-	-	-	-	-	-	-	855

SAWW $ 1,140.02
Maximum Rate $855.00
Maximum Rate Chart
Permanent Partial Disability
Compensation Rate - 70% of Wage
Minimum Rate $35.00 per week
Amputation - 30% of Award - Added
no counsel fee
25 Weeks Additional for Enucleation
of Eye

1/1/2015
TOTAL PERMANENT DISABILITY- 70% of Wages - Maximum $855.00 - Minimum $228.00 - 450 Weeks, Plus Additional Benefits as Set Forth in R.S. 34:15-12(b)
TEMPORARY DISABILITY - 70% of Wages - Maximum $855.00 - Minimum $228.00 - Maximum 400 Weeks
DEATH BENEFITS - 70% of Wages - 450 Weeks Plus Spouse's Statutory Benefits - Maximum Rate $855.00
FUNERAL ALLOWANCE - Not to Exceed $3,500.00

SCHEDULE OF DISABILITIES AND MAXIMUM BENEFITS EXCLUSIVE OF AMPUTATION AND ENUCLEATION

EFFECTIVE 1/1/2016

PER-CENT	HAND 245 WEEKS	ARM 330 WEEKS	FINGERS - SEE FOOTNOTE					LEG 315 WEEKS	FOOT 230 WEEKS	TOES		EYE 200 WEEKS	HEARING		PARTIAL TOTAL BASED ON 600 WEEKS	PER-CENT
			THUMB 75 WEEKS	FIRST 50 WEEKS	SECOND 40 WEEKS	THIRD 30 WEEKS	FOURTH 20 WEEKS			GREAT TOE 40 WEEKS	OTHER TOE 15 WEEKS		1 EAR 60 WEEKS	2 EARS 200 WEEKS		
1	2.4500 568.40	3.3000 765.60	0.7500 174.00	0.5000 116.00	0.4000 92.80	0.3000 69.60	0.2000 46.40	3.1500 730.80	2.3000 533.60	0.4000 92.80	0.1500 34.80	2.0000 464.00	0.6000 139.20	2.0000 464.00	6.0000 1,392.00	1
1 1/2	3.6750 852.60	4.9500 1,148.40	1.1250 261.00	0.7500 174.00	0.6000 139.20	0.4500 104.40	0.3000 69.60	4.7250 1,096.20	3.4500 800.40	0.6000 139.20	0.2250 52.20	3.0000 696.00	0.9000 208.80	3.0000 696.00	9.0000 2,088.00	1 1/2
2	4.9000 1,136.80	6.6000 1,531.20	1.5000 348.00	1.0000 232.00	0.8000 185.60	0.6000 139.20	0.4000 92.80	6.3000 1,461.60	4.6000 1,067.20	0.8000 185.60	0.3000 69.60	4.0000 928.00	1.2000 278.40	4.0000 928.00	12.0000 2,784.00	2
2 1/2	6.1250 1,421.00	8.2500 1,914.00	1.8750 435.00	1.2500 290.00	1.0000 232.00	0.7500 174.00	0.5000 116.00	7.8750 1,827.00	5.7500 1,334.00	1.0000 232.00	0.3750 87.00	5.0000 1,160.00	1.5000 348.00	5.0000 1,160.00	15.0000 3,480.00	2 1/2
3	7.3500 1,705.20	9.9000 2,296.80	2.2500 522.00	1.5000 348.00	1.2000 278.40	0.9000 208.80	0.6000 139.20	9.4500 2,192.40	6.9000 1,600.80	1.2000 278.40	0.4500 104.40	6.0000 1,392.00	1.8000 417.60	6.0000 1,392.00	18.0000 4,176.00	3
3 1/2	8.5750 1,989.40	11.5500 2,679.60	2.6250 609.00	1.7500 406.00	1.4000 324.80	1.0500 243.60	0.7000 162.40	11.0250 2,557.80	8.0500 1,867.60	1.4000 324.80	0.5250 121.80	7.0000 1,624.00	2.1000 487.20	7.0000 1,624.00	21.0000 4,872.00	3 1/2
4	9.8000 2,273.60	13.2000 3,062.40	3.0000 696.00	2.0000 464.00	1.6000 371.20	1.2000 278.40	0.8000 185.60	12.6000 2,923.20	9.2000 2,134.40	1.6000 371.20	0.6000 139.20	8.0000 1,856.00	2.4000 556.80	8.0000 1,856.00	24.0000 5,568.00	4
5	12.2500 2,842.00	16.5000 3,828.00	3.7500 870.00	2.5000 580.00	2.0000 464.00	1.5000 348.00	1.0000 232.00	15.7500 3,654.00	11.5000 2,668.00	2.0000 464.00	0.7500 174.00	10.0000 2,320.00	3.0000 696.00	10.0000 2,320.00	30.0000 6,960.00	5
7 1/2	18.3750 4,263.00	24.7500 5,742.00	5.6250 1,305.00	3.7500 870.00	3.0000 696.00	2.2500 522.00	1.5000 348.00	23.6250 5,481.00	17.2500 4,002.00	3.0000 696.00	1.1250 261.00	15.0000 3,480.00	4.5000 1,044.00	15.0000 3,480.00	45.0000 10,440.00	7 1/2
10	24.5000 5,684.00	33.0000 7,656.00	7.5000 1,740.00	5.0000 1,160.00	4.0000 928.00	3.0000 696.00	2.0000 464.00	31.5000 7,308.00	23.0000 5,336.00	4.0000 928.00	1.5000 348.00	20.0000 4,640.00	6.0000 1,392.00	20.0000 4,640.00	60.0000 13,920.00	10
12 1/2	30.6250 7,105.00	41.2500 9,570.00	9.3750 2,175.00	6.2500 1,450.00	5.0000 1,160.00	3.7500 870.00	2.5000 580.00	39.3750 9,135.00	28.7500 6,670.00	5.0000 1,160.00	1.8750 435.00	25.0000 5,800.00	7.5000 1,740.00	25.0000 5,800.00	75.0000 17,400.00	12 1/2
15	36.7500 8,526.00	49.5000 11,484.00	11.2500 2,610.00	7.5000 1,740.00	6.0000 1,392.00	4.5000 1,044.00	3.0000 696.00	47.2500 10,962.00	34.5000 8,004.00	6.0000 1,392.00	2.2500 522.00	30.0000 6,960.00	9.0000 2,088.00	30.0000 6,960.00	90.0000 20,880.00	15
17 1/2	42.8750 9,947.00	57.7500 13,398.00	13.1250 3,045.00	8.7500 2,030.00	7.0000 1,624.00	5.2500 1,218.00	3.5000 812.00	55.1250 12,789.00	40.2500 9,338.00	7.0000 1,624.00	2.6250 609.00	35.0000 8,120.00	10.5000 2,436.00	35.0000 8,120.00	105.0000 25,755.00	17 1/2
20	49.0000 11,368.00	66.0000 15,312.00	15.0000 3,480.00	10.0000 2,320.00	8.0000 1,856.00	6.0000 1,392.00	4.0000 928.00	63.0000 14,616.00	46.0000 10,672.00	8.0000 1,856.00	3.0000 696.00	40.0000 9,280.00	12.0000 2,784.00	40.0000 9,280.00	120.0000 29,970.00	20
22 1/2	55.1250 12,789.00	74.2500 17,226.00	16.8750 3,915.00	11.2500 2,610.00	9.0000 2,088.00	6.7500 1,566.00	4.5000 1,044.00	70.8750 16,443.00	51.7500 12,006.00	9.0000 2,088.00	3.3750 783.00	45.0000 10,440.00	13.5000 3,132.00	45.0000 10,440.00	135.0000 34,635.00	22 1/2
25	61.2500 14,210.00	82.5000 19,140.00	18.7500 4,350.00	12.5000 2,900.00	10.0000 2,320.00	7.5000 1,740.00	5.0000 1,160.00	78.7500 18,270.00	57.5000 13,340.00	10.0000 2,320.00	3.7500 870.00	50.0000 11,600.00	15.0000 3,480.00	50.0000 11,600.00	150.0000 39,720.00	25
27 1/2	67.3750 15,631.00	90.7500 22,143.00	20.6250 4,785.00	13.7500 3,190.00	11.0000 2,552.00	8.2500 1,914.00	5.5000 1,276.00	86.6250 20,097.00	63.2500 14,674.00	11.0000 2,552.00	4.1250 957.00	55.0000 12,760.00	16.5000 3,828.00	55.0000 12,760.00	165.0000 45,251.00	27 1/2
30	73.5000 17,052.00	99.0000 24,189.00	22.5000 5,220.00	15.0000 3,480.00	12.0000 2,784.00	9.0000 2,088.00	6.0000 1,392.00	94.5000 23,058.00	69.0000 16,008.00	12.0000 2,784.00	4.5000 1,044.00	60.0000 13,920.00	18.0000 4,176.00	60.0000 13,920.00	180.0000 51,216.00	30
33 1/3	81.6667 18,946.67	110.0000 27,114.00	25.0000 5,800.00	16.6667 3,866.67	13.3333 3,093.33	10.0000 2,320.00	6.6667 1,546.67	105.0000 25,755.00	76.6667 17,786.67	13.3333 3,093.33	5.0000 1,160.00	66.6667 15,466.67	20.0000 4,640.00	66.6667 15,466.67	200.0000 81,200.00	33 1/3
35	85.7500 19,894.00	115.5000 28,565.00	26.2500 6,090.00	17.5000 4,060.00	14.0000 3,248.00	10.5000 2,436.00	7.0000 1,624.00	110.2500 27,183.75	80.5000 18,676.00	14.0000 3,248.00	5.2500 1,218.00	70.0000 16,240.00	21.0000 4,872.00	70.0000 16,240.00	210.0000 85,260.00	35
37 1/2	91.8750 22,417.50	123.7500 31,102.50	28.1250 6,525.00	18.7500 4,350.00	15.0000 3,480.00	11.2500 2,610.00	7.5000 1,740.00	118.1250 29,426.25	86.2500 20,010.00	15.0000 3,480.00	5.6250 1,305.00	75.0000 17,400.00	22.5000 5,220.00	75.0000 17,400.00	225.0000 104,400.00	37 1/2
40	98.0000 23,934.00	132.0000 33,660.00	30.0000 6,960.00	20.0000 4,640.00	16.0000 3,712.00	12.0000 2,784.00	8.0000 1,856.00	126.0000 31,782.00	92.0000 22,448.00	16.0000 3,712.00	6.0000 1,392.00	80.0000 18,560.00	24.0000 5,568.00	80.0000 18,560.00	240.0000 111,360.00	40
45	110.2500 27,183.75	148.5000 39,198.00	33.7500 7,830.00	22.5000 5,220.00	18.0000 4,176.00	13.5000 3,132.00	9.0000 2,088.00	141.7500 36,873.75	103.5000 25,354.50	18.0000 4,176.00	6.7500 1,566.00	90.0000 20,880.00	27.0000 6,264.00	90.0000 20,880.00	270.0000 140,940.00	45
50	122.5000 30,725.00	165.0000 45,261.00	37.5000 8,700.00	25.0000 5,800.00	20.0000 4,640.00	15.0000 3,480.00	10.0000 2,320.00	157.5000 42,438.00	115.0000 28,520.00	20.0000 4,640.00	7.5000 1,740.00	100.0000 24,444.00	30.0000 6,960.00	100.0000 24,444.00	300.0000 174,300.00	50
55	134.7500 34,553.75	181.5000 73,689.00	41.2500 9,570.00	27.5000 6,380.00	22.0000 5,104.00	16.5000 3,828.00	11.0000 2,552.00	173.2500 48,483.75	126.5000 31,938.50	22.0000 5,104.00	8.2500 1,914.00	110.0000 27,114.00	33.0000 7,656.00	110.0000 27,114.00	330.0000 210,870.00	55
60	147.0000 38,675.00	198.0000 80,388.00	45.0000 10,440.00	30.0000 6,960.00	24.0000 5,568.00	18.0000 4,176.00	12.0000 2,784.00	189.0000 76,734.00	138.0000 35,610.00	24.0000 5,568.00	9.0000 2,088.00	120.0000 29,970.00	36.0000 8,352.00	120.0000 29,970.00	360.0000 250,920.00	60
65	159.2500 43,089.00	214.5000 99,528.00	48.7500 11,310.00	32.5000 7,540.00	26.0000 6,032.00	19.5000 4,524.00	13.0000 3,016.00	204.7500 83,128.50	149.5000 39,546.00	26.0000 6,032.00	9.7500 2,262.00	130.0000 33,034.00	39.0000 9,048.00	130.0000 33,034.00	390.0000 294,450.00	65
66 2/3	163.3333 44,622.65	220.0000 102,080.00	50.0000 11,600.00	33.3333 7,733.33	26.6667 6,186.67	20.0000 4,640.00	13.3333 3,093.33	210.0000 85,260.00	153.3333 40,919.99	26.6667 6,186.67	10.0000 2,320.00	133.3333 34,093.32	40.0000 9,280.00	133.3333 34,093.32	400.0000 325,200.00	66 2/3
70	171.5000 47,792.50	231.0000 107,184.00	52.5000 12,180.00	35.0000 8,120.00	28.0000 6,496.00	21.0000 4,872.00	14.0000 3,248.00	220.5000 102,312.00	161.0000 43,740.00	28.0000 6,496.00	10.5000 2,436.00	140.0000 36,284.00	42.0000 9,744.00	140.0000 36,284.00	420.0000 341,460.00	70
75	183.7500 74,602.50	247.5000 129,195.00	56.2500 13,050.00	37.5000 8,700.00	30.0000 6,960.00	22.5000 5,220.00	15.0000 3,480.00	236.2500 109,620.00	172.5000 48,187.50	30.0000 6,960.00	11.2500 2,610.00	150.0000 39,720.00	45.0000 10,440.00	150.0000 39,720.00	450.0000 391,950.00	75
80	196.0000 79,576.00	264.0000 137,808.00	60.0000 13,920.00	40.0000 9,280.00	32.0000 7,424.00	24.0000 5,568.00	16.0000 3,712.00	252.0000 131,544.00	184.0000 74,704.00	32.0000 7,424.00	12.0000 2,784.00	160.0000 43,368.00	48.0000 11,136.00	160.0000 43,368.00	480.0000 418,080.00	80
85	208.2500 84,549.50	280.5000 162,970.50	63.7500 14,790.00	42.5000 9,860.00	34.0000 7,888.00	25.5000 5,916.00	17.0000 3,944.00	267.7500 139,765.50	195.5000 79,373.00	34.0000 7,888.00	12.7500 2,958.00	170.0000 47,200.00	51.0000 11,832.00	170.0000 47,200.00	510.0000 444,210.00	85
90	220.5000 102,312.00	297.0000 172,557.00	67.5000 15,660.00	45.0000 10,440.00	36.0000 8,352.00	27.0000 6,264.00	18.0000 4,176.00	283.5000 164,713.50	207.0000 84,042.00	36.0000 8,352.00	13.5000 3,132.00	180.0000 51,216.00	54.0000 12,528.00	180.0000 51,216.00	540.0000 470,340.00	90
95	232.7500 107,996.00	313.5000 200,326.50	71.2500 16,530.00	47.5000 11,020.00	38.0000 8,816.00	28.5000 6,612.00	19.0000 4,408.00	299.2500 173,864.25	218.5000 101,384.00	38.0000 8,816.00	14.2500 3,306.00	190.0000 77,140.00	57.0000 13,224.00	190.0000 77,140.00	570.0000 496,470.00	95
100	245.0000 127,890.00	330.0000 210,870.00	75.0000 17,400.00	50.0000 11,600.00	40.0000 9,280.00	30.0000 6,960.00	20.0000 4,640.00	315.0000 201,285.00	230.0000 106,720.00	40.0000 9,280.00	15.0000 3,480.00	200.0000 81,200.00	60.0000 13,920.00	200.0000 81,200.00	600.0000 XXXXXXXX	100

Footnote: Hand or Thumb and First and Second Fingers (on 1 Hand) or 4 Fingers (on 1 Hand)

EXPLANATION: The percent columns on the outside of the chart represent percentage of disability. The remaining columns show this percentage in terms of weeks and total benefits. The top figure in each box represents weeks, and the lower figure is dollar benefits.

WCC-231 (10/15)

NEW JERSEY MANUFACTURERS INSURANCE COMPANY
301 SULLIVAN WAY, WEST TRENTON, N.J. 08628

WEEKS		90	90	97	103	109	115	121	127	133	139	145	151	157	163	169	175									
			96	102	108	114	120	126	132	138	144	150	156	162	168	174	180									
MAX. DOLLAR AMT.		20,880	23,424	24,954	26,556	28,230	29,970	31,782	33,660	35,610	37,632	39,720	41,880	44,112	46,410	48,780	51,216									
90	20% of SAWW	232																								
91 TO 96	21% of SAWW	244	244																							
97 TO 102	22% of SAWW	244	244	255																						
103 TO 108	23% of SAWW	244	244	255	267																					
109 TO 114	24% of SAWW	244	244	255	267	279																				
115 TO 120	25% of SAWW	244	244	255	267	279	290																			
121 TO 126	26% of SAWW	244	244	255	267	279	290	302																		
127 TO 132	27% of SAWW	244	244	255	267	279	290	302	313																	
133 TO 138	28% of SAWW	244	244	255	267	279	290	302	313	325																
139 TO 144	29% of SAWW	244	244	255	267	279	290	302	313	325	337															
145 TO 150	30% of SAWW	244	244	255	267	279	290	302	313	325	337	348														
151 TO 156	31% of SAWW	244	244	255	267	279	290	302	313	325	337	348	360													
157 TO 162	32% of SAWW	244	244	255	267	279	290	302	313	325	337	348	360	372												
163 TO 168	33% of SAWW	244	244	255	267	279	290	302	313	325	337	348	360	372	383											
169 TO 174	34% of SAWW	244	244	255	267	279	290	302	313	325	337	348	360	372	383	395										
175 TO 180	35% of SAWW	244	244	255	267	279	290	302	313	325	337	348	360	372	383	395	406									
181 TO 210	35% of SAWW	-	-	-	-	-	-	-	-	-	-	-	-	-	-	-	-	406								
211 TO 240	40% of SAWW	-	-	-	-	-	-	-	-	-	-	-	-	-	-	-	-	-	464							
241 TO 270	45% of SAWW	-	-	-	-	-	-	-	-	-	-	-	-	-	-	-	-	-	-	522						
271 TO 300	50% of SAWW	-	-	-	-	-	-	-	-	-	-	-	-	-	-	-	-	-	-	-	581					
301 TO 330	55% of SAWW	-	-	-	-	-	-	-	-	-	-	-	-	-	-	-	-	-	-	-	-	639				
331 TO 360	60% of SAWW	-	-	-	-	-	-	-	-	-	-	-	-	-	-	-	-	-	-	-	-	-	697			
361 TO 390	65% of SAWW	-	-	-	-	-	-	-	-	-	-	-	-	-	-	-	-	-	-	-	-	-	-	755		
391 TO 420	70% of SAWW	-	-	-	-	-	-	-	-	-	-	-	-	-	-	-	-	-	-	-	-	-	-	-	813	
421 TO 600	75% of SAWW	-	-	-	-	-	-	-	-	-	-	-	-	-	-	-	-	-	-	-	-	-	-	-	-	871

SAWW $ 1,161.04
Maximum Rate $871.00
Maximum Rate Chart
Permanent Partial Disability
Compensation Rate - 70% of Wage
Minimum Rate $35.00 per week
Amputation - 30% of Award - Added
no counsel fee
25 Weeks Additional for Enucleation of Eye

1/1/2016

TOTAL PERMANENT DISABILITY- 70% of Wages - Maximum $871.00 - Minimum $232.00 - 450 Weeks, Plus Additional Benefits as Set Forth in R.S. 34:15-12(b)

TEMPORARY DISABILITY - 70% of Wages - Maximum $871.00 - Minimum $232.00 - Maximum 400 Weeks

DEATH BENEFITS - 70% of Wages - 450 Weeks Plus Spouse's Statutory Benefits - Maximum Rate $871.00

FUNERAL ALLOWANCE - Not to Exceed $3,500.00

SCHEDULE OF DISABILITIES AND MAXIMUM BENEFITS EXCLUSIVE OF AMPUTATION AND ENUCLEATION

EFFECTIVE 1/1/2017

PER-CENT			FINGERS - SEE FOOTNOTE						TOES			HEARING			PER-CENT
	HAND 245 WEEKS	ARM 330 WEEKS	THUMB 75 WEEKS	FIRST 50 WEEKS	SECOND 40 WEEKS	THIRD 30 WEEKS	FOURTH 20 WEEKS	LEG 315 WEEKS	FOOT 230 WEEKS	GREAT TOE 40 WEEKS	OTHER TOE 15 WEEKS	EYE 200 WEEKS	1 EAR 60 WEEKS	2 EARS 200 WEEKS	PARTIAL TOTAL BASED ON 600 WEEKS	
1	2.4500 585.55	3.3000 788.70	0.7500 179.25	0.5000 119.50	0.4000 95.60	0.3000 71.70	0.2000 47.80	3.1500 752.85	2.3000 549.70	0.4000 95.60	0.1500 35.85	2.0000 478.00	0.6000 143.40	2.0000 478.00	6.0000 1,434.00	1
1 1/2	3.6750 878.33	4.9500 1,183.05	1.1250 268.88	0.7500 179.25	0.6000 143.40	0.4500 107.55	0.3000 71.70	4.7250 1,129.28	3.4500 824.55	0.6000 143.40	0.2250 53.78	3.0000 717.00	0.9000 215.10	3.0000 717.00	9.0000 2,151.00	1 1/2
2	4.9000 1,171.10	6.6000 1,577.40	1.5000 358.50	1.0000 239.00	0.8000 191.20	0.6000 143.40	0.4000 95.60	6.3000 1,505.70	4.6000 1,099.40	0.8000 191.20	0.3000 71.70	4.0000 956.00	1.2000 286.80	4.0000 956.00	12.0000 2,868.00	2
2 1/2	6.1250 1,463.88	8.2500 1,971.75	1.8750 448.13	1.2500 298.75	1.0000 239.00	0.7500 179.25	0.5000 119.50	7.8750 1,882.13	5.7500 1,374.25	1.0000 239.00	0.3750 89.63	5.0000 1,195.00	1.5000 358.50	5.0000 1,195.00	15.0000 3,585.00	2 1/2
3	7.3500 1,756.65	9.9000 2,366.10	2.2500 537.75	1.5000 358.50	1.2000 286.80	0.9000 215.10	0.6000 143.40	9.4500 2,258.55	6.9000 1,649.10	1.2000 286.80	0.4500 107.55	6.0000 1,434.00	1.8000 430.20	6.0000 1,434.00	18.0000 4,302.00	3
3 1/2	8.5750 2,049.43	11.5500 2,760.45	2.6250 627.38	1.7500 418.25	1.4000 334.60	1.0500 250.95	0.7000 167.30	11.0250 2,634.98	8.0500 1,923.95	1.4000 334.60	0.5250 125.48	7.0000 1,673.00	2.1000 501.90	7.0000 1,673.00	21.0000 5,019.00	3 1/2
4	9.8000 2,342.20	13.2000 3,154.80	3.0000 717.00	2.0000 478.00	1.6000 382.40	1.2000 286.80	0.8000 191.20	12.6000 3,011.40	9.2000 2,198.80	1.6000 382.40	0.6000 143.40	8.0000 1,912.00	2.4000 573.60	8.0000 1,912.00	24.0000 5,736.00	4
5	12.2500 2,927.75	16.5000 3,943.50	3.7500 896.25	2.5000 597.50	2.0000 478.00	1.5000 358.50	1.0000 239.00	15.7500 3,764.25	11.5000 2,748.50	2.0000 478.00	0.7500 179.25	10.0000 2,390.00	3.0000 717.00	10.0000 2,390.00	30.0000 7,170.00	5
7 1/2	18.3750 4,391.63	24.7500 5,915.25	5.6250 1,344.38	3.7500 896.25	3.0000 717.00	2.2500 537.75	1.5000 358.50	23.6250 5,646.38	17.2500 4,122.75	3.0000 717.00	1.1250 268.88	15.0000 3,585.00	4.5000 1,075.50	15.0000 3,585.00	45.0000 10,755.00	7 1/2
10	24.5000 5,855.50	33.0000 7,887.00	7.5000 1,792.50	5.0000 1,195.00	4.0000 956.00	3.0000 717.00	2.0000 478.00	31.5000 7,528.50	23.0000 5,497.00	4.0000 956.00	1.5000 358.50	20.0000 4,780.00	6.0000 1,434.00	20.0000 4,780.00	60.0000 14,340.00	10
12 1/2	30.6250 7,319.38	41.2500 9,858.75	9.3750 2,240.63	6.2500 1,493.75	5.0000 1,195.00	3.7500 896.25	2.5000 597.50	39.3750 9,410.63	28.7500 6,871.25	5.0000 1,195.00	1.8750 448.13	25.0000 5,975.00	7.5000 1,792.50	25.0000 5,975.00	75.0000 17,925.00	12 1/2
15	36.7500 8,783.25	49.5000 11,830.50	11.2500 2,688.75	7.5000 1,792.50	6.0000 1,434.00	4.5000 1,075.50	3.0000 717.00	47.2500 11,292.75	34.5000 8,245.50	6.0000 1,434.00	2.2500 537.75	30.0000 7,170.00	9.0000 2,151.00	30.0000 7,170.00	90.0000 21,510.00	15
17 1/2	42.8750 10,247.13	57.7500 13,802.25	13.1250 3,136.88	8.7500 2,091.25	7.0000 1,673.00	5.2500 1,254.75	3.5000 836.50	55.1250 13,174.88	40.2500 9,619.75	7.0000 1,673.00	2.6250 627.38	35.0000 8,365.00	10.5000 2,509.50	35.0000 8,365.00	105.0000 26,499.00	17 1/2
20	49.0000 11,711.00	66.0000 15,774.00	15.0000 3,585.00	10.0000 2,390.00	8.0000 1,912.00	6.0000 1,434.00	4.0000 956.00	63.0000 15,057.00	46.0000 10,994.00	8.0000 1,912.00	3.0000 717.00	40.0000 9,560.00	12.0000 2,868.00	40.0000 9,560.00	120.0000 30,840.00	20
22 1/2	55.1250 13,174.88	74.2500 17,745.75	16.8750 4,033.13	11.2500 2,688.75	9.0000 2,151.00	6.7500 1,613.25	4.5000 1,075.50	70.8750 16,939.13	51.7500 12,368.25	9.0000 2,151.00	3.3750 806.63	45.0000 10,755.00	13.5000 3,226.50	45.0000 10,755.00	135.0000 35,649.00	22 1/2
25	61.2500 14,638.75	82.5000 19,717.50	18.7500 4,481.25	12.5000 2,987.50	10.0000 2,390.00	7.5000 1,792.50	5.0000 1,195.00	78.7500 18,821.25	57.5000 13,742.50	10.0000 2,390.00	3.7500 896.25	50.0000 11,950.00	15.0000 3,585.00	50.0000 11,950.00	150.0000 40,890.00	25
27 1/2	67.3750 16,102.63	90.7500 21,698.25	20.6250 4,929.38	13.7500 3,286.25	11.0000 2,629.00	8.2500 1,971.75	5.5000 1,314.50	86.6250 20,703.38	63.2500 15,116.75	11.0000 2,629.00	4.1250 985.88	55.0000 13,145.00	16.5000 3,943.50	55.0000 13,145.00	165.0000 46,584.00	27 1/2
30	73.5000 17,566.50	99.0000 24,885.00	22.5000 5,377.50	15.0000 3,585.00	12.0000 2,868.00	9.0000 2,151.00	6.0000 1,434.00	94.5000 22,639.50	69.0000 16,491.00	12.0000 2,868.00	4.5000 1,075.50	60.0000 14,340.00	18.0000 4,302.00	60.0000 14,340.00	180.0000 52,710.00	30
33 1/3	81.6667 19,518.34	110.0000 27,898.00	25.0000 5,975.00	16.6667 3,983.34	13.3333 3,186.66	10.0000 2,390.00	6.6667 1,593.34	105.0000 26,499.00	76.6667 18,323.34	13.3333 3,186.66	5.0000 1,195.00	66.6667 15,933.34	20.0000 4,780.00	66.6667 15,933.34	200.0000 83,630.00	33 1/3
35	85.7500 20,494.25	115.5000 29,404.50	26.2500 6,273.75	17.5000 4,182.50	14.0000 3,346.00	10.5000 2,509.50	7.0000 1,673.00	110.2500 27,969.75	80.5000 19,239.50	14.0000 3,346.00	5.2500 1,254.75	70.0000 16,730.00	21.0000 5,019.00	70.0000 16,730.00	210.0000 87,790.00	35
37 1/2	91.8750 21,980.63	123.7500 32,006.25	28.1250 6,721.88	18.7500 4,481.25	15.0000 3,585.00	11.2500 2,688.75	7.5000 1,792.50	118.1250 30,279.38	86.2500 20,613.75	15.0000 3,585.00	5.6250 1,344.38	75.0000 17,925.00	22.5000 5,377.50	75.0000 17,925.00	225.0000 107,550.00	37 1/2
40	98.0000 24,622.00	132.0000 34,644.00	30.0000 7,170.00	20.0000 4,780.00	16.0000 3,824.00	12.0000 2,868.00	8.0000 1,912.00	126.0000 32,706.00	92.0000 22,012.00	16.0000 3,824.00	6.0000 1,434.00	80.0000 19,120.00	24.0000 5,736.00	80.0000 19,120.00	240.0000 114,720.00	40
45	110.2500 27,969.75	148.5000 40,351.50	33.7500 8,066.25	22.5000 5,377.50	18.0000 4,302.00	13.5000 3,226.50	9.0000 2,151.00	141.7500 37,955.25	103.5000 26,086.50	18.0000 4,302.00	6.7500 1,613.25	90.0000 21,510.00	27.0000 6,453.00	90.0000 21,510.00	270.0000 145,260.00	45
50	122.5000 31,817.50	165.0000 46,584.00	37.5000 8,962.50	25.0000 5,975.00	20.0000 4,780.00	15.0000 3,585.00	10.0000 2,390.00	157.5000 43,683.00	115.0000 29,345.00	20.0000 4,780.00	7.5000 1,792.50	100.0000 25,148.00	30.0000 7,170.00	100.0000 25,148.00	300.0000 179,400.00	50
55	134.7500 35,566.25	181.5000 75,867.00	41.2500 9,858.75	27.5000 6,572.50	22.0000 5,258.00	16.5000 3,943.50	11.0000 2,629.00	173.2500 49,897.50	126.5000 32,867.50	22.0000 5,258.00	8.2500 1,971.75	110.0000 27,898.00	33.0000 7,887.00	110.0000 27,898.00	330.0000 216,810.00	55
60	147.0000 39,813.00	198.0000 82,764.00	45.0000 10,755.00	30.0000 7,170.00	24.0000 5,736.00	18.0000 4,302.00	12.0000 2,868.00	189.0000 79,002.00	138.0000 36,654.00	24.0000 5,736.00	9.0000 2,151.00	120.0000 30,840.00	36.0000 8,604.00	120.0000 30,840.00	360.0000 258,120.00	60
65	159.2500 44,351.50	214.5000 102,531.00	48.7500 11,651.25	32.5000 7,767.50	26.0000 6,214.00	19.5000 4,660.50	13.0000 3,107.00	204.7500 85,585.50	149.5000 40,710.50	26.0000 6,214.00	9.7500 2,330.25	130.0000 33,998.00	39.0000 9,321.00	130.0000 33,998.00	390.0000 303,030.00	65
66 2/3	163.3333 45,927.32	220.0000 105,160.00	50.0000 11,950.00	33.3333 7,966.66	26.6667 6,373.34	20.0000 4,780.00	13.3333 3,186.66	210.0000 87,780.00	153.3333 42,123.32	26.6667 6,373.34	10.0000 2,390.00	133.3333 35,090.66	40.0000 9,560.00	133.3333 35,090.66	400.0000 334,800.00	66 2/3
70	171.5000 49,187.00	231.0000 110,418.00	52.5000 12,547.50	35.0000 8,365.00	28.0000 6,692.00	21.0000 5,019.00	14.0000 3,346.00	220.5000 105,399.00	161.0000 45,020.00	28.0000 6,692.00	10.5000 2,509.50	140.0000 37,348.00	42.0000 10,038.00	140.0000 37,348.00	420.0000 351,540.00	70
75	183.7500 75,807.50	247.5000 133,155.00	56.2500 13,443.75	37.5000 8,962.50	30.0000 7,170.00	22.5000 5,377.50	15.0000 3,585.00	236.2500 112,927.50	172.5000 49,593.00	30.0000 7,170.00	11.2500 2,688.75	150.0000 40,890.00	45.0000 10,755.00	150.0000 40,890.00	450.0000 403,200.00	75
80	196.0000 81,928.00	264.0000 142,032.00	60.0000 14,340.00	40.0000 9,560.00	32.0000 7,648.00	24.0000 5,736.00	16.0000 3,824.00	252.0000 135,576.00	184.0000 76,912.00	32.0000 7,648.00	12.0000 2,868.00	160.0000 44,638.00	48.0000 11,472.00	160.0000 44,638.00	480.0000 430,080.00	80
85	208.2500 87,048.50	280.5000 167,739.00	63.7500 15,236.25	42.5000 10,157.50	34.0000 8,126.00	25.5000 6,094.50	17.0000 4,063.00	267.7500 144,049.50	195.5000 81,719.00	34.0000 8,126.00	12.7500 3,047.25	170.0000 48,578.00	51.0000 12,189.00	170.0000 48,578.00	510.0000 456,960.00	85
90	220.5000 105,399.00	297.0000 177,606.00	67.5000 16,132.50	45.0000 10,755.00	36.0000 8,604.00	27.0000 6,453.00	18.0000 4,302.00	283.5000 169,533.00	207.0000 86,526.00	36.0000 8,604.00	13.5000 3,226.50	180.0000 52,710.00	54.0000 12,906.00	180.0000 52,710.00	540.0000 483,840.00	90
95	232.7500 111,254.50	313.5000 205,969.50	71.2500 17,028.75	47.5000 11,352.50	38.0000 9,082.00	28.5000 6,811.50	19.0000 4,541.00	299.2500 178,951.50	218.5000 104,443.00	38.0000 9,082.00	14.2500 3,405.75	190.0000 79,420.00	57.0000 13,623.00	190.0000 79,420.00	570.0000 510,720.00	95
100	245.0000 131,810.00	330.0000 216,810.00	75.0000 17,925.00	50.0000 11,950.00	40.0000 9,560.00	30.0000 7,170.00	20.0000 4,780.00	315.0000 206,955.00	230.0000 109,940.00	40.0000 9,560.00	15.0000 3,585.00	200.0000 83,600.00	60.0000 14,340.00	200.0000 83,600.00	600.0000 XXXXXXXX	100

Footnote: Hand or Thumb and First and Second Fingers (on 1 Hand) or 4 Fingers (on 1 Hand)

EXPLANATION: The percent columns on the outside of the chart represent percentage of disability. The remaining columns show this percentage in terms of weeks and total benefits. The top figure in each box represents weeks, and the lower figure is dollar benefits.

NEW JERSEY MANUFACTURERS INSURANCE COMPANY
301 SULLIVAN WAY, WEST TRENTON, N.J. 08628

WCC-231 (10/16)

WEEKS		90	90	97	103	109	115	121	127	133	139	145	151	157	163	169	175									
			96	102	108	114	120	126	132	138	144	150	156	162	168	174	180									
MAX. DOLLAR AMT.		21,510	24,096	25,674	27,324	29,046	30,840	32,706	34,644	36,654	38,736	40,890	43,110	45,402	47,766	50,202	52,710									
90	20% of SAWW	239																								
91 TO 96	21% of SAWW	251	251																							
97 TO 102	22% of SAWW	251	251	263																						
103 TO 108	23% of SAWW	251	251	263	275																					
109 TO 114	24% of SAWW	251	251	263	275	287																				
115 TO 120	25% of SAWW	251	251	263	275	287	299																			
121 TO 126	26% of SAWW	251	251	263	275	287	299	311																		
127 TO 132	27% of SAWW	251	251	263	275	287	299	311	323																	
133 TO 138	28% of SAWW	251	251	263	275	287	299	311	323	335																
139 TO 144	29% of SAWW	251	251	263	275	287	299	311	323	335	347															
145 TO 150	30% of SAWW	251	251	263	275	287	299	311	323	335	347	359														
151 TO 156	31% of SAWW	251	251	263	275	287	299	311	323	335	347	359	370													
157 TO 162	32% of SAWW	251	251	263	275	287	299	311	323	335	347	359	370	382												
163 TO 168	33% of SAWW	251	251	263	275	287	299	311	323	335	347	359	370	382	394											
169 TO 174	34% of SAWW	251	251	263	275	287	299	311	323	335	347	359	370	382	394	406										
175 TO 180	35% of SAWW	251	251	263	275	287	299	311	323	335	347	359	370	382	394	406	418									
181 TO 210	35% of SAWW	-	-	-	-	-	-	-	-	-	-	-	-	-	-	-	-	418								
211 TO 240	40% of SAWW	-	-	-	-	-	-	-	-	-	-	-	-	-	-	-	-	-	478							
241 TO 270	45% of SAWW	-	-	-	-	-	-	-	-	-	-	-	-	-	-	-	-	-	-	538						
271 TO 300	50% of SAWW	-	-	-	-	-	-	-	-	-	-	-	-	-	-	-	-	-	-	-	598					
301 TO 330	55% of SAWW	-	-	-	-	-	-	-	-	-	-	-	-	-	-	-	-	-	-	-	-	657				
331 TO 360	60% of SAWW	-	-	-	-	-	-	-	-	-	-	-	-	-	-	-	-	-	-	-	-	-	717			
361 TO 390	65% of SAWW	-	-	-	-	-	-	-	-	-	-	-	-	-	-	-	-	-	-	-	-	-	-	777		
391 TO 420	70% of SAWW	-	-	-	-	-	-	-	-	-	-	-	-	-	-	-	-	-	-	-	-	-	-	-	837	
421 TO 600	75% of SAWW	-	-	-	-	-	-	-	-	-	-	-	-	-	-	-	-	-	-	-	-	-	-	-	-	896

SAWW $ 1,195.08
Maximum Rate $896.00
Maximum Rate Chart
Permanent Partial Disability
Compensation Rate - 70% of Wage
Minimum Rate $35.00 per week
Amputation - 30% of Award - Added
no counsel fee
25 Weeks Additional for Enucleation
of Eye

1/1/2017

TOTAL PERMANENT DISABILITY - 70% of Wages - Maximum $896.00 - Minimum $239.00 - 450 Weeks, Plus Additional Benefits as Set Forth in R.S. 34:15-12(b)

TEMPORARY DISABILITY - 70% of Wages - Maximum $896.00 - Minimum $239.00 - Maximum 400 Weeks

DEATH BENEFITS - 70% of Wages - 450 Weeks Plus Spouse's Statutory Benefits - Maximum Rate $896.00

FUNERAL ALLOWANCE - Not to Exceed $3,500.00

SCHEDULE OF DISABILITIES AND MAXIMUM BENEFITS EXCLUSIVE OF AMPUTATION AND ENUCLEATION

EFFECTIVE 1/1/2018

			FINGERS - SEE FOOTNOTE							TOES			HEARING			
PER-CENT	HAND 245 WEEKS	ARM 330 WEEKS	THUMB 75 WEEKS	FIRST 50 WEEKS	SECOND 40 WEEKS	THIRD 30 WEEKS	FOURTH 20 WEEKS	LEG 315 WEEKS	FOOT 230 WEEKS	GREAT TOE 40 WEEKS	OTHER TOE 15 WEEKS	EYE 200 WEEKS	1 EAR 60 WEEKS	2 EARS 200 WEEKS	PARTIAL TOTAL BASED ON 600 WEEKS	PER-CENT
1	2.4500 590.45	3.3000 795.30	0.7500 180.75	0.5000 120.50	0.4000 96.40	0.3000 72.30	0.2000 48.20	3.1500 759.15	2.3000 554.30	0.4000 96.40	0.1500 36.15	2.0000 482.00	0.6000 144.60	2.0000 482.00	6.0000 1,446.00	1
1 1/2	3.6750 885.68	4.9500 1,192.95	1.1250 271.13	0.7500 180.75	0.6000 144.60	0.4500 108.45	0.3000 72.30	4.7250 1,138.73	3.4500 831.45	0.6000 144.60	0.2250 54.23	3.0000 723.00	0.9000 216.90	3.0000 723.00	9.0000 2,169.00	1 1/2
2	4.9000 1,180.90	6.6000 1,590.60	1.5000 361.50	1.0000 241.00	0.8000 192.80	0.6000 144.60	0.4000 96.40	6.3000 1,518.30	4.6000 1,108.60	0.8000 192.80	0.3000 72.30	4.0000 964.00	1.2000 289.20	4.0000 964.00	12.0000 2,892.00	2
2 1/2	6.1250 1,476.13	8.2500 1,988.25	1.8750 451.88	1.2500 301.25	1.0000 241.00	0.7500 180.75	0.5000 120.50	7.8750 1,897.88	5.7500 1,385.75	1.0000 241.00	0.3750 90.38	5.0000 1,205.00	1.5000 361.50	5.0000 1,205.00	15.0000 3,615.00	2 1/2
3	7.3500 1,771.35	9.9000 2,385.90	2.2500 542.25	1.5000 361.50	1.2000 289.20	0.9000 216.90	0.6000 144.60	9.4500 2,277.45	6.9000 1,662.90	1.2000 289.20	0.4500 108.45	6.0000 1,446.00	1.8000 433.80	6.0000 1,446.00	18.0000 4,338.00	3
3 1/2	8.5750 2,066.58	11.5500 2,783.55	2.6250 632.63	1.7500 421.75	1.4000 337.40	1.0500 253.05	0.7000 168.70	11.0250 2,657.03	8.0500 1,940.05	1.4000 337.40	0.5250 126.53	7.0000 1,687.00	2.1000 506.10	7.0000 1,687.00	21.0000 5,061.00	3 1/2
4	9.8000 2,361.80	13.2000 3,181.20	3.0000 723.00	2.0000 482.00	1.6000 385.60	1.2000 289.20	0.8000 192.80	12.6000 3,036.60	9.2000 2,217.20	1.6000 385.60	0.6000 144.60	8.0000 1,928.00	2.4000 578.40	8.0000 1,928.00	24.0000 5,784.00	4
5	12.2500 2,952.25	16.5000 3,976.50	3.7500 903.75	2.5000 602.50	2.0000 482.00	1.5000 361.50	1.0000 241.00	15.7500 3,795.75	11.5000 2,771.50	2.0000 482.00	0.7500 180.75	10.0000 2,410.00	3.0000 723.00	10.0000 2,410.00	30.0000 7,230.00	5
7 1/2	18.3750 4,428.38	24.7500 5,964.75	5.6250 1,355.63	3.7500 903.75	3.0000 723.00	2.2500 542.25	1.5000 361.50	23.6250 5,693.63	17.2500 4,157.25	3.0000 723.00	1.1250 271.13	15.0000 3,615.00	4.5000 1,084.50	15.0000 3,615.00	45.0000 10,845.00	7 1/2
10	24.5000 5,904.50	33.0000 7,953.00	7.5000 1,807.50	5.0000 1,205.00	4.0000 964.00	3.0000 723.00	2.0000 482.00	31.5000 7,591.50	23.0000 5,543.00	4.0000 964.00	1.5000 361.50	20.0000 4,820.00	6.0000 1,446.00	20.0000 4,820.00	60.0000 14,460.00	10
12 1/2	30.6250 7,380.63	41.2500 9,941.25	9.3750 2,259.38	6.2500 1,506.25	5.0000 1,205.00	3.7500 903.75	2.5000 602.50	39.3750 9,489.38	28.7500 6,928.75	5.0000 1,205.00	1.8750 451.88	25.0000 6,025.00	7.5000 1,807.50	25.0000 6,025.00	75.0000 18,075.00	12 1/2
15	36.7500 8,856.75	49.5000 11,929.50	11.2500 2,711.25	7.5000 1,807.50	6.0000 1,446.00	4.5000 1,084.50	3.0000 723.00	47.2500 11,387.25	34.5000 8,314.50	6.0000 1,446.00	2.2500 542.25	30.0000 7,230.00	9.0000 2,169.00	30.0000 7,230.00	90.0000 21,690.00	15
17 1/2	42.8750 10,332.88	57.7500 13,917.75	13.1250 3,163.13	8.7500 2,108.75	7.0000 1,687.00	5.2500 1,265.25	3.5000 843.50	55.1250 13,285.13	40.2500 9,700.25	7.0000 1,687.00	2.6250 632.63	35.0000 8,435.00	10.5000 2,530.50	35.0000 8,435.00	105.0000 26,709.00	17 1/2
20	49.0000 11,809.00	66.0000 15,906.00	15.0000 3,615.00	10.0000 2,410.00	8.0000 1,928.00	6.0000 1,446.00	4.0000 964.00	63.0000 15,183.00	46.0000 11,086.00	8.0000 1,928.00	3.0000 723.00	40.0000 9,640.00	12.0000 2,892.00	40.0000 9,640.00	120.0000 31,080.00	20
22 1/2	55.1250 13,285.13	74.2500 17,894.25	16.8750 4,066.88	11.2500 2,711.25	9.0000 2,169.00	6.7500 1,626.75	4.5000 1,084.50	70.8750 17,080.88	51.7500 12,471.75	9.0000 2,169.00	3.3750 813.38	45.0000 10,845.00	13.5000 3,253.50	45.0000 10,845.00	135.0000 35,919.00	22 1/2
25	61.2500 14,761.25	82.5000 19,882.50	18.7500 4,518.75	12.5000 3,012.50	10.0000 2,410.00	7.5000 1,807.50	5.0000 1,205.00	78.7500 18,978.75	57.5000 13,857.50	10.0000 2,410.00	3.7500 903.75	50.0000 12,050.00	15.0000 3,615.00	50.0000 12,050.00	150.0000 41,190.00	25
27 1/2	67.3750 16,237.38	90.7500 21,870.75	20.6250 4,970.63	13.7500 3,313.75	11.0000 2,651.00	8.2500 1,988.25	5.5000 1,325.50	86.6250 20,876.63	63.2500 15,243.25	11.0000 2,651.00	4.1250 994.13	55.0000 13,255.00	16.5000 3,976.50	55.0000 13,255.00	165.0000 46,929.00	27 1/2
30	73.5000 17,713.50	99.0000 25,083.00	22.5000 5,422.50	15.0000 3,615.00	12.0000 2,892.00	9.0000 2,169.00	6.0000 1,446.00	94.5000 22,828.50	69.0000 16,629.00	12.0000 2,892.00	4.5000 1,084.50	60.0000 14,460.00	18.0000 4,338.00	60.0000 14,460.00	180.0000 53,100.00	30
33 1/3	81.6667 19,681.67	110.0000 28,118.00	25.0000 6,025.00	16.6667 4,016.67	13.3333 3,213.33	10.0000 2,410.00	6.6667 1,606.67	105.0000 26,709.00	76.6667 18,476.67	13.3333 3,213.33	5.0000 1,205.00	66.6667 16,066.67	20.0000 4,820.00	66.6667 16,066.67	200.0000 84,200.00	33 1/3
35	85.7500 20,665.75	115.5000 29,725.50	26.2500 6,326.25	17.5000 4,217.50	14.0000 3,374.00	10.5000 2,530.50	7.0000 1,687.00	110.2500 28,180.25	80.5000 19,400.50	14.0000 3,374.00	5.2500 1,265.25	70.0000 16,870.00	21.0000 5,061.00	70.0000 16,870.00	210.0000 88,410.00	35
37 1/2	91.8750 22,164.38	123.7500 32,253.75	28.1250 6,778.13	18.7500 4,518.75	15.0000 3,615.00	11.2500 2,711.25	7.5000 1,807.50	118.1250 30,515.63	86.2500 20,786.25	15.0000 3,615.00	5.6250 1,355.63	75.0000 18,075.00	22.5000 5,422.50	75.0000 18,075.00	225.0000 108,225.00	37 1/2
40	98.0000 24,818.00	132.0000 34,908.00	30.0000 7,230.00	20.0000 4,820.00	16.0000 3,856.00	12.0000 2,892.00	8.0000 1,928.00	126.0000 32,958.00	92.0000 22,196.00	16.0000 3,856.00	6.0000 1,446.00	80.0000 19,280.00	24.0000 5,784.00	80.0000 19,280.00	240.0000 115,440.00	40
45	110.2500 28,190.25	148.5000 40,648.50	33.7500 8,133.75	22.5000 5,422.50	18.0000 4,338.00	13.5000 3,253.50	9.0000 2,169.00	141.7500 38,238.75	103.5000 26,293.50	18.0000 4,338.00	6.7500 1,626.75	90.0000 21,690.00	27.0000 6,507.00	90.0000 21,690.00	270.0000 148,340.00	45
50	122.5000 31,862.50	165.0000 46,929.00	37.5000 9,037.50	25.0000 6,025.00	20.0000 4,820.00	15.0000 3,615.00	10.0000 2,410.00	157.5000 44,005.50	115.0000 29,375.00	20.0000 4,820.00	7.5000 1,807.50	100.0000 25,348.00	30.0000 7,230.00	100.0000 25,348.00	300.0000 180,600.00	50
55	134.7500 35,834.75	181.5000 76,411.50	41.2500 9,941.25	27.5000 6,627.50	22.0000 5,302.00	16.5000 3,976.50	11.0000 2,651.00	173.2500 50,267.25	126.5000 33,120.50	22.0000 5,302.00	8.2500 1,988.25	110.0000 28,118.00	33.0000 7,953.00	110.0000 28,118.00	330.0000 218,460.00	55
60	147.0000 40,107.00	198.0000 83,358.00	45.0000 10,845.00	30.0000 7,230.00	24.0000 5,784.00	18.0000 4,338.00	12.0000 2,892.00	189.0000 79,569.00	138.0000 36,930.00	24.0000 5,784.00	9.0000 2,169.00	120.0000 31,080.00	36.0000 8,676.00	120.0000 31,080.00	360.0000 259,920.00	60
65	159.2500 44,679.25	214.5000 103,174.50	48.7500 11,748.75	32.5000 7,832.50	26.0000 6,266.00	19.5000 4,699.50	13.0000 3,133.00	204.7500 86,199.75	149.5000 41,008.50	26.0000 6,266.00	9.7500 2,349.75	130.0000 34,258.00	39.0000 9,399.00	130.0000 34,258.00	390.0000 304,980.00	65
66 2/3	163.3333 46,267.32	220.0000 105,820.00	50.0000 12,050.00	33.3333 8,033.33	26.6667 6,426.67	20.0000 4,820.00	13.3333 3,213.33	210.0000 88,410.00	153.3333 42,433.32	26.6667 6,426.67	10.0000 2,410.00	133.3333 35,357.32	40.0000 9,640.00	133.3333 35,357.32	400.0000 336,800.00	66 2/3
70	171.5000 49,551.50	231.0000 111,111.00	52.5000 12,652.50	35.0000 8,435.00	28.0000 6,748.00	21.0000 5,061.00	14.0000 3,374.00	220.5000 108,060.50	161.0000 45,353.00	28.0000 6,748.00	10.5000 2,530.50	140.0000 37,828.00	42.0000 10,122.00	140.0000 37,828.00	420.0000 353,640.00	70
75	183.7500 77,358.75	247.5000 134,145.00	56.2500 13,556.25	37.5000 9,037.50	30.0000 7,230.00	22.5000 5,422.50	15.0000 3,615.00	236.2500 113,636.25	172.5000 48,960.50	30.0000 7,230.00	11.2500 2,711.25	150.0000 41,190.00	45.0000 10,845.00	150.0000 41,190.00	450.0000 406,350.00	75
80	196.0000 82,516.00	264.0000 143,088.00	60.0000 14,460.00	40.0000 9,640.00	32.0000 7,712.00	24.0000 5,784.00	16.0000 3,856.00	252.0000 136,584.00	184.0000 77,464.00	32.0000 7,712.00	12.0000 2,892.00	160.0000 44,968.00	48.0000 11,568.00	160.0000 44,968.00	480.0000 433,440.00	80
85	208.2500 87,673.25	280.5000 168,861.00	63.7500 15,363.75	42.5000 10,242.50	34.0000 8,194.00	25.5000 6,145.50	17.0000 4,097.00	267.7500 145,120.50	195.5000 82,305.50	34.0000 8,194.00	12.7500 3,072.75	170.0000 48,938.00	51.0000 12,291.00	170.0000 48,938.00	510.0000 460,530.00	85
90	220.5000 108,060.50	297.0000 178,794.00	67.5000 16,267.50	45.0000 10,845.00	36.0000 8,676.00	27.0000 6,507.00	18.0000 4,338.00	283.5000 170,667.00	207.0000 87,147.00	36.0000 8,676.00	13.5000 3,253.50	180.0000 53,100.00	54.0000 13,014.00	180.0000 53,100.00	540.0000 487,620.00	90
95	232.7500 111,852.75	313.5000 207,537.00	71.2500 17,171.25	47.5000 11,447.50	38.0000 9,158.00	28.5000 6,868.50	19.0000 4,579.00	299.2500 180,148.50	218.5000 105,098.50	38.0000 9,158.00	14.2500 3,434.25	190.0000 78,990.00	57.0000 13,737.00	190.0000 78,990.00	570.0000 514,710.00	95
100	245.0000 132,790.00	330.0000 218,460.00	75.0000 18,075.00	50.0000 12,050.00	40.0000 9,640.00	30.0000 7,230.00	20.0000 4,820.00	315.0000 208,930.00	230.0000 110,630.00	40.0000 9,640.00	15.0000 3,615.00	200.0000 84,200.00	60.0000 14,460.00	200.0000 84,200.00	600.0000 XXXXXXXX	100

Footnote: Hand or Thumb and First and Second Fingers (on 1 Hand) or 4 Fingers (on 1 Hand)

EXPLANATION: The percent columns on the outside of the chart represent percentage of disability. The remaining columns show this percentage in terms of weeks and total benefits. The top figure in each box represents weeks, and the lower figure is dollar benefits.

WCC-231 (10/17)

NEW JERSEY MANUFACTURERS INSURANCE COMPANY
301 SULLIVAN WAY, WEST TRENTON, N.J. 08628

WEEKS		90	90 96	97 102	103 108	109 114	115 120	121 126	127 132	133 138	139 144	145 150	151 156	157 162	163 168	169 174	175 180									
MAX. DOLLAR AMT.		21,690	24,288	25,878	27540	29,274	31,080	32,958	34,908	36,930	39,024	41,190	43,428	45,738	48,120	50,574	53,100									
90	20% of SAWW	241																								
91 TO 96	21% of SAWW	253	253																							
97 TO 102	22% of SAWW	253	253	265																						
103 TO 108	23% of SAWW	253	253	265	277																					
109 TO 114	24% of SAWW	253	253	265	277	289																				
115 TO 120	25% of SAWW	253	253	265	277	289	301																			
121 TO 126	26% of SAWW	253	253	265	277	289	301	313																		
127 TO 132	27% of SAWW	253	253	265	277	289	301	313	325																	
133 TO 138	28% of SAWW	253	253	265	277	289	301	313	325	337																
139 TO 144	29% of SAWW	253	253	265	277	289	301	313	325	337	349															
145 TO 150	30% of SAWW	253	253	265	277	289	301	313	325	337	349	361														
151 TO 156	31% of SAWW	253	253	265	277	289	301	313	325	337	349	361	373													
157 TO 162	32% of SAWW	253	253	265	277	289	301	313	325	337	349	361	373	385												
163 TO 168	33% of SAWW	253	253	265	277	289	301	313	325	337	349	361	373	385	397											
169 TO 174	34% of SAWW	253	253	265	277	289	301	313	325	337	349	361	373	385	397	409										
175 TO 180	35% of SAWW	253	253	265	277	289	301	313	325	337	349	361	373	385	397	409	421									
181 TO 210	35% of SAWW	-	-	-	-	-	-	-	-	-	-	-	-	-	-	-	-	421								
211 TO 240	40% of SAWW	-	-	-	-	-	-	-	-	-	-	-	-	-	-	-	-	-	481							
241 TO 270	45% of SAWW	-	-	-	-	-	-	-	-	-	-	-	-	-	-	-	-	-	-	542						
271 TO 300	50% of SAWW	-	-	-	-	-	-	-	-	-	-	-	-	-	-	-	-	-	-	-	602					
301 TO 330	55% of SAWW	-	-	-	-	-	-	-	-	-	-	-	-	-	-	-	-	-	-	-	-	662				
331 TO 360	60% of SAWW	-	-	-	-	-	-	-	-	-	-	-	-	-	-	-	-	-	-	-	-	-	722			
361 TO 390	65% of SAWW	-	-	-	-	-	-	-	-	-	-	-	-	-	-	-	-	-	-	-	-	-	-	782		
391 TO 420	70% of SAWW	-	-	-	-	-	-	-	-	-	-	-	-	-	-	-	-	-	-	-	-	-	-	-	842	
421 TO 600	75% of SAWW	-	-	-	-	-	-	-	-	-	-	-	-	-	-	-	-	-	-	-	-	-	-	-	-	903

SAWW $ 1,203.43
Maximum Rate $903.00
Maximum Rate Chart
Permanent Partial Disability
Compensation Rate - 70% of Wage
Minimum Rate $35.00 per week
Amputation - 30% of Award - Added
no counsel fee
25 Weeks Additional for Enucleation of Eye

1/1/2018
TOTAL PERMANENT DISABILITY - 70% of Wages - Maximum $903.00 - Minimum $241.00 - 450 Weeks, Plus Additional Benefits as Set Forth in R.S. 34:15-12(b)
TEMPORARY DISABILITY - 70% of Wages - Maximum $903.00 - Minimum $241.00 - Maximum 400 Weeks
DEATH BENEFITS - 70% of Wages - 450 Weeks Plus Spouse's Statutory Benefits - Maximum Rate $903.00
FUNERAL ALLOWANCE - Not to Exceed $3,500.00

G. Order Approving Settlement ("OAS")

State of New Jersey Department of Labor and Workforce Development DIVISION OF WORKERS' COMPENSATION WC-100 (r. 8/27/2015)	**ORDER** ☐ JUDGMENT ☐ APPROVING SETTLEMENT	CASE NO'S.: VICINAGE:

PETITIONER	NAME:	
	DATE OF BIRTH	MEDICARE ELIGIBLE: ☐ YES ☐ NO
	ADDRESS:	

VS

RESPONDENT	NAME:
	ADDRESS:
ATTORNEY FOR RESPONDENT	NAME:
	ADDRESS:
	TELEPHONE NUMBER (AREA CODE)
	APPEARING

ATTORNEY FOR PETITIONER	FEDERAL EMPLOYER NUMBER
	NAME
	ADDRESS:
	TELEPHONE NUMBER (AREA CODE):
	APPEARING:
INSURANCE CARRIER	NAME ☐ RESPONDENT IS SELF-INSURED ☐ TPA
	ADDRESS:
	CLAIM NUMBER
	DATE OF ACCIDENT OR OCCUPATIONAL EXPOSURE
	DESCRIBE (Briefly):

ADMINISTRATIVE DISMISSALS
(List Other Insurance Carriers to be dismissed from case, without prejudice):

Weekly Wages : $ ________ **Rate(s):** $ ________ / $ ________

IF RE-OPENED PETITION, INDICATE FOR LAST AWARD:

Date: ________ **Award:** ________ **Permanent Paid:** $ ________ **Temporary Paid:** $ ________

THIS MATTER HAVING COME BEFORE THE COURT ON THIS ________ **DAY OF** ________ , ________

☐ **ORDER FOR JUDGMENT**

It appearing that the Petitioner suffered a compensable injury on the above mentioned date while in the employ of respondent; It is Ordered and Adjudged that Petitioner be awarded compensation benefits, payable as indicated on Page 2.

☐ **ORDER APPROVING SETTLEMENT**

The parties having settled the matter and a finding by the Court having been made that the terms of the settlement are fair and just; It is Ordered that this settlement be approved and the petitioner be paid as indicated on page 2.

PERMANENT DISABILITY (Describe Percentages below followed by the Nature and Extent of Injury and Members involved):

% of

State of New Jersey Department of Labor and Workforce Development DIVISION OF WORKERS' COMPENSATION WC-100 (r 8/27/2015)	**ORDER** ☐ JUDGMENT ☐ APPROVING SETTLEMENT	CASE NO'S.: VICINAGE:

DISABILITY AWARDED:

TEMPORARY: ________ weeks at $ ________ = $ ________ less $ ________ paid = Balance due $ ________

PERMANENT: ________ weeks at $ ________ = $ ________ less $ ________ paid = Balance due $ ________

Credits: ☐ Bonafide Voluntary Tender ☐ Non Bonafide Voluntary Tender ☐ Reopener Credit ☐ N.J.S.A. 34:15-40 ☐

MEDICAL BILLS (Doctors and/or Institutions) AND/OR MISCELLANEOUS INFORMATION:

☐ ORDER FOR CHILD SUPPORT ☐ MEDICARE ADDENDUM ATTACHED ☐ ADDENDUM ATTACHED

ALLOWANCES	REIMBURSE	TAX IDENTIFICATION NUMBER	TOTAL AMT. ALLOWED	PAYABLE BY PETITIONER	PAYABLE BY RESPONDENT
MEDICAL FEE ALLOWED: *(report and/or testimony)*					
INTERPRETER:					
ATTORNEY(S) FEE:					
STENOGRAPHIC SERVICE					
MISCELLANEOUS FEES: *(list below)*					

☐ **The Court finds the parties adequately considered Medicare interest, be that as it may, should a Medicare issue arise, this Court retains jurisdiction.**

WE HEREBY CONSENT TO THE ENTRY AND FORM OF THIS ORDER AND ACKNOWLEDGE RECEIPT OF COPY:

THE COURT FINDS THIS SETTLEMENT FAIR AND JUST.

PETITIONER'S ATTORNEY

JUDGE OF COMPENSATION DATE

PETITIONER (where applicable)

JUDGE'S NAME

RESPONDENT'S ATTORNEY

THE ORIGINAL OF THIS DOCUMENT, SIGNED BY THE JUDGE OF COMPENSATION, WILL BE MAINTAINED ON FILE IN THE DIVISION OF WORKERS' COMPENSATION, PURSUANT TO N.J.S.A. 34:15-121 et. seq.

State of New Jersey
Department of Labor and Workforce Development
DIVISION OF WORKERS' COMPENSATION
WC-168 r. 8/27/2015

CASE EXHIBIT LISTING

FOR: ☐ PETITIONER ☐ RESPONDENT

CASE NO'S.:

VICINAGE:

Judge: ______________________________

Petitioner: ______________________________ **Respondent:** ______________________________

Petitioner Attorney: ______________________________ **Respondent Attorney:** ______________________________

Hearing Date	*No.*	*ID*	*Ev.*	*Description*	Retained *Court*	*Atty.*	*Reporter*
					☐	☐	
					☐	☐	
					☐	☐	
					☐	☐	
					☐	☐	
					☐	☐	
					☐	☐	
					☐	☐	
					☐	☐	
					☐	☐	
					☐	☐	
					☐	☐	
					☐	☐	
					☐	☐	
					☐	☐	
					☐	☐	
					☐	☐	
					☐	☐	

H. Application for Review or Modification of Award

State of New Jersey Department of Labor and Workforce Development Division of Workers' Compensation PO Box 381 Trenton, New Jersey 08625-0381 WC-368 r.8/26/2015	APPLICATION FOR REVIEW OR MODIFICATION OF FORMAL AWARD ☐ ORIGINAL ☐ AMENDED FILING	Case No.: Vicinage: **Case Number Required**

PETITIONER

SOCIAL SECURITY NUMBER	
NAME:	
ADDRESS	
DATE OF BIRTH	SEX:

☐ A guardian or other representative is filing on behalf of the petitioner. See additional page for details.

ATTORNEY FOR PETITIONER

TAX IDENTIFICATION NUMBER	
NAME	
ADDRESS	
TELEPHONE NUMBER:	FAX NUMBER

VS

RESPONDENT

NAME:
ADDRESS

☐ If uninsured, individual corporate officers, or others, are also named as respondent(s). See Supplemental Page for details.

INSURANCE CARRIER / TPA

NAME
ADDRESS
CARRIER CLAIM NUMBER:

☐ See Supplemental Page for additional carriers

TO THE DIVISION OF WORKERS' COMPENSATION: ____________________ *(Name of Petitioner or Respondent)*, pursuant to N.J.S.A. 34:15-27 seeks modification and review of the award entered on ______________, for the following reasons:

☐ See Attached For Additional Information

As to Claim Petitioner:	Date of Injury:	Date of Last Comp. Pd:	Present Employment Status:	Claim Petitions filed since last award:

This is the __________ (Number) Application for Review or Modification of this award.

☐ Demand is hereby made for all records of medical treatment, examinations and diagnostic studies. [N.J.A.C. 12:235-3.8 (c)]

ARE YOU MEDICARE ELIGIBLE OR A MEDICARE BENEFICIARY?	☐ YES	☐ NO
WERE YOU ELIGIBLE FOR MEDICAID BENEFITS AT THE TIME OF THE WORK INJURY?	☐ YES	☐ NO
DID YOU BECOME ELIGIBLE FOR MEDICAID BENEFITS AFTER THE WORK INJURY?	☐ YES	☐ NO

Summary of Changes (*Complete only if filing an Amended pleading*):

STATE OF NEW JERSEY, COUNTY OF ____________________

Subscribed and sworn or affirmed to before me this ______ day of ______________ , ________

________________________________ ________________________________
Applicant

Please be advised that information collected from the filing of this Application for Review or Modification of Formal Award may be used by the Division of Workers' Compensation for record keeping, record access/distribution, and case scheduling purposes. Petitions filed with the Division are public documents and may be inspected and copied except where prohibited by Section 34:15-128 of the Workers' Compensation Statute.

The Privacy Act, 5 U.S.C. §552a, the Social Security Act, 42 U.S.C. § 405, and N.J.S.A. 34:15-1 et seq. authorize the Division of Workers' Compensation to request that the Applicant supply the Division with his or her Social Security Number for record keeping purposes and cross-matches with the Social Security Administration, Workforce New Jersey, Temporary Disability Insurance and any other proper public purpose.

DIVISION OF WORKERS' COMPENSATION

State of New Jersey Department of Labor and Workforce Development Division of Workers' Compensation PO Box 381 Trenton, New Jersey 08625-0381 WC-368supp r. 8/26/2015	**APPLICATION FOR REVIEW OR MODIFICATION OF FORMAL AWARD** **SUPPLEMENTAL PAGE**	Case No.: ________ Vicinage: ________

ADDITIONAL CARRIERS

NAME:	NAME
ADDRESS	ADDRESS
CARRIER CLAIM NUMBER	CARRIER CLAIM NUMBER:
PERIOD OF COVERAGE: FROM: TO:	PERIOD OF COVERAGE FROM: TO:

GUARDIAN OR REPRESENTATIVE

NAME
ADDRESS:
RELATIONSHIP TO PETITIONER

INDIVIDUAL CORPORATE OFFICERS/PARTNERS/LLC MEMBERS

NAME	NAME
ADDRESS	ADDRESS

I. Order Approving Settlement with Dismissal ("Section 20")

State of New Jersey
Department of Labor and Workforce Development
DIVISION OF WORKERS' COMPENSATION
WC(DO)-370 Interactive(r. 4/24/13)

ORDER APPROVING SETTLEMENT WITH DISMISSAL
N.J.S.A. 34:15-20

CASE NO'S.:

VICINAGE:

PETITIONER
NAME
DATE OF BIRTH — MEDICARE ELIGIBLE: ☐ YES ☐ NO
ADDRESS:

VS

RESPONDENT
NAME
ADDRESS

ATTORNEY FOR RESPONDENT
NAME
ADDRESS:
TELEPHONE NUMBER (AREA CODE)
APPEARING

ATTORNEY FOR PETITIONER
FEDERAL EMPLOYER NUMBER
NAME:
ADDRESS
TELEPHONE NUMBER (AREA CODE)
APPEARING

INSURANCE CARRIER
NAME ☐ SELF-INSURED ☐ TPA
ADDRESS
CLAIM NUMBER

This is a lump sum settlement between the parties in the amount of $______________ pursuant to N.J.S.A. 34:15-20 which has the effect of a dismissal with prejudice, being final as to all rights and benefits of the petitioner and is a complete and absolute surrender and release of all rights arising out of this/these claim petitions(s). The payment hereunder shall be recognized as a payment of workers' compensation benefits for insurance rating purposes only.

The parties agree that this settlement [☐ does (complete page 2) / ☐ does not] contemplate a complete and absolute surrender and release of any and all rights by the petitioner's dependents as defined by N.J.S.A. 34:15-13 arising out of this/these claim petition(s).

☐ **Order for Child Support Attached** ☐ **Addendum attached**

☐ **Further Agreed:** ______________________________

ALLOWANCES	REIMBURSE	TAX IDENTIFICATION NUMBER	TOTAL AMT. ALLOWED	PAYABLE BY PETITIONER	PAYABLE BY RESPONDENT
MEDICAL FEE ALLOWED: *(report and/or testimony)*					
ATTORNEY(S) FEE:					
STENOGRAPHIC SERVICE:					
MISCELLANEOUS FEES:					

Reason(s) for Section 20 (check all that apply):
Contested issues regarding: ☐ **JURISDICTION** ☐ **LIABILITY** ☐ **CAUSAL RELATIONSHIP** ☐ **DEPENDENCY**

WE HEREBY CONSENT TO THE ENTRY AND FORM OF THIS ORDER AND ACKNOWLEDGE RECEIPT OF COPY

____
PETITIONER'S ATTORNEY

____
PETITIONER (where applicable)

____
RESPONDENT'S ATTORNEY

After considering the circumstances, I find this settlement fair and just.

____
JUDGE OF COMPENSATION DATE

____
JUDGE'S NAME

THE ORIGINAL OF THIS DOCUMENT, SIGNED BY THE JUDGE OF COMPENSATION, WILL BE MAINTAINED ON FILE IN THE DIVISION OF WORKERS' COMPENSATION, PURSUANT TO N.J.S.A. 34:15-131 et. seq.

State of New Jersey Department of Labor and Workforce Development DIVISION OF WORKERS' COMPENSATION WC(DO)-370 Interactive(r. 4/24/13)	**ORDER APPROVING SETTLEMENT WITH DISMISSAL** **N.J.S.A. 34:15-20** **Page 2**	CASE NO'S.: VICINAGE:

The parties agree that this settlement does contemplate a complete and absolute surrender and release of any and all rights by the petitioner's dependents as defined by N.J.S.A. 34:15-13 arising out of this/these claim petitioner(s).

As the spouse or other person who may be defined as a dependent under N.J.S.A. 34:15-13 or the guardian or representative of such a person, I (we) consent to the entry of this order and recognize that this agreement is a complete and absolute surrender of any rights that I (we) may have pursuant to N.J.S.A. 34:15-13, should petitioner die as a result of the injuries, conditions, or exposures alleged in this/these claim petition(s).

Name Date

On Behalf of

Name Date

On Behalf of

Name Date

On Behalf of

Name Date

On Behalf of

Name Date

On Behalf of

Name Date

On Behalf of

I certify that the above is (are) the only individual(s) who is (are) dependent(s) as defined in N.J.S.A. 34:15-13 at the present time.

Petitioner Date

WE HEREBY CONSENT TO THE ENTRY AND FORM OF THIS ORDER AND ACKNOWLEDGE RECEIPT OF COPY

PETITIONER'S ATTORNEY

PETITIONER (where applicable)

RESPONDENT'S ATTORNEY

After considering the circumstances, I find this settlement fair and just.

JUDGE OF COMPENSATION DATE

JUDGE'S NAME

THE ORIGINAL OF THIS DOCUMENT, SIGNED BY THE JUDGE OF COMPENSATION, WILL BE MAINTAINED ON FILE IN THE DIVISION OF WORKERS' COMPENSATION, PURSUANT TO N.J.S.A. 34:15-121 et. seq.

J. Second Injury Fund Verified Petition

State of New Jersey Department of Labor & Workforce Development DIVISION OF WORKERS' COMPENSATION Office of Special Compensation Funds	SECOND INJURY FUND VERIFIED PETITION SCF-161 (R 12-07)	C.P. NO'S.: VICINAGE:

PETITIONER

SOCIAL SECURITY NUMBER: ☐ SSN Unavailable
NAME:
ADDRESS:

ATTORNEY FOR PETITIONER

FEDERAL EMPLOYER IDENTIFICATION NUMBER:
NAME:
ADDRESS:
TELEPHONE NO:

VS

RESPONDENT

NAME:
ADDRESS:

INSURANCE CARRIER

NAME: Indicate if ☐ Self- Insured or ☐ Uninsured
ADDRESS:

TO THE COMMISSIONER OF LABOR AND WORKFORCE DEVELOPMENT OF THE STATE OF NEW JERSEY:

Petitioner hereby alleges eligibility for benefits from the Second Injury Fund pursuant to N.J.S.A. 34:15-95 et seq., and respectfully states the following:

Date of Birth:	Age:	Sex:	Marital Status:	Number of Dependents: (If one or more, see Page 3)
Educational Background:			Special Skills:	
Employment History: (List all former employers, dates of employment and job descriptions; use additional sheets as required.				
Pre-Existing Medical Conditions: (List physical and/or psychiatric conditions which pre-existed your last compensable accident of exposure or dates of onset)				
Description and Date of Last Compensable Accident or Occupational Disease Exposure:				
Gross Weekly Wages for Last Compensable Injury:			Weekly Benefit Rate for Last Compensable Injury:	

Brief Description of Treatment Received For Last Compensable Injury or Disease:

Current Medical Conditions: (List physical and/or psychiatric conditions which have been caused, aggravated or accelerated by the last compensable accident or exposure or dates of onset:

If you have initiated an action at law against a third party for all or any portion of the injury or disease you sustained as a result of your last compensable injury or disease, please provide the name and address of such third party, the status of your action, and, if concluded, the gross settlement amount of such action.

Provide below your current monthly income from the following sources:		
Social Security Retirement:	$	If receiving Social Security retirement benefits, provide the date of your entitlement:
Social Security Disability:	$	If receiving Social Security Disability benefits, provide the date of your entitlement:
Auxiliary Social Security:	$	If receiving Auxiliary Social Security, provide the date of your entitlement:
Black Lung Benefits:	$	If receiving Black Lung benefits, provide the date of your entitlement:
Retirement Pension Benefits:	$	If receiving Retirement Pension, provide the date you began receiving same:
Disability Retirement Benefits:	$	If receiving Disability Retirement Benefits, provide the date you began receiving same:
Veterans Administration Benefits:	$	If receiving Veterans Administration Benefits, provide the date you began receiving same:
Temporary Disability Benefits:	$	If receiving Temporary Disability Benefits, provide the dates of such benefits:
Unemployment Benefits:	$	If receiving Unemployment Benefits, provide the dates of such benefits:

Are you currently eligible for benefits from Medicare? ☐ No ☐ Yes If Yes, have you applied for or received Medicare benefits?

Please provide the names and dates of birth of all dependents cited on Page 1.

Prior Compensation Awards: (Please list all claim petition numbers, dates of injury or last exposure, percentages of disability and body parts and attach any copies of Judgments in your possession:

Are you currently employed or engaged in a business activity? ☐ No ☐ Yes If Yes, please provide the following information:	
Name, Address and Telephone of Employer:	
Job Title and Nature of the duties performed:	
Number of hours worked per week:	Gross Weekly Wage or Earnings:

I believe that I am totally and permanently disabled as the result of a combination of my pre-existing physical and/or psychiatric conditions and my last compensable injury or disease. Further, I believe that the exclusionary provisions of N.J.S.A. 34:15-95 do not apply to my case. Accordingly, I hereby petition for Second Injury Fund benefits under the provisions of N.J.S.A. 34:15-95, *et seq.* Therefore I hereby, on my oath, affirm that I have read the foregoing and am familiar with the contents thereof and that the matters set forth are true to the best of my knowledge and belief.

______________________________ *(Petitioner Signature)*

______________________________ *(Date)*

STATE OF NEW JERSEY

COUNTY OF ______________________

Subscribed and sworn before me on this _______ day of

________________ , __________.

____

The Privacy Act, 5 U.S.C. §522a, the Social Security Act, 42 U.S.C. § 405, and N.J.S.A. 34:15-1 *et seq.* authorize the Division of Workers' Compensation to request that the Petitioner supply the Division with his or her Social Security number for record keeping purposes and cross-matches with the Social Security Administration, Workforce New Jersey, Temporary Disability Insurance and any other proper public purpose.

NOTE: Attach copies of all proposed expert witnesses' reports. Pursuant to Division Rules, do not attach hospital records. Attach index of medical records only.

K. Fact Sheet #15, Disability Retirement Benefits, a publication of the N.J. Division of Pension and Benefits

BD-0114-0117 **Fact Sheet #15**

A PUBLICATION OF THE NEW JERSEY DIVISION OF PENSIONS AND BENEFITS

Disability Retirement Benefits

Public Employees' Retirement System • Teachers' Pension and Annuity Fund

Ordinary Disability and Accidental Disability Retirement for PERS or TPAF members is **only** for those enrolled *on or before* May 21, 2010 (membership **Tier 1**, **Tier 2**, and **Tier 3**).

Under the provisions of N.J.S.A. 43:15A-42.1 (PERS) and N.J.S.A. 18A:66-39.1 (TPAF), Tier 4 and 5 members *may* be eligible for disability insurance coverage. See your employer or Fact Sheet #85, *Long Term Disability for PERS and TPAF Tiers 4 and 5*, for more information.

ORDINARY DISABILITY

The processing of Ordinary Disability retirement benefits normally takes six to eight months. To qualify for Ordinary Disability retirement benefits you must:

- have separated from employment as a result of the alleged disabling condition;
- have an active pension account (active membership ceases after discontinuance of pension contributions for more than two consecutive years[1] or withdrawal of member contributions from the retirement system);
- have 10 or more years of New Jersey service credit in the pension system **(the purchase of out-of-state, military, and U.S. government civilian service cannot be used to attain the 10 years)**;
- be considered permanently and totally disabled at the time you separate from service (you must prove that you are physically or mentally incapacitated from performing your normal or assigned job duties, or any other position that your employer may assign);
- provide any and all medical reports or corroborating evidence on file that supports your disability (the required documentation must be received within six months of the date of filing the disability application. If the documentation is not received, the retirement will be cancelled and the member will need to complete a new disability application for a future date); and
- complete the *Authorization for Release of Information* (*HIPAA*).

The regulations governing the retirement systems require two physician reports (or one physician report and one hospital record) to be supplied when you apply for disability retirement. In addition, you may be required to be examined by physicians selected by the retirement system.

Please Note: The initial independent medical examination (IME) will be scheduled at no cost to you. However, if you fail to attend or cancel the initial IME, you will be required to pay for any subsequent medical examinations arranged by the Division. In addition, if additional medical documentation is submitted after the initial IME, you will be required to pay for any subsequent review and reports. Payment is required before the Division will schedule another IME, reviews, or reports; failure to provide payment within 90 days will result in the dismissal of the disability retirement case.

[1] *Special rules apply for former members who discontinue service after two years and terminate employment because of a disability. At the time the member separates from service, they must be considered permanently and totally disabled. Contact the Division of Pensions and Benefits for more information.*

If you qualify for an Ordinary Disability retirement, the annual benefit is equal to 43.6 percent of your Final Average Salary (FAS).

"Final Average Salary" means your average salary for the 36 months (or 30 months for members paid on a 10-month basis) immediately preceding your retirement on which pension contributions were taken. If your last 36 months are not your highest years of salary, your allowance may be calculated using your three highest fiscal years (July 1 to June 30) of salary. If this is the case, please indicate on your online retirement application that you had higher fiscal years of salary (paper applications are no longer accepted and all members must file using the Member Benefits Online System (MBOS)). For more information about registering for MBOS, visit our Web site at: *www.nj.gov/treasury/pensions*

Calculation Example: In the 36 months prior to retirement, a member's average salary was $45,000. After approval of Ordinary Disability retirement benefits, the member would be entitled to an annual benefit of $19,620 ($45,000 X 0.436) under the Maximum Option (see Fact Sheet #5, *Pension Options*, for an explanation of other options that provide for survivor benefits).

The retirement benefit is not reduced by any Social Security or private insurance benefits that may be payable. However, any Workers' Compensation award you receive may be reduced. See your employer for details.

Ordinary Disability retirement benefits are subject to federal tax to the same extent as other pensions, but are not subject to New Jersey State income tax until you reach age 65.

ACCIDENTAL DISABILITY

The processing of Accidental Disability retirement benefits normally takes six to eight months. To qualify for Accidental Disability retirement benefits you must:

- have separated from employment as a result of the alleged disabling condition;
- have an active pension account (active membership ceases after discontinuance of pension contributions for more than two consecutive years);
- be considered permanently and totally disabled at the time you separate from service (you must prove that you are physically or mentally incapacitated from performing your normal or assigned job duties or any other position that your employer may assign) as a "direct result of a traumatic event" (see definition below) that happened during and as a direct result of carrying out your regular or assigned job duties;
- be an active member of the PERS or TPAF on the date of the "traumatic event";
- file an application for Accidental Disability retirement within five years of the date of the "traumatic event";
- be examined by physicians selected by the retirement system at no cost to you (see exceptions to cost below);
- provide any and all medical reports to support the application for disability including but not limited to, accident reports, witness reports, and corroborating evidence on file for any and all accidents for which you are filing; and
- complete the *Authorization for Release of Information* (*HIPAA*).

Please Note: The initial independent medical examination (IME) will be scheduled at no cost to you. However, if you fail to attend or cancel the initial IME, you will be required to pay for any subsequent medical examinations arranged by the Division. In addition, if additional medical documentation is submitted after the initial IME, you will be required to pay for any subsequent review and reports. Payment is required before the Division will schedule another IME, reviews, or reports; failure to provide payment within 90 days will result in the dismissal of the disability retirement case.

'Direct Result of a Traumatic Event' has been defined by the courts as an occurrence that is:

- identifiable as to time and place;
- undesigned and unexpected;
- caused by a circumstance external to the member (not the result of pre-existing disease that is aggravated or accelerated by the work);
- occurred during and as a result of the member's regular or assigned duties;
- was not the result of the member's willful negligence; and
- results in the member's permanent and total incapacitation from performing his or her usual or any other duty.

When there is an issue of mental incapacity caused by a non-physical event, the member must also establish that the event that forms the basis for an accidental disability was objectively capable of causing a reasonable person in similar circumstances to suffer a disabling mental injury, based on a finding that the disability resulted from "direct personal experience of a terrifying or horror-inducing event that involves actual or threatened death or serious injury, or a similarly serious threat to the physical integrity of the member or another person."

If you qualify for an Accidental Disability retirement, the annual benefit is equal to 72.7 percent of your base salary at the time of the traumatic event.

Calculation Example: On the date of the traumatic event that caused the member's disability, a member's annual salary was $45,000. After approval of Accidental Disability retirement benefits, the member would be entitled to an annual benefit of $32,715 ($45,000 X 0.727) under the Maximum Option (see Fact Sheet #5, *Pension Options*, for an explanation of other options that provide for survivor benefits).

If you are receiving periodic Workers' Compensation benefits, your Accidental Disability retirement benefits will be reduced dollar for dollar by the periodic benefits paid after your retirement date.

The retirement benefit is not reduced by any Social Security or private insurance benefits that may be payable.

The Division of Pensions and Benefits reports your Accidental Disability retirement benefit as exempt from federal income tax; your benefits are not subject to New Jersey State income tax until you reach age 65.

If you apply for Accidental Disability retirement and are found by the Board of Trustees to be permanently and totally disabled, but not because of a traumatic event or the event was not the primary cause of your disability, you will be retired on an Ordinary Disability if you have 10 years of New Jersey service in the retirement system. You may be offered a Service or Early Retirement depending on your age and service credit at the time the application is received.

APPLYING FOR DISABILITY RETIREMENT BENEFITS

Paper applications are no longer accepted. **The disability retirement application must be submitted online using the Member Benefits Online System (MBOS).** Before you can begin using the system, you must be registered with MBOS. Registration is free. To begin the MBOS registration process go to our Web site at: *www.nj.gov/treasury/pensions/mbosregister.shtml*

Filing for a disability retirement includes forms for your physicians to complete and a release for any hospital records related to your disability. Applicants for disability retirement must submit all supporting hospital and physician records using the forms linked from the online application. Two forms of medical documentation are required and **specific forms available from the Division of Pensions and Benefits must be used:** the Division requires any hospital/medical records and one (1) of OUR treating physician statement forms. If no other hospital/medical records are available, the Division requires two (2) of OUR treating physician statement forms — one each from two different physicians. These Division of Pensions and Benefits forms are available online at:

Medical Examination By Personal or Treating Physician:
www.nj.gov/treasury/pensions/epbam/exhibits/pdf/bd0021.pdf

Authorization to Disclose Hospital Records:
www.nj.gov/treasury/pensions/epbam/exhibits/pdf/.pdf

Authorization for Release of Information (HIPAA):
www.nj.gov/treasury/pensions/epbam/exhibits/pdf/hipaa-form.pdf

Supporting documents should be submitted to:

Division of Pensions and Benefits
Disability Review Unit
PO Box 295
Trenton, NJ 08625-0295

All medical information is kept confidential and used only by the Board of Trustees in reviewing the claim.

You must pay for the cost of any medical documentation that may be required to prove your claim. For example, if you had a hospital stay due to your disability and the hospital charges for the duplication of medical records from your stay, you would be responsible for any cost involved.

ADDITIONAL PROVISIONS OF DISABILITY RETIREMENT

In order to be eligible to receive either Ordinary or Accidental Disability retirement benefits, you must terminate all retirement system covered employment prior to your retirement date.

If you have been terminated for cause or have a settlement agreement, which sets forth the terms of your departure in lieu of the termination for cause, you and your employer MUST provide that information to us at the time you are filing for disability. It must be shown that you have separated from employment as a result of the disabling condition. The Division reviews disability applications to determine they are eligible for processing. If it is determined that the reason for termination is not from the disability, you may be deemed ineligible to apply for a disability retirement.

Your employer has the right to apply for an Involuntary Disability retirement on your behalf. Along with the retirement application **State employers must provide** an official letter from the Department's highest authority; **Local employers must provide** a copy of a resolution adopted by the governing body, stating that, in the employing authority's opinion, the employee is "totally and permanently disabled" from fulfilling his or her job duties (include any pertinent medical records).

> **Please Note:** An employer submitting an Involuntary Disability retirement application must select the Maximum Option and list the member's beneficiary as "estate." If the retirement is approved by the Board of Trustees, the member may change the option selection and beneficiary designation within 30 days. The member cannot change the date of retirement under an Involuntary Disability retirement.

The approval of Workers' Compensation or Social Security disability benefits has no bearing on your application for disability retirement from the retirement system.

If you retire with an outstanding loan balance, your monthly loan repayment schedule will continue into retirement until the loan balance plus interest has been repaid.

Once the Board of Trustees approves a member for a disability retirement allowance, the member's retirement application cannot be withdrawn, cancelled, or amended to a later retirement date than the date specified in the approved retirement application.

Group Life Insurance

Most members of the retirement system are covered by group life insurance. If you are covered immediately prior to your retirement, you are entitled to reduced coverage in retirement as follows:

PERS Members

If you retire on a disability retirement, you are covered by group life insurance in the amount of 1½ times your final salary until age 60. At age 60 your life insurance coverage automatically reduces to 3/16 of your final salary.

"Final Salary" for PERS group life insurance benefits is calculated using the salary on which pension contributions were based in the last 12 months immediately preceding your retirement.

TPAF Members

- If you retire on a disability retirement with contributory and noncontributory group life insurance, you are covered by group life insurance in the amount of 1¾ times your final salary until age 60, when your life insurance coverage automatically reduces to 7/16 of your final salary.
- If you retire on a disability retirement with noncontributory group life insurance *only*, you are covered by group life insurance in the amount of 1½ times your final salary until age 60, when your life insurance coverage automatically reduces to 3/16 of your final salary.

"Final Salary" for TPAF group life insurance benefits is calculated using the salary on which pension contributions were based in the last 12 months immediately preceding your retirement or the highest contractual year.

Conversion

When your group life insurance is reduced, you have 31 days to convert the amount of insurance reduced to private individual insurance coverage. Please see Fact Sheet #13, *Conversion of Group Life Insurance,* for more information.

Health Benefits

Fact Sheet #11, *Enrolling in Health Benefits Coverage When You Retire*, provides information about continuing your State Health Benefits Program or School Employees' Health Benefits Program coverage in retirement.

If you are not covered by the State Health Benefits Program or School Employees' Health Benefits Program, contact your employer about continuing your coverage.

Employment after Retirement

A disability retirement allowance may be adjusted if you have earnings from any occupation or employment (public or non-public) after retirement. If the pension portion of your retirement allowance, when added to the earnings from other employment, exceeds what your former position currently pays, the law requires that the disability pension be reduced dollar for dollar by the excess earnings above what the former position currently pays. PERS and TPAF disability retirees are subject to an annual earnings test and the Division of Pensions and Benefits may request copies of your federal tax returns, *Form W-2,* and completion of federal *Form 4506T.*

If you were granted a disability retirement but are no longer disabled, before you can return to active service in a PERS or TPAF eligible title with any public employer, you must first prove to the satisfaction of the Board of Trustees that you are no longer disabled. A disability retiree must:

1. Make a written request to return to active service to the Division of Pensions and Benefits;
2. Submit a physician's report to the Division certifying that you are no longer disabled and can return to employment. The physician should be one with the same specialty as the physician who originally certified that you were disabled;
3. Be examined by a physician appointed by the Board of Trustees; and
4. Be approved for return to active service by the Board of Trustees.

If approved to return to active service in a position covered by the PERS or TPAF, your original account and membership tier are restored — provided that you work the minimum number of hours or earn the minimum annual salary required for enrollment in your original membership tier ($1,500 for Tier 1 or Tier 2 PERS members; $500 for Tier 1 or Tier 2 TPAF members; for Tier 3 PERS and TPAF members the minimum salary is subject to annual adjustment). When membership is restored, pension contributions resume and you are treated as an active member in all respects.

Upon subsequent retirement, you must meet the retirement qualifications of your PERS or TPAF membership tier and file for retirement with the Division of Pensions and Benefits before any benefits can be paid. You will receive a benefit based on total service.

Additional restrictions may apply if you return to employment after retirement. Please refer to Fact Sheet #86, *Post-Retirement Employment Restrictions*, for more information.

Cost-of-Living Adjustments

Under N.J.S.A. 43:3B-2, Cost-of-Living Adjustments (COLA) are suspended for all current and future retirees of all retirement systems. No further COLA increases will be granted. The law does not reduce any COLA increases that have already been added to retiree benefits. See Fact Sheet #18, *Cost-of-Living Adjustments*, for more information.

Fact Sheets and Forms

The fact sheets, forms, and other publications mentioned are available on the Division of Pensions and Benefits Web site. Our homepage address is: *www.nj.gov/treasury/pensions*

Member Benefits Online System

Active employees and retirees can access information about their benefits using the Member Benefits Online System (MBOS). MBOS is a set of Internet based applications that allow registered members quick and safe access to specific information about their own pension. You can log on or register for MBOS at: *www.nj.gov/treasury/pensions* (select "Online Member Services - MBOS").

This fact sheet has been produced and distributed by:
New Jersey Division of Pensions and Benefits • PO Box 295 • Trenton, New Jersey 08625-0295
(609) 292-7524 • For the hearing impaired: TRS 711 (609) 292-6683
URL: **http://www.nj.gov/treasury/pensions** • E-mail: **pensions.nj@treas.nj.gov**

Notes

Made in the USA
Monee, IL
29 June 2026

56050308R00138